A QUESTION OF QUALITIES

Writing **Architecture** series

A project of the Anyone Corporation; Cynthia Davidson, editor

THE MIT PRESS

CAMBRIDGE, MASSACHUSETTS

LONDON, ENGLAND

A QUESTION OF QUALITIES

ESSAYS IN ARCHITECTURE

JEFFREY KIPNIS

EDITED BY ALEXANDER MAYMIND

MIT Press books may be purchased at special quantity discounts for business or sales promotional use. For information, please email special_sales@mitpress.mit.edu or write to Special Sales Department, The MIT Press, 55 Hayward Street, Cambridge, MA 02142.

This book was set in Filosofia and Trade Gothic by the MIT Press. Printed and bound in the United States of America.

Library of Congress Cataloging-in-Publication Data

Kipnis, Jeffrey

[Essays. Selections]

A question of qualities : essays in architecture / Jeffrey Kipnis; edited by Alexander Maymind.

pages cm

Includes bibliographical references and index.

ISBN 978-0-262-51955-7 (pbk. : alk. paper)

1. Architecture, Modern—20th century—Themes, motives.

2. Architecture, Modern—21st century—Themes, motives.

I. Maymind, Alexander, editor of compilation. II. Kipnis, Jeffrey. A question of qualities. III. Title.

NA680.K518 2013

724.6—dc23

2012046609

10 9 8 7 6 5 4 3 2

CONTENTS

PREFACE

I first heard about Jeffrey Kipnis when I was an undergraduate at The Ohio State University. Rumor had it that he was the Knowlton School of Architecture's eccentric, the professor whose candidness and unique mannerisms continually violated social and academic customs. Kipnis, it seemed, taught only one course: a contemporary theory seminar for graduate students that was off limits to undergraduates. Older students said that the seminar was more like happy hour in Jeff's living room, where academic formalities were replaced by extended conversation and argument, inside jokes, and highly entertaining stories. I took all this to be preposterous exaggeration, yet, intrigued by the conflicting accounts that Kipnis was both a "genius" and something I won't repeat here, I began steadily to collect and read his essays. The summer of my junior year, I attempted to offset the mind-numbingly banal days of a corporate internship by reading Kipnis at night. I quickly discovered that his writing evidenced a keen ability to situate difficult philosophic and cultural concerns in relation to architecture's own disciplinary questions. This did not seem to be the work of an eccentric personality. In one sense, I realized it would be necessary to get beyond the personality so that I could see the writing as something other.

To do this I needed to enroll myself in the infamous seminar. Back at school that fall, I asked to be admitted to the yearlong graduate-level class. Upon seeing my highlighted photocopies of his essays, Jeff said I could enroll, but only if I could find four other undergrads willing to join as well. This was easy, since for those students the seminar was considered a rite of passage.

After my summer of intense reading, my own interest was something else: to clear Jeff the personality out of the writing. This turned out to be more difficult than I expected, given his approach to teaching.

The class was fundamentally different from any I had experienced. Once a week Jeff would shuffle up to the front of the class, flop into a rolling chair, and lead a circuitous discussion that inevitably invoked contemporary architects, projects, diagrams, ideas, and arguments, all while maintaining a steady flow of ancillary material—from art to philosophy, television, film, music, yesterday's news—to supplement the narrative. His diverse range of topics consistently foregrounded architecture as both an intellectual discourse and a lived, affective experience. His uncanny ability to situate it in an intellectually rigorous yet accessible manner transformed abstract, hermetic discourse into a working set of ideas that opened up material initially foreign to me. It became clear that his undeclared intent was to instill a distinct method of thinking about architecture. These insights, taken from the seminar, allowed me to see his writing, and the very idea of writing, in a different context. At heart, his criticism is nonformal. It is not about the material or language of architecture, but about its affect. The mobile and fluid materiality of language that Jeff sees in poetry is apparent in his essays, notable for their rationality but also for their written affects; affects that distinguish his writing not only from his "personality" but also from other critics'.

It is this difference that this collection of essays attempts to present. While they constitute a very partial record of Kipnis's contribution to architectural thought, they reflect this unique aspect of his work: his emphasis on being first a writer and second a critic. While the essays address the projects of some of the most recognized architects working today, this is not the central point of the book. Instead, the essays evidence a critical voice interested not in final value judgments but rather in explication, exegesis, and provocation—in writing per se. His best writing has a clarity of argumentation that is profoundly pleasurable to read, as if one's own understanding of the ideas at hand was suddenly expanded to recognize an entirely other version of the same story. Arguably, that "other version" underpins many of Jeff's ambitions, not only for writing but also for architecture itself.

Kipnis is the rarest of teachers. Part shaman, part "overlord," part mentor, his total efforts and their far-reaching effects are nearly impossible to quantify. Similarly, the eleven critical and theoretical essays in this volume demonstrate a manner of writing that is not so much about architecture as it is an affect of architecture itself.

Alexander Maymind
New York City, 2012

1 A QUESTION OF QUALITIES

Prologue

The fifth installment of Rizzoli's documentation of the evolution of Morphosis finds the practice at the peak of its powers, enjoying critical and professional success.[1] Thom Mayne, who according to legend lived in his car for months on end during the 1980s to keep his studio on life support, is now a Pritzker laureate with offices in Los Angeles and New York. And the studio, once famous for restaurants, houses, and other miniatures, now bustles with teams working on banks, civic buildings, schools, and a centerpiece high-rise in Paris. But more important, the current architecture has not just maintained the vigor of the early work but grown stronger by all measures—bolder, less fussy, conceptually more adroit.

The reasons Morphosis's later projects have neither lapsed into mannerism nor become watered down are more a matter of luck than of genius. They boil down to two. First, the more physical the stuff Mayne has to work with and the thornier the architectural problem, the better his architecture gets. Second, he has never quite known what he is after in his architecture in the sense of a clearly preconceived philosophy, vision, or cause. Like a creature drawn to its habitat, Mayne gravitates intuitively toward awkward complication. Hence his fascination with any contraption possessed of a lot of incongruent parts working in unlikely collaboration to do something, such as his perennial favorites, Diderot's machines and the Apollo Lunar Module. One gets the impression, both from the work and from reading and listening to the architect, that these exemplars spark an intuition about architectural situations that might feel right to him, even if he does not know in advance what architecture's counterpart to the machines might be. And it is toward such situations that he strives by fits and starts in his work.

Neither a graceless sensibility nor a superior performance alone is a wholly sufficient description, for Mayne is neither a bricoleur nor an engineer. What he seeks is to engender distinct instances in his work in which the two—sensibility and performance—come to depend intimately on one another. All the more because, even if most of us in the discipline can identify a notable architectural performance when we encounter one, none of us to my knowledge has ever convincingly established the terms and conditions for one in advance. In that sense, despite the use of the term as neodeterminist jargon today, *performance* in architecture is closer to theater and music than to science or engineering, as much if not more a question of elusive qualities than of measurable effects.

In Morphosis's early projects, there simply was not enough intrinsic material, nor were the problems sufficiently demanding. In retrospect, the most popular contrivances that at the time seemed to be the elements of a Morphosis style—the mecho-tech fetish, the indulgent detailing, the fixation on conceiving layered sections and plans even when literal layering was not possible, the concoction of superfluous material with which to supplement basic architecture, and most of all the obsession with abstruse, conceptual representations of projects in excess models and drawings—were but compensations for missing essential ingredients, preparatory studies in strategy and technique for a time if and when . . . And as the work itself began to supply these potentials, the architect began to jettison the early confections one after another without hesitation, without regret.

To grasp this later work—let us not yet say "understand"—then, our task in commentary cannot be just to track Mayne's journey but to follow his example. Rather than wrestle this architecture into a preconceived critical framework, we too must jettison those ideas and impressions that we perfected in the response to Morphosis's early work, to see what else comes our way.

I. Causes and Concepts

Though much has been written about Morphosis, no one—including myself—has to my mind satisfactorily articulated any allegiance of the later works—say those projects after the Blades House (1997)—to a cause, that is, to an intellectual, cultural, or political enterprise that would guide the divergence of a building's qualities away from custom, as could otherwise be said of comparable speculative practices such as those of OMA or Peter Eisenman. On the other hand, neither have critics found Morphosis's works to be as purely inspired as those of Frank Gehry, Jean Nouvel, or Herzog & de Meuron.

While comprehension of Morphosis's early architecture fell well within the competence of a critique of part-to-whole relations, the aptitude of that discourse began to wane with the Diamond Ranch High School (1996). The school offers ample evidence—too much, in fact—of a number of incommensurable, partial discourses that neither coalesce into a new synthesis nor remain resolute in their differences as collage. To cite three examples: a revised relation of building to ground; a reimagined relationship between the prevailing architectural standards of the institution and its program; and a psychologically aggressive use of form, construction, and materials given that the destined primary users are adolescents. It is as if three distinct agencies—place (as ground), soul (as program), and body (as building)—coexist in the same space and time, vying with one another for face—as they did in Eve. Such discomfited coexistences might even be related to the psychoanalytic theme of the *partial object*—that which cannot be assimilated into the subject's narcissistic illusion of completeness.

In any case, in the recent projects—built between 1999 and 2008—the failure of any coherent discourse to take command of the work has only become more apparent. While commentary continues to detect a palpable presence of conceptual ambitions in these works and so instinctively avoids a merely phenomenological account of them, somehow those ambitions elude specification. Perhaps the problem resides less in some mystery unique to Morphosis's architecture than in our prevailing model of a conceptual discourse, which in recent years has been reformulated from one to two variables: concepts and effects—staged separately in writing and building. This model assumes that concepts emerge out of the critical conversations generated by works, whether buildings or projects, to find best expression in writing. Buildings, the scene of architecture's irreducible and irreproducible effects, are a preeminent measure of certain concepts as their best demonstration. In the conceptual framework, this role of buildings is paramount but not unique, as it is in a phenomenological framework. The entire repertoire of material practices in the field carries this potential; for example, Rem Koolhaas's Parc de la Villette proposal, or even a single drawing such as the structural perspective of Le Corbusier's Maison Dom-ino, with no evidence whatsoever that realization would have significantly contributed much more of value to the discourse.

In addition, the unpredictable, promiscuous effects engendered by any building make it the instrument par excellence of improvisation. As such, the building both provides a rich source of new conceptual germ and acts as an instrument of play that continuously enriches the treasury of architecture's effects, always keeping it larger than any subset emphasized by a particular discourse. The situation is similar to the relationship between a musical performance and a score within a critical context, with at least one crucial difference: that the "score" of a work of architecture aspires to receive but one performance.[2]

The conceptual model has grown into a sophisticated tool that avoids most of the obvious pitfalls that once hampered it. Neither concept nor effect is subordinate to the other. Rather, they are conjugates; one cannot ask which came first or which is more important, any more than one can ask whether length or width is more important to the area of a rectangle. Nor does either pretend to timelessness or independence from context, but they are wed through discourse into a coevolution under the selective pressures of a complex of influences which they in turn inflect.[3]

Due to the ramifications of inspired practices such as those already mentioned, the conceptual discourse has more or less relaxed its initial anxieties about such issues as talent, genius, originality, authorship, masterpieces, and so forth. While its critique of the indefensible belief system from which these notions first sprang remains vigilant, new insights into the complex processes they identify obligate discourse to reinstate them in revised version to its conception of creativity in respect of cultural industry. It is as barren to think of Beethoven, Einstein, and Le Corbusier as but ones among many as it is to think of them as gods, worse still to believe that their renown is nothing more than the conspiracy of some insidious publicity machine. These names are not the identities of people but the coordinates given to catastrophic bifurcations in various phase spaces, coordinates that of necessity are "written" in an identity; but that is a discussion better taken up elsewhere.

Given the difficulties of pinning down the discourse of Morphosis's work, is it conceivable for there to arise in certain buildings an ineffable component of conceptual discourse—that is, aspects of the architecture that are in every way intellectual, in every way discursive, even available to paraphrase, but that are not, at least for the time being, best expressed in words, drawings, or models? The idea of "uncertainty" in quantum physics is certainly an example of such ineffability, a concept-as-effect that later found best expression in mathematics, but whose life in words even today remains an impoverished caricature. Then again, the example itself is too threadbare because of its arcane rarity. What we need is more ordinary evidence of cultural concepts that appear first and best as effects. To look for such evidence, we take our cue not from physics but from social theory, music, psychology, and art history.

For anyone committed to architecture as a conceptual discourse, ineffability is a hazardous proposition on a number of fronts, not least of which is the danger of a naïve interpretation that would mistake it as an invitation to relapse into an anti-intellectual posture in which the "experience itself" of a building stands as a sufficient arbiter of the architecture's achievement. Nothing could be further from the aim, given that the single most important achievement of discourse in the arts has been to refute once and for all the very possibility of a virgin "experience itself," unaligned with any agenda and uncolored by manifold influences.

Also hazardous would be the assumption that the proposition calls into question the essential role of writing in the discipline. If architectural production is a cultural industry (distinct, for example, from an entertainment or service business), then written discourse—whether conceptual, phenomenological, or otherwise—provides its medium of exchange and constructs its accounting system, enabling the burgeoning of both intellectual wealth and material effects, much as money and double-entry accounting do for business. Simply put, there is no architecture without writing.

On the other hand, we should not overestimate the derangement such a proposition would pose to the current model of discourse were it to find a compelling argument. If any change is required, it would take place not as a revolution, but as further development of a successful approach with which to grasp architecture's manifold relations to life. We have already noticed the conceptual model's capacity to appreciate most speculative projects, from those with an explicit affiliation with an expressed *intellectual* agenda to those relying entirely on *inspiration*. In the end, the elusiveness of Morphosis's recent work compels us to question the place of *intuition* in the conceptual model of architectural discourse.

Social theorist Roberto Mangabeira Unger posits that each of us already holds answers to questions that none of us yet knows how to ask, providing a powerful formulation of intuition for a conceptual discourse. Careful not to arrest the artful turbulence he seeks to exalt, his thought calls attention to those eddies that occur in the mists of the nether lagoon where mind merges into body, intensifications that are yet neither ideas nor sensations and that mostly dissipate into oblivion for lack of sustenance.

Unger's intuition-answers cannot be formulated into words, because if they could, the questions toward which they point would not be obscure but already intelligible. So the energies, matters, and forms necessary to grant some extension to these fugitive awakenings can only be found in one or another of the arts—in the unlikely event that they can be found at all. But should they indeed acquire such a provisional body, then they also acquire the power to stir awareness in a few of us at a time (as is always the case with the arts) and perhaps, eventually, even to give rise to a new state of self-consciousness, one either able to find a better expression of the concept in another medium, such as words, or able to apprehend that what seemed a provisional moment is already best expression.

Clearly, these intuition-answers are no more available to the artist as knowledge, ideas, or concepts than they are to his or her audience. One should not expect that learning about the architect's own ideas, sources, or the combinatorial processes used to generate the ultimate arrangements will yield any real insight into the discourse of the work. Indeed, one should instead expect a certain kind of confusion, even some frustration and embarrassment, to attend any explanation of why what was done was done. Nor, on the other hand, can such work be expected to generate the immediate, visceral impact of an inspired work, the greatness and poignancy of which relate more to the powers of theater than to thought. All that we could know at its nascence is that for the artist and his or her audience, no matter how few or great in number, the work would feel somehow more real, or better still, somehow more right.

If at first the conceptual project in the arts daydreamed that it was destined one day to replace entirely the life of matter with the life of ideas, that foolishness has long since passed. Rather, we are coming to understand what history seems in retrospect to have been trying to teach us for some time, that the place of conceptual discourse in the arts is to husband new cultivars of material practices that in turn can grow into new species, even new genera, empowering a proliferating catalog of talent, genius, and intuition, each of which enlarges the existential territory available to each and all of us. And the larger that territory gets, the more freedom we have to move.

For those with some interest in early modern music, the notion of intuitions as answers to as-yet-unposable questions seems to promise immediate benefits in the face of a prolonged thorn in the side of music's discourse—the comprehension of the work of Charles Ives vis-à-vis his contemporary modern masters, Igor Stravinsky and Arnold Schoenberg. Like Frank Lloyd Wright, Le Corbusier, and Mies van der Rohe, the three composers constitute the seminal triumvirate in their discipline's modernism. The foundations of music's theoretical discourse are far better grounded than those of architecture because of the success of the former's early history of harmonic and formal codification. Stravinsky's inspired inventions in orchestration and performance technique, polytonality, and polyrhythms are well grasped in the discourse for their unparalleled expansion of music's theatrical powers, a contribution facilitated because the most important of his works took the form of ballet. The *Rite of Spring*, in concert with Vaslav Nijinsky's radical choreography, captures in music the violence, sexuality, and schizoid frenzy that would come to be the heart of modernity. The intellectual achievements of Schoenberg, such as his inventions of *Sprechstimme* and his serial twelve-tone theory, are also thoroughly comprehended by music's discourse and appreciated for its capacity to capture the thought, mood, and timbre of modernity's intellectual proclivities.

If the recent work of Morphosis befuddles contemporary architectural discourse, the work of Ives rendered music's discourse virtually dumb for a century. To be sure, there has been an abundance of admiration and appreciation, and certainly no dearth of biographies, exegeses of notebooks, manuscript scores, source materials, and formal and harmonic analyses, but none has taught us how to listen to the music, to discover its immediacy with the same success with which we now hear an Anton Webern or see a Jackson Pollock. Once unapproachable, the works of these latter artists are now consumed as if their projects were always obvious and never required explanation. Not so for Ives.

It is fascinating to learn that the complex rhythm schemes and microtonalities in Ives's music derive from the way amateur singers in churches or other gatherings sing—slightly off key or out of rhythm—or to discover that, just beneath an alien wash of atonality in the music, there are often several familiar march, folk, and jazz tunes playing at the same time. But this knowledge does little to catalyze an intimate awakening to it, because the music seeks neither to represent those events in the manner of theater nor to reflect on them in an intellectual vein. Even today, most listeners—schooled or not—find Ives's music frustrating, confused, addled, embarrassing, or inept. For a few, though, Ives began to write music which told not the facts or the feelings of their lives, but a truth of it to which they had no other access. Is this evidence of intuition-answers, of a new conceptual subjectivity yet to arrive? Perforce, that must remain an "unanswered question,"[4] but the parallel with Mayne's relative position in the discourse of architecture is striking.

II. The Qualities of Effects

One gets the impression that *artless* does not play well in San Francisco. Morphosis's San Francisco Federal Building may be neither as rough-hewn nor as unself-conscious as that term implies, but it is a damned artless building for a town where even a little disheveling of its self-image is as welcome as a hangnail. On the front side facing the hills, an immense perforated sunscreen cascades off the roof, splits as it slides down the facade, and spills into the forecourt like a tattered crepe veil. From the opposite side, the sunscreen is visible only on the top, where it forms a sketchy trough that caps the building. From certain perspectives, the trough looks like the characteristic cross bar of a great ceremonial gate, but perhaps that is just a mirage stirred by thoughts of San Francisco's Chinatown. Otherwise, the facade on this side presents a quiet, blue-glass curtain wall utterly incongruous with the front and featureless save for a troop of vertical glass fins deployed across the entire surface that promises to do something serious for the building.

When I traveled to San Francisco to view the building with Mayne, he spoke exclusively about the various energy-saving gains his team has managed to achieve, and as we entered he started in on them again, digressing for a moment to a detail or a formal relation, but only half-heartedly. His mind remains preoccupied with the research his office has put into the building's systems and the pleasure he takes in the complications that have resulted. While the scurry of rapid-fire thought fragments that constitute his conversation can sometimes be hard to follow, there is nothing disingenuous about them. I trust his claims and his sincere enthusiasm for the research process and the result; indeed, for a moment, he almost has me convinced that these environmental considerations are not just a measure of the building, but the raison d'être for its architecture.

But something is not quite right; as I scan the building, what I see does not easily reconcile with what I hear. I recognize—as would anyone who follows the office's work—the crenellated sunscreen as a familiar formal motif that appears, for example, in the Diamond Ranch High School, the University of Cincinnati Recreation Center, and the Hypo Alpe-Adria Bank. In fact, some version of it is evident in most of the recent work. Mayne typically uses it as a device to join building to landscape, whether literally, as in the high school, or figuratively, as in the extension of the football field in the recreation center. Rather than honor the ground, however, the device seems more to want to gather site and building into a totality larger than that already given. Sketches suggest that in San Francisco, too, the architect would have preferred that the screen merge into the ground of the forecourt.

For whatever reason, however, the screen as built does not meet the ground but hovers above as a low-slung covered walkway. I prefer this separation for its inference that the figuring of the ground is less a representation than a transubstantiation of landscape and architecture into a third state, one that belongs neither to ground nor to building, an actual *morphosis* in

1.1
Morphosis, San Francisco Federal Building, 2007.
© Iwan Baan.

the literal sense. Not only does it make ambiguous the question of origin—whence emanates the surface?—but in so doing it also helps an overall massing that might have landed heavy-metal, like the Caltrans building in Los Angeles, to alight instead as ephemeral. The effect, even if serendipitous, is all the more engaging given that this Federal Building sits just across the street from the famous U.S. Court of Appeals for the Ninth Circuit. Completed in 1905 by architect James Knox Taylor and considered one of the most ornate public buildings in the country, the Beaux-Arts courthouse—nicknamed the Dowager Queen—stands on the ground with a decidedly different attitude about architecture and governance.

As I walk through the lobby and the remainder of the building's interior, I am pleased to find much more: amenities, of course—a breathtaking public belvedere, artwork by James Turrell—but, more to my interests, other familiar Morphosis motifs and themes, such as the curious translucent bars that skewer through the lobby to the exterior, and the invigorating space that has long been a hallmark of the practice. In short, a full palette of architectural ambition, experiential and conceptual, is in evidence despite the more practical issues that so captivate the architect. Only after we leave the building to depart does Mayne stop and reflect. In the tone of a denouement, he points out a specific episode and allows, "I guess if there were one place in the building that possessed the architectural qualities I am after, it would be there—where so many of the discreet systems converge." He is calling to my attention a cluster of stuff orbiting around the entry that consists of portions of skewers and sunscreen, elements of structure, and a faceted form serving as a three-dimensional portico. The gravity that gathers the clutter into a constellation turns out, on closer inspection, to be a subtle set of painterly tricks with form, materials, and construction. The cant of the concrete columns, for example, echoes the diagonals of the exposed strutwork holding the sunscreen, while folds of the screen mirror precisely the faceting of the portico polyhedron, as if the former had only just peeled from the latter. The precarious sense that the two once adhered is reinforced by the construction of each surface. The perforated metal panels of the screen and the composite panels of the portico are identical in scale and rhythm, recalling the volumetric coherence Cézanne achieved with his patch technique in the late paintings. Like glazing, the building materials themselves augment the effect, as the contrast between the reflective silver screen and the matte, blue-gray portico causes the latter to appear to be the screen's shadow-become-form.

A tour through the building would discover a surprising number of such formal and material devices, but it begs the more fundamental question: Why refer them to painting at all? One cannot pretend to be unaware of architecture's envy of its sister art's libertine spirit. Paint is so rich, beautiful, light, compliant, one cannot but indulge its excesses. Paint anything—any subject, scene, or the obscene—or nothing at all, and, if the wiles of paint's talent are insufficient, no problem. Just attach a newspaper, a tire, a chair, or a broken plate to the canvas, or for that matter, forget the canvas.

Mayne's public lecture on the San Francisco Federal Building offers some suggestions. As always, his presentation contains a scattering of evocative images shown in passing and without comment. In the case of this work, most of these allude to textiles, fabrics, or clothing, perhaps to reinforce the sense that the building has been casually dressed, especially when compared to its counterpart across the street. Aside from an obligatory Diderot weaving machine, he shows Robert and Shana Parke-Harrison's surreal photograph *Reclamation*, depicting two men pulling an immense carpet of lawn over an endless rocky landscape as if it were a bedspread. The image immediately widens

1.2
Morphosis, San Francisco Federal Building, 2007.
© Iwan Baan.

the circulation between building and landscape set into motion by the screen to include lawn and fabric.

Then appears a Jim Dine bathrobe print, *Cardinal*. At first, the unavoidable comparison between the bathrobe and judicial robes seems just to be the punch line of Mayne's silent rant on government, textiles, and casual dress. But the picture contains far more potent effects that compel us to drag painting back into a discussion of architecture. It is so supersaturated with orange that the color itself seems to be off-gassing from the robe as a spirit vapor. We glimpse the vapor a moment or two after it has briefly condensed into an ethereal body to try on the robe, just as it begins to evanesce into the dark atmospheric ground.

One can glean many unexpected reverberations between *Cardinal* and the Federal Building, such as the formal and behavioral parallels between the sunscreen and the color mist, but the central issue this picture raises is Mayne's desire to achieve such an incredible level of coherence in architecture.

Over centuries, painters have concocted extraordinary philters out of geometries, application techniques, and material effects, to brew incompatible elements, forms, and spaces into ensembles infused with an unimaginable coherence. Such compositions have long cast a spell over the imagination of architects, who not only envy their power to unify such disparate conditions, but also fantasize about potential new powers of *organizational*

1.4
Morphosis, San Francisco Federal Building, 2007.
© Iwan Baan.

performance, those uniquely architectural scintillations that occur when composition meets program. A door may allow entry into a building as its function, but the processional leading to a cathedral's door transports us from hell to heaven.

Celebrated but still sloppily theorized by architecture's own discourse, such effects are often treated as achievements best understood through other disciplines—art history, psychology, semiotics, sociology, even metaphysics for god's sake. Even worse, they are gathered under the ham-handed catchall of function, though they occur in the overtones of utility. Every other art practice owns its own discourse of "entry," for example, from painting to literature to music.[5] Were that to be true for architecture, perhaps we would be better able to appreciate the achievement of the entry to the Federal Building.

Though not as operatic as a cathedral door, the Federal Building's entry transports those who pass through it across an ontological distance every bit as great. The decisive question is, from where to where? If there were a simple answer, then intuition would have completed its transmutation into concept, but there are clues. Though the building establishes axial approaches to grand facades on both its front and back, these are strictly visual devices to gather the extended urban field under the influence of the building, and thus they belong to the ambition for new kinds of architectural coherence. On the other hand, the anticipated entries at the termini of these axes have been denied. Rather, one enters unheralded into the short side of the building off a side street, a location more common to service entries.

For those inclined to such things, the architecture of this entry can be said to engage in sharp formal banter with the pedimented corner entries to the Italianate courthouse across the street, indifferent to those passing through them. The Federal Building entry itself is composed as a gnarl, an atonal overture of all the forces, systems, and devices that unfold throughout the edifice. So the journey of all who enter the building—bureaucrat and constituent—starts not in the profane but the mundane. But where does it end? To describe the feelings of exhilaration, anonymity, and liberation that attend the entry begs the question, much as would identifying a pasture by extolling the bucolic feelings it stirs. The answer is a real place, just not yet a real concept.

Mayne's fascination with new modes of coherence and new performative organizations reminds us that even if we are moved by his work to speculate about the possibility of an intuitive-conceptual architecture, we should not mistake that to mean that the work is not disciplined by intellect and research. To the contrary, unlike the situation for any practice confident of its conceptual horizons and therefore already aware of the broad direction of its investigations, frenetic research surfaces as the sine qua non of Morphosis's process, as it would be for anyone compelled to a destination but unsure quite what that is.

Mayne makes his need for information clear: "We begin every project by asking questions outside our narrow area of expertise. Guided by the project itself, we query a wide range of cultural, urban, political, and ecological knowledge with the hope of discovering ideas to stimulate the relevance and creativity of our designs. To allow this research to gain a foothold in the design, we reject any predictable or a priori impulse in its early stages. Resolution emerges slowly as our understanding of the project allows us to accommodate increasingly complex inputs, ideas and challenges."[6] This is why institutional programs and larger buildings with increased functional and financial demands have proved so instrumental to the development of Morphosis's architecture. Gather together the twenty or so page-length project prescriptions that preface each project in *Morphosis: Buildings and Projects 1999–2008*, and one has a log of the practice's cravings for information, any information that might help it find a way. Aside from the energy concerns, urban analysis, and history

of the courthouse mentioned in the discussion of the San Francisco Federal Building, we find notes about the history of the
dome as a symbol of authority (Alaska State Capitol), the relationship between theoretical cosmologists and observational astronomers (Cahill Center for Astronomy and Astrophysics), the
doctrine of *Stare decisis* in Western law (Wayne Lyman Morse U.S.
Courthouse), recombinant DNA (Broad Art Museum), et cetera,
et cetera. Concomitant with those cravings is an equally vora-
cious appetite for the latest digital design technology, for every
advance in CAD, CAM, rapid prototyping, and project scripting,
as a means of gaining an increasing virtuosity over effects.

To be sure, one can detect some residue or another of much
of the information gathered in each project, and, equally, each
project reflects the architect's ever-increasing power to digitally
manipulate design and construction. But if there is any purchase
to the issue of intuition that concerns us, then neither the research nor the bravura technique can answer the question "What
does this architecture do?" at the level of a conceptual discourse
any more than such broad notions as new coherence or performative organization. Rather, they initiate movement toward the
marriage of complexity and suppleness that intuition requires
for best expression.

But the magnum opus of Mayne's gift for new coherences
must be the Cincinnati Recreation Center. The brief called for
a large building to house a long and complicated list of facilities:
basketball courts, gyms, pools, fitness center, café, and other
spaces. But the more interesting problem for Mayne was the
given site conditions, whose chaos provided the perfect opportunity for him to advance his investigation of new coherences.
Not only was the building to be located within a stone's throw
of several large, clashing iconic buildings, such as a beloved but
bland football stadium, a colossal French Enlightenment fantasy
by Michael Graves, and a strange round layer-cake-like thing by

1.5
Morphosis, University of Cincinnati Campus
Recreation Center, 2005. © Roland Halbe.

Charles Gwathmey, but it was also obligated by an operative master plan to help realize a fairy-tale "Main Street," as if the campus itself were a small town.

In a tour de force of analysis, invention, and improvisation, Mayne generated the practice's most accomplished work of architectural discourse to date. The scheme deploys a ground surface that flows from the stadium as if the football field itself overflowed onto the campus landscape, a scene reminiscent of the ParkeHarrisons' photograph. Functionally, this surface is the roof of the rec center, but architecturally it serves as the key device to affect a new level of connectivity within the campus.

In an extraordinary stroke of luck, the university nearly doubled the size of the original commission by adding more programs: a major student housing block and a large wing of additional classrooms. Nothing could have been better for Mayne's architecture. He gave each of these large subprograms its own discreet formal identity, running the risk of further increasing the cacophony of the campus. But then he immersed them in form and material in the fluid ground surface, catalyzing a reaction which dissolves all the disjointed elements and relations on the campus into a single perceptual and conceptual unity, while at the same time distributing a new network of pedestrian circulation from the building as part of the campus infrastructure.

III. In Defense of Style

The Cincinnati Recreation Center is perhaps the most accomplished exercise in a new coherence to be achieved in the discipline in recent years. Yet this achievement operates entirely at a manifest conceptual level. As one might a text, one reads the *tropes* (the football field turns into a new ground, the curvature of the classroom wing appears to be part of the original stadium architecture and at the same time mimics the Eisenman DAAP building nearby), *the formal relations* (the curve of the classroom

wing echoes the curvatures of the Gwathmey building and another across the street by Moore, Ruble & Yudell, the new housing block completes the forecourt to the Graves palazzo), and *the
material effects* (the exterior of the entire project, including the
roof, is made to match a ubiquitous slate-gray cladding specified by the master plan, amplifying the "soup" effect). In these
terms, the discursive contribution is as available to the intellect
in drawings and models as in the actual construction, with no
other reason to experience the building itself than to appreciate
the idea's consummate realization as best expression.

But there is another dimension to the building. An interesting feature of the enormous construction is the utter absence of
any iconic architectural presence of the nominal program, the
recreation center itself. Were it not for the expansive roofscape
and signage, one might not know it was there. The only strong
formal presences that are visible belong to the added program—
the housing and the classrooms. Like the entry to the Federal
Building, the anonymity of the recreation center heralds an in-
difference, neither hostile nor hospitable, to all of its users.

Entering the recreation center from "Main Street" immerses
one in a startling shift of magnitude and sensibility, as if transported from small town to future metropolis. The cartoon pleasantries of the campus, with its tree-lined walkways, garden
follies, and folksy street, are not just a different place from the
vast, infrastructural interior of the recreation center; they are a
different world. For the most part, commentary dismisses these
differences today as mere questions of style, yet it is in this world
shift that the conceptual achievement of a new coherence might
engender new organizational performances, giving rise to the
first answers to unaskable questions. For the concept-intuition,
effects are not enough; it is the qualities of effects that matter.

In *Renaissance and Baroque*, Heinrich Wölfflin broaches
the issue of why architecture changes style, offering a strong

argument to dispatch the two standard answers that neverthe-less still dominate the question today: that style responds to a zeitgeist as an expression of an age, or that style changes in re-sponse to boredom, to the jading effect of repetition. To advance his counter theory, he enlists the notion of painterliness to de-scribe baroque architecture's flaccidity as against Renaissance architecture's taut articulation. He associates these two distinct stylistic postures with what he suggests is architecture's higher vocation, to provide an ever more subtle model of the corporeal body in its relation to mind. It is fundamental that his is a the-ory of active participation rather than passive response, making style not merely decoration but the very instrument by which ar-chitecture effects changes in us and our world.

According to Wölfflin, the Renaissance's attention to part/whole harmonies yields exquisite awareness of the concinnities of our articulated anatomy when considered as an ideality. The baroque, on the other hand, portrays the ecstasies of an eccen-tric, fleshy body in motion, laboring against gravity:

> *While the Renaissance permeated the whole body with its feeling [of effortless, light-hearted resilience] . . . , the baroque luxuriated in unarticulated mass. One is more aware of the matter than the structure of the body and its articulation. . . . But this is only one aspect, for massiveness is complemented everywhere by violent and impetuous movement. . . . This movement became ever faster and more hasty. . . . At the same time, the limbs no longer move independently; the rest of the body is also drawn partially into the movement. This emotion of wild, ecstatic delight cannot be expressed uniformly by the whole body; emotion breaks out with violence in certain organs, while the rest of the body remains subject only to gravity.[7]*

Wölfflin's thesis is all the more interesting because it was written the same year that Freud, drawing on his work in Paris with the hypnotist Jean-Martin Charcot, made public his interpretation of the difference between hysterical and organic paralysis—an insight that the poet W. H. Auden deemed among the most important in history. Marveling at the power of hypnosis to temporarily relieve a hysterical paralysis of a patient's hand, Freud observed that only the hand below the wrist showed signs of atrophy from lack of use, while in a patient with organic paralysis, any anatomist would expect to see such atrophy as well in the arm muscles that control the hand. Freud proposed that in the hysteric, it was not the patient's anatomical hand but his mind's image of his hand that was paralyzed.

Let us suppose for sake of argument that the "hand" in the case of the hysteric would be a manifest discursive concept having found best expression (though erroneous from the point of view of anatomy) in the word. Indeed, it is so powerfully expressed that through language as its vector, a cultural discourse of the body has entered and taken over the body as if by metempsychosis, the transmigration of the soul—hence the interest of Auden the poet. Unconscious hysteria, on the other hand, would suggest something closer to the notion of an intuition-concept, because the patient's body would somehow have had to intuit the possibility of hysterical paralysis before it could be known as discursive knowledge.

Following the likes of Baruch Spinoza, Friedrich Nietzsche, and Fyodor Dostoevsky, Freud and many others after him would go on to braid the two great but incompatible existential strands of Western civilization—the clear reasoning of Enlightenment and the occult passions of the romantic—into that single, monstrous rope we are and call modern. From then on, we not only would have a single mind and body, but many minds—conscious and unconscious—and many bodies, all incoherent, all incommensurate, yet somehow converging into a singular manifold. The artistic, scientific, and philosophical intricacies of the psychosomatic would so burgeon in the twentieth century that today we have indeterminate numbers and kinds of bodies, from chemical bodies, elementary particle bodies, and savant bodies to bodies without organs and bodies that are eco-confederacies of hundreds of independent species.[8] What, then, is the legacy of Wölfflin's body in Morphosis's architecture?

IV. In Praise of Confusion

The naïveté of Wölfflin's conjecture lies in his assumption that there is a body as such that we can better discover through architecture. Since 1900, we have learned that there is a body, but it is not a thing—though, crucially, "it" always feels like one. Body is an agile, sensate multiplicity, ever roiling anew under a blitz of influences from discourses and practices each with a distinct palette of effects that leaves telltale traces. Not a sum, therefore, nor even a product nor a process, but a production. We have felt it as a concept-intuition for a long time across a dazzling range of cases: a cubist painting does not represent a revised understanding of the body; it revises the body.

Given the theoretical problems that the notion of the body has faced and the obvious relevance of the forces that shaped it, such as language, economics, technology, art, and social relations, discourse has for the most part turned its attention away from the body to undertake deeper studies of those impinging forces. Existential phenomenology was the one line of discourse to mount an effort to defend the body as the singular preintellectual possibility of all ensuing intellection, reaching its pinnacle in the writings of the French philosopher Maurice Merleau-Ponty. These writings have exercised considerable influence over many architects, including Mayne.

But one thinker, Gilles Deleuze, did grapple head-on with the confounded state of the modern body and its relationship to various practices. In his book *Francis Bacon: The Logic of Sensation*, the French philosopher states his case for the specificity of each discipline and its discourse: "The task of painting is defined as the attempt to render visible forces that are not themselves visible. Likewise, music attempts to render sonorous forces that are not themselves sonorous. That much is clear."[9] The extension we require, then, is obvious; the task of architecture is to render sensate the insensate forces to which it is most attuned. Force here includes the simple and obvious—weight, pressure, attraction—but also the more complex: history, politics, affects.

Then, in the chapter entitled "Hysteria," Deleuze takes up the relationship between this view of artistic specificity and the sensate body, positioning the argument against Merleau-Ponty's phenomenology:

> The phenomenological hypothesis is perhaps insufficient [to the problem of specificity] because it merely invokes the lived body. . . . [But] painting gives us eyes all over: in the ear, in the stomach, in the lungs. . . . But in the end, why should all this be peculiar to painting? . . . Why could not music also extricate pure presences, but through an ear that has become a polyvalent organ for sonorous bodies? And why not poetry and theater? . . . This problem concerning the essence of each art, and possibly their clinical essence, is less difficult than it seems to be. Certainly music traverses our bodies in profound ways, putting an ear in the stomach, in the lungs, and so on. It knows all about waves and nervousness.[10]

To give this passage its due, it is essential to read it not as a metaphorical description but as a description of fact, one that comes to rest just at the verge of a new account of our body. To any readers accepting the challenge, the word *confused* may never air, but will always linger just out of earshot, precisely because "confusion" is its creative conceptual adventure. Our manifold, sensate body is nothing other than a con-fusion of all the bodies we have named and all those that architects have and will produce. Here it may be useful to recall that when the verb *confuse* first appeared in the fourteenth century, it meant *to mix or mingle things so as to render the elements indistinguishable*. Only in 1800 did an additional sense of the word take root: *discomfit in mind*.

But let us trust that etymological evolution and not choose between the two senses of the term; let us instead embrace them both, for have we not been talking about both from the very beginning of these reflections? After all, what is it to create a "new coherence" other than *to mix or mingle things so as to render the elements indistinguishable*, and what can an answer that does not yet know its question feel like other than *a discomfiting in mind*? Thus the legacy of Wölfflin's body: confusion; and to find an affirmation of that body, then, is Morphosis's adventure.

Epilogue: A Brief Note on the Phare Tower in Paris

It is meaningless coincidence, a mere trick of the text, that Morphosis's first major high-rise, the Phare Tower, should appear in the context of this essay to have anything to do with the body, that the fact of it being sliced flat on one side and voluptuous on the other should remind us of Damien Hirst's *Mother and Child (Divided)*. Even if it seems to harbinger a shift in the architect's sensibility—less robotic, more organic—that swerve has been under way for some time and is already conspicuous in the Wayne Lyman Morse Courthouse. In fact, Morphosis's work has been moving inexorably toward this design for more than a decade in its desire to accumulate as design influences as many of the urban flows and contextual forces as possible, to melt together

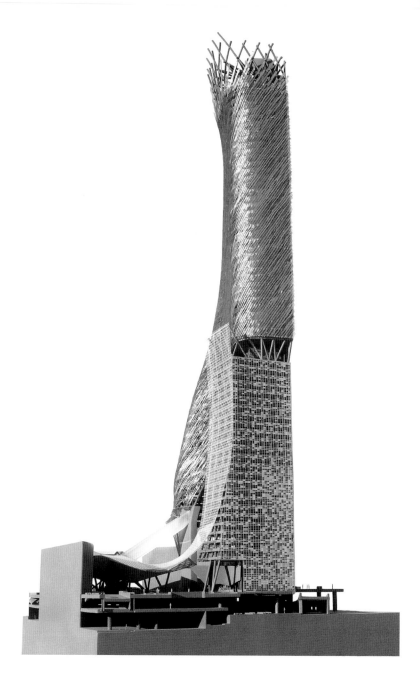

1.6
Morphosis, Phare Tower, Paris. Model.
Photo: Michael Powers.

1.7
Damien Hirst, *Mother and Child (Divided)*,
Exhibition Copy 2007 (original 1993), 2007.
Photographed by Prudence Cuming Associates.
© 2013 Damien Hirst and Science Ltd. All rights
reserved, DACS / ARS, NY.

1.8
John Hejduk, House of Suicide, 1980–1982.
Collection Centre Canadian d'Architecture / Canadian
Center for Architecture, Montreal.

ground and building, and to make the building as intelligent as possible in its response to energy concerns by taking advantage of advanced design technology, such as the digital scripting of the skin, to optimize the building's response to sun and wind.

Moreover, should one have desired in passing to comment on the hypnotic, slightly disquieting corporeal qualities of the Phare Tower and the effects it might have on Parisians, not to mention those it will have on the unfortunate assortment of formal types that today circumscribe La Défense, one need not call on the body theories of Wölfflin, Freud, or Deleuze. It would have been enough simply to call out the tower's evocative reminiscence of John Hejduk's powerful architecture, whose aura could extend far into its environs wherever it might be located.

I do not know if Unger, Wölfflin, Deleuze, or Mayne are in any sense correct, or even what it would mean for them to be correct, but I feel that they are on a right track. I do know that no one with any sensitivity who encounters the work of Morphosis, Hejduk, Eisenman, Koolhaas, or any of the others mentioned in these remarks can sustain a credible argument that architecture should conceive itself strictly as a service. It seems beyond doubt that architecture entails ideas that shape who we are and who we are to become. Those ideas evolve in the discipline through an intricate circulation of vectors that includes written concepts and material, formal, and spatial effects that we call discourse. The singular architecture of Morphosis compels us to recognize the unique intelligence of intuition and the qualities it seeks out, and to incorporate these vectors, too, among the indispensable components of a conceptual framework.

2 EXILE ON RINGSTRASSE; EXCITATIONS ON MAIN STREET

I. Exile on Ringstrasse

What really matters about the architecture of Coop Himmelb(l)au is not what it means nor how it looks, but how it behaves. With behavior in mind, then, where do we begin? Two of Vienna's greats, Sigmund Freud and Otto Rank, suggest that birth trauma might be a good place to start, especially if the behavior in question is anxious or unruly. Let us see.

Pregnancy and Gestation

1960: Hans Hollein produces *Die Stadt* (The City), a drawing that seems to haunt the unconscious of Coop Himmelb(l)au to this day. '62: The Soviet Union and United States move to the brink of nuclear war over Cuba. '63: Hollein and Walter Pichler attack the functionalism of Arbeitsgruppe 4, and follow with an influential series of joint and individual conceptual projects and texts. '63–'68: The extraordinary Günther Feuerstein rekindles and fans the flames of experimental architecture in Austria with his club seminars, reintroducing historical discourse and the discredited modern internationalists with the same vigor as he approaches the then-current speculations of Superstudio and Archigram. Under his influence, students Wolf D. Prix and Helmut Swiczinsky travel to the Architectural Association in London. '65: Hans Hollein, Günther Feuerstein, Sokratis Dimitriou, Gustav Peichl, and Walter Pichler seize control of *Der Bau* from the technocratic functionalists and reintroduce historical, intellectual, and cultural discourse to the journal, reviving interest in Adolf Loos, Otto Wagner, Josef Hoffmann, Rudolph M. Schindler, Frederick Kiesler, Konstantin Melnikov, and others. '66: David Greene's Living Pod, Michael Webb's Cushicle, and other inflatables proliferate. '67: *Sergeant Pepper's Lonely Hearts Club Band*. Pot. Acid. *Bonnie and Clyde*.[1]

Labor Pains

January 1968: Hollein's explosive manifesto "Alles ist Architektur" appears in *Bau*. March '68: the group Utopie organizes the seminal inflatables exhibition, "Structures Gonflables," that draws a surreal but compelling equation between inflatable architecture and radical situationist-inspired political action.[2]

March 1968: Coop Himmelb(l)au is born from an inflatable uterus, The Cloud, amid the trauma. Vietnam War—the Tet offensive, My Lai massacre, General Nguyen Ngoc Loan shoots a Viet Cong prisoner in the head on the front page of every newspaper in the world. Worldwide antiwar demonstrations. U.S. civil rights riots. May. Red Army Faction. Martin Luther King Jr. and Bobby Kennedy assassinated, Andy Warhol shot. *Electric Ladyland. Beggars Banquet. Cheap Thrills. 2001: A Space Odyssey. Barbarella. Schamlos. Moos auf den Steinen*. Saddam Hussein seizes control of Iraq. Alexander Dubček's Prague Spring blossoms only to be smothered within months by 200,000 Warsaw Pact troops and 5,000 tanks. The Chicago Seven, Black Panthers. Student bloodbath in Mexico 10 days before the Summer Olympics. Marcel Duchamp and Yuri Gagarin die. Mao Zedong orders all intellectuals out of the cities to work in farms. The "concept album" kills the 45 rpm single.[3]

Vienna is one of the few European capitals that is mostly quiet during the May uprisings in Paris, London, New York, and elsewhere throughout the world, though Günter Brus began serving a

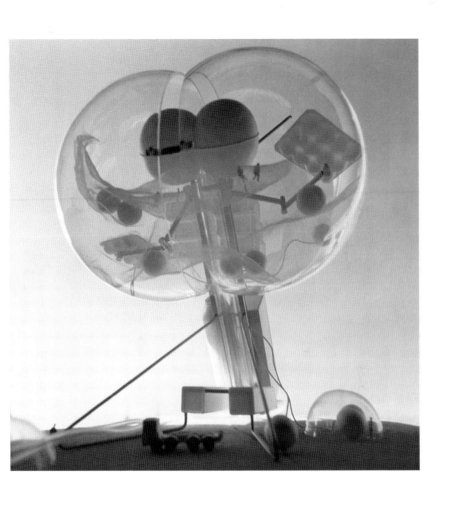

2.1
Coop Himmelb(l)au, The Cloud, 1968. Model. © Coop
Himmelb(l)au.

six-month prison sentence for the crime of "degrading symbols of the state" during the Kunst und Revolution event. Hollein and Peter Noever publish *Svobodair*, a tongue-in-cheek work of conceptual architecture in which a canister of Environmental Control Spray produces "good moods," thereby solving the problems of architecture's collaboration with offices and other suffocating social settings. 1969: a man on the moon, Woodstock, the first ATM. Altamont. The Internet begins.[4]

So, do we now understand the architecture of Coop Himmelb(l)au? The inflatables and public actions perhaps, maybe a little. The Cloud, Villa Rosa. Heart City—The White Suit. Action. Basel Kontakt. Supersommer. House with Flying Roof. How could they avoid it? The strange equation of happenings, street actions, inflatables, and pods was everywhere, in every major city, at the Osaka World's Fair, in movies, on TV. In a world paralyzed by fear, these were a better future become the present: plastic, technological, mobile, informal, personal, free of history's wrinkles and dust, free of corruption, of ideology, of arrogance, of fear. Free of gravity, in both senses of the word.

New York (1998):

> *"The Inflatable Moment"* . . . *celebrates a time when, if you didn't have an idea, you just didn't show up. You'd be too embarrassed. How different from today's climate of fear, when showing up with an idea could get you fired.*
>
> *Inflatable architecture, the show's subject, was a terrible idea, as it happens. . . . Yes, but so what? In those days, a terrible idea was better than no idea. At times, a bad idea was even better than a good idea. Architects at that moment were exploring the relationship between metaphor and material reality. There's nothing like a bad idea for showing up the difference between them.*[5]

But, then, why are they still at it today? When the madness of those times, delicious and horrifying, finally began to ebb, why did Coop Himmelb(l)au not disperse and fade away, as did most of the other architectural visionaries—Archigram, Utopie, Superstudio, Missing Link? Certainly, by the time they built the beautiful but oh-so-well-mannered exhibition pavilion/lounge for Cincinnati Milacron in 1974, the realities of the profession and fatal limitations of plastics and pods could not be ignored.

Clients were going to be wealthy, powerful, and politically established, buildings were not going to move or bounce, program was not going away, and neither the shape of a building nor the material it was made of were in and of themselves going to free anyone from anything. And more to the point, if they could not figure out how to cope with those realities without abandoning their naïve ambitions, there were plenty of architects with no qualms and ready to work.

Ever since, that has been what Coop Himmelb(l)au has been doing. In retrospect, Prix and Swiczinsky were less about inflatables as such than about any architecture capable of clearing a new space liberated from the burden of stale clichés and dead ideologies. Some indication of the direction that the practice would head also comes from the Cincinnati Milacron pavilion, not from the project itself but from its documentation. A short clip of the opening shows young Swiczinsky and Prix inside the space, talking, drinking, smoking cigarettes. If the image seems innocently staged, its message is prophetic, because from that point forward the two would concentrate strictly on the new sensations their architectural space could produce.

Maybe it was a mistake, then, to start with the traumas of their birth; perhaps we should have started earlier, with their heritage. But how far back: the Allied occupation, the Anschluss, Freud, the fin de siècle? No, none of these; too obvious, too broad. To 1857, then, when Franz Joseph wills into existence the

Ringstrasse? An ancient city wall disappears, only to be replaced by an urban manifestation of the strangely convoluted, porous barrier between ego and id/superego. Today, the Ringstrasse seems to draw the line between the possibilities of a confident Vienna that values the present as a step toward the future, and a bourgeois Vienna that wallows in petty gratifications and clichés of the past.

But how Coop Himmelb(l)au's work is in any sense Viennese is a different question. A city of imponderables, Vienna's spirit oscillates between extremes of depth and shallowness, between profound humanity and base antipathy. On the one hand, it has nurtured some of Western civilization's most humane talents, from Wolfgang Amadeus Mozart to Kurt Gödel, but on the other, it is notorious for the animosity it has shown toward the likes of Freud, Oskar Kokoschka, Gustav Mahler, Lise Meitner, Frederick Kiesler, Arnold Schönberg, Elfriede Jelinek, and others, all of whom it today claims with pride.

No wonder the psyches of some of its most adventurous architects are so knotted. After all, though buildings may be its paint and the city its canvas, it is the heart and will of collective life that is always the true subject matter of architecture. There is no such thing as a private house any more than there is such a thing as a private language—as Ludwig Wittgenstein taught us. Thus, whatever leap any architect hopes to make to a new space, it will always be to a new collective space that can only be reached from the old space the architect is formed in, knows, lives, and leaps from.

That Coop Himmelb(l)au is Viennese, therefore, must inhabit our thoughts even if we can never understand what that means, and it makes this first retrospective of their work in Vienna not just one exhibition among many.[6] All the more because it is at the MAK, toward which their work has always been destined. Yet, though all of the historical and psychological turmoil is ingrained in the architecture of Coop Himmelb(l)au, does it explain anything? Does it help us better grasp its behavior? Or have we made the mistake of confusing insights into the lives of the architects with insights into the performance of their architecture? To get inside these buildings requires a different strategy.

II. Excitations on Main Street

Strolling through the exhibition, one cannot help being struck by the sheer quantity of invention Coop Himmelb(l)au has produced, suggesting that Prix and Swiczinsky indulge an insatiable appetite for novelty. Because of that and the raucous audacity of their architecture, Coop Himmelb(l)au is often treated by international critics like some kind of rock and roll practice: born of raw talent, fueled by iconoclasm, sustained by bravado, and rescued by daring leaps of building technique, a bunch of guys always on the lookout for a bigger amplifier. That view is no doubt reinforced by the offhand image so carefully cultivated by front man Prix in lectures and other public appearances, not to mention the fact that a call to the studio inevitably yields a few seconds of the Stones' "Gimme Shelter" while one waits on hold. To be sure, when they nail it, their architecture is visceral—nothing to explain, no panel discussions necessary. Like lightning storms, hard drugs, fast cars, and kickin' music, it sends waves of commotion through us. Depending on the particular nervous system under assault, those waves either thrill or agonize, nothing in between. But unlike the selfish rush of a line of coke or hauling ass on the autobahn, the euphoria of Coop Himmelb(l)au's architecture belongs to a different order of time, space, and collective life.[7]

Though trite, the comparison with life in the fast lane does call attention to certain assumptions implicit in the work: that it wants to produce sensations instead of interpretations, that it prefers now to then, and that it thrives on the promiscuous energies of the city as such, with little patience for pastoral serenity or the pleasantries of place. Above all, a Coop Himmelb(l)au building refuses predetermination, refuses, that is, to be justified by allegiance to precedent or context or even the program that gives rise to it. Above all, their buildings want to appear in the world as unaligned moments able to stake their architectural claims entirely on the potentialities they bring to a situation.

Because it will not gratify conventional expectations, the architecture of Coop Himmelb(l)au causes us to grab onto anything to help understand it, and so we all—expert and layperson alike—often resort to visual analogy: it looks like an insect! a wing! an act of violence! a hurricane! All of these are evocative, even true. They capture well, for example, the work's avoidance of familiar architectural signs and symbols, its tempestuous passions and urge to take flight from the ground, and its reliance on process-based gestural abstraction. On the other hand, such analogies underestimate the coherent architectural intelligence that has run through the work from its beginning, the single thread that elevates its excitations from the realm of erotic pleasure to the realm of political exhilaration, all the while making use of the fact that the two—the erotic and the political—are but front and back of the one mirror we see ourselves in. Thus, these analogies do very little to help us probe the deeper aspirations vested in the work.

For instance, a cursory overview of the four decades of work deriving from such visual analogies suggests that it settles loosely into four stylistic periods: bubbles (1968–1980), wings (1980–1990), wrecks (1990–1997), and fog banks (1997–present). For convenience, let us use The Cloud, the Open House, the Groninger Museum, and the Musée des Confluences in Lyon to represent each period respectively. Though each appears unrelated to the others, they are in fact the first evidence of a single genetic thread passing through all, like DNA through related species, a thread that evolves over time at the

2.2
Coop Himmelb(l)au, The Open House, Malibu,
1988–1989. © Coop Himmelb(l)au.

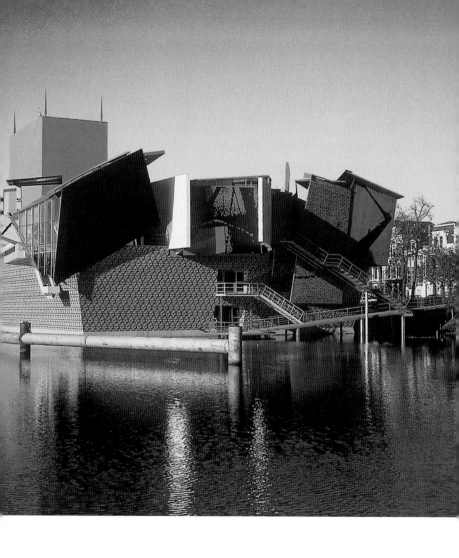

2.3
Coop Himmelb(l)au, Groninger Museum, Groningen,
1994. © Coop Himmelb(l)au.

intersection between the increasing skill and sophistication of the practitioners and the changes that occur around them in technology, in the discipline, and in the world at large.

To comb out that thread, we need to look for hints and clues, such as unexpected similarities between projects, as if we were biologists doing comparative anatomy. For example, certain views of the models of the Open House and the Musée des Confluences appear virtually identical, though the two buildings are vastly different and separated by decades.

Oddly enough, aspects of the Groninger Museum and the Open House are also very similar, though Groninger seems irreconcilable with Lyon. The Cloud just appears to defeat any such study. But then, if we compare it with Lyon by looking more closely at the two interiors, we find another, different set of familial traits. In each, sinuous tissues of circulation that call to mind Kiesler's seminal Endless House swirl like puffs of cigarette smoke around smaller forms, forming spheres in The Cloud and more incongruous figures in Lyon. Place ZAK—Zukunftsakademie, Haslau, Austria, between them, and it is as if it is the missing link in the evolution of the one into the other.[8]

More and more, The Cloud, the Open House, and Lyon unfold as increasingly complex variations on a theme: a diaphanous membrane that envelopes independent objects scattered in its interior amid circuitous paths of circulation.

What, then, are we to make of the menagerie of awkward, off-balance prisms and cones that seem to show up out of nowhere in the mid-1990s and come to dominate such works as the Expo.02 Forum Arteplage in Biel?

Sometimes opaque, sometimes transparent, they are almost always cinched at the waist into doubled cones and other figures strangely reminiscent of chess pieces. Once we get the hang of spotting them, they show up everywhere, as far back as the early 1990s and up to the current day. We find them in every possible

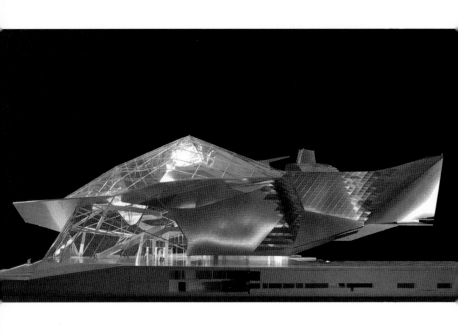

2.4
Coop Himmelb(l)au, Musée des Confluences, Lyon,
2001–2010. Model. © Markus Pillhofer/Vienna.

size and orientation, in whole and part; over, under, sideways, and down. Clip out the right side of the double cone in Biel and it becomes the form of the housing complex added to the Gasometer redevelopment in Vienna, while the fog banks of Lyon and BMW Welt drift over clusters of these figures as if on a miniature city. As basic formal material goes, these shapes come to be in the work of Coop Himmelb(l)au what the I, IV, and V chords in open G tuning are to Keith Richards's guitar playing, and it is astonishing how many riffs and how much expressive range each artist can extract from such a simple set.

The basic geometries of these shapes may tempt us to recall Paul Cézanne's remark about the invisible scaffolding of cones and cylinders that underlies nature, but that would be a mistake. There are no smaller, simpler parts to these; they are not forms but animate figures. We cannot unstack or divide them without killing them; their poses are irreducible, their dance unstoppable. The mongrel fruit of an illicit union between the contemporary urban body and the modern building (which, we must admit, always has had a stick up its ass), they are architectural hip-hop; they lighten us up, make us smile. But sculptural energy is just the beginning of their capacities.

A first clue to the more occult powers of these figures comes again from circulation. In Lyon, in addition to the sinuous ribbons already mentioned, we find a sharp hairpin staircase, whose switchback landing floats in midair, staging views into the space—exactly as the switchback staircase does in the Open House. The acute angle formed by these staircases finds its way into the plan of Groninger, where it carves the floor away from the wall to create dizzying overlooks.

The rich effects produced by the discontinuities inherent in that acute angle make it one of the keys to this architecture, wherever it is found: it is visually provocative, giving rise to all the metaphors of violence and damage one finds in the discussion of Coop Himmelb(l)au. It cuts into the space that surrounds it or compresses it when juxtaposed incongruently to another form or object. Whether walking on it as circulation or next to it as form, we are always on edge, off balance, a little afraid, subject to a confusing overload of sensations as exciting vistas distract our attention from sharp turns and unexpected confrontations. That very sense of edginess and fear of the unknown awaiting us around a sharp corner provoked the reactionary English critic Roger Scruton to whine about the modern city and long nostalgically for onion-domed corners gently curved to allay our fears about what was coming, that is, about the future. The thrill of an unknown future in a fearless city that thrives on adventure, on the other hand, is what Prix and Swiczinsky are all about.

These strange figures, then, are the result of an evolution in which the floating single-celled spheres inside The Cloud slowly merge with the zigzag and winding circulation devices into new organisms, architecturalizations of the city not just as image but as sounds, rhythms, and sensations. As we move nearer to the discomforts of their bizarre adjacencies and beyond into their interstitial voids, we feel them and hear them as they thicken the space from a passive vacuum to a viscous fluid that pushes and pulls us with pressures, currents, and eddies; sex as city, city as sex.

But there is another dimension to the long continuous thread that is as important to the behavior of these works as the formal relations, one that operates out of sight. In the Falkestrasse rooftop remodeling, forces flow along a spider web of steel from a spring beam whose curvature strains to hold the roof taut. The arch of the beam in the rooftop office derives not from structural principles but from the design process that generated it—one of the notorious "psychograms," a kind of automatic drawing Prix and Swiczinsky borrowed from early avant-garde practices to free themselves from habits and preconceptions. Frantic spasms of the wrist rather than a desire to generate any

2.5
Coop Himmelb(l)au, Expo.02, Forum Arteplage, Biel,
1999–2002. © Gerald Zugmann / www.zugmann.com.

particular image gave rise to those projects whose contours seem winglike.

Coop Himmelb(l)au's psychogram technique began as a way to free architecture from clichés, a renunciation of design methods seen by Prix and Swiczinsky as serving discredited institutions and authorities. But their vow to will the psychogram into building without simplification required them to push structure and materials to new frontiers. By forcing themselves out of their own comfort levels with building, they learned how to amplify the dynamic tensions of a space, must as Jimi Hendrix learned how to use feedback. Indeed, the use of strain for artistic effect is well known in music. When Marvin Gaye arrived to record "I Heard It through the Grapevine," producer Norman Whitfield transposed the music, forcing the singer to sing above his range of comfort. Gaye was furious, but the angry, bereft sound achieved is today legend. Perhaps a better musical analogy is to be found in *The Rite of Spring*, where Igor Stravinsky strained the orchestra to its limits, pushing its instruments to the extreme heights and depths of their ranges and contorting the musicians into uncomfortable positions. The carnal sounds and bestial rhythms he discovered changed music forever by transforming the erotic into the political, as evidenced by the riot that erupted within the audience at its debut. Why political? Because the audience came to the concert more or less like members of a political party, a complacent group who convened to let the familiarities of ballet confirm their shared values and sentiments. When the music and dance refused to behave, arousing ecstasy in some, revulsion in others, and passions in all, the self-satisfied unity atomized into unforeseeable groups held together by unpredictable feelings and thoughts, each member reborn as a reflecting individual.[9]

Larger buildings and more complex programs eventually exhausted the usefulness of the psychogram, but its material lessons were well learned. Coop Himmelb(l)au emerged from its tutelage to stand as the field's most accomplished experts in the use of a building's raw physicality to stir intoxicating martinis of contemporary space. As we enter the UFA Cinema Center in Dresden, we feel the leaning glass envelope glibly refuse gravity's demands; in Munich, where a massive cloud of steel and glass floats overhead on impossibly few columns, we hear the songs of the vortices of force pour through the steel of BMW Welt's gigantic double cone.

Above all, what makes Coop Himmelb(l)au's space feel like now is that the cumulative effect of all of the intensities and sensations is not weight, but exhilarating buoyancy that feels like license, like liberty. The first thing you want to do in a Coop Himmelb(l)au building is to light a cigarette, maybe have a drink and talk to someone—even if you don't drink or smoke. That is no small achievement when one considers that the greatest of all of architecture's social achievements—from the ancient to the neomodern—is to impose silence, which it can solicit with miraculous range: contemplation, awe, reverie, amazement, wonder, tranquillity, stillness. But silence and repose, no matter how serene, no matter how blissful, are still the stuff of obedience.

Epilogue: The MAK Installation

These few remarks have strived to call attention to the thread of coherence that runs through the apparent variety in the four decades of Coop Himmelb(l)au's work on display in order to foreground the intelligence of the architecture and to demonstrate its unfaltering commitment to a political project achieved through sensations produced by architectural space. But the occasional metaphor likening that thread to DNA has been employed for an ulterior motive. DNA enjoys an unequaled power to respond creatively to new circumstances, but it also endows a profound coherence upon the extraordinary diversity of species that fill the niches of any ecosystem. Every animal that walks, crawls, or flies on earth, including you and me, shares the same body plan—essentially that of a worm. The ulterior motive, therefore, is to suggest that when all of Coop Himmelb(l)au's work is brought together, its internal coherence begins spontaneously to link the works together into a new kind of urban network whose more complex space might be as liberating as the buildings themselves.

To call attention to that possibility, rather than to focus on the chronology of individual buildings, the curators of the exhibition have gathered the work together on a great chessboard. The idea of the chess table derived from a lecture by Prix on the unacceptable state of urban planning and architecture's responsibility to proffer viable alternatives, a lecture in which the grid of the chessboard transformed into a digital field to represent the incapacity of old regimes to meet the spatial demands or to take advantage of the spatial possibilities of the digital age, while the three chess pieces—the queen, the bishop, and the knight—represented the power of architecture to make creative leaps of imagination and respond affirmatively to the new situation, and of course echoed Coop Himmelb(l)au's hip-hop shapes.

To organize the city, the curators turned to the architects' competition-winning urban plan for Melun-Sénart, "The Heart of the City," as a guide. It asks, if the Melun-Sénart scheme had been realized, how it might feel to be there today. Cities, after all, evolve over time, nurture striking changes in building form and construction technology, and endure extreme disjunctions in scales and sensibilities. The installation constitutes an explicit critique by Coop Himmelb(l)au of urban planning today, with its anemic catalogs of formal typology, materials, ornamentation, and trite clichés of public space, by demonstrating how easy it would be to make something much better, if only we had the courage.

3 ... AND THEN, SOMETHING MAGICAL

*The Nelson-Atkins Museum of Art has picked American architect
Steven Holl, widely considered a rising star in the profession, to
design an $80 million addition to the original 1933 building. . . .
"At the end of the day, this stood out as something that was magical,"
Nelson-Atkins director Marc Wilson said of the Holl scheme.*
—Kansas City Star, July 8, 1999

Even if you have never been to Kansas City and your only experience of Steven Holl and Chris McVoy's[1] design for an addition
to the Nelson-Atkins Museum comes from the photographs you
are browsing, you can still sense how prophetic Marc Wilson's
remark was. There *is* something magical about the architecture.
Most obviously, the Bloch Building enchants the night as its
stark floes of frozen light, afloat on swells of landscape, draft
the darkness into a chiaroscuro so vast that it cannot exist, still
so real that you can touch it. Yet that act of wizardry is but one of
many the architecture performs, and, if the most stunning, not
nearly the most fascinating.

For those familiar with the Nelson-Atkins collection, the
building's operatic night countenance may bring to mind a similar drama of darkness and light staged in Caravaggio's painting
Saint John the Baptist in the Wilderness. If so, then another of the
powers of the building will have already begun to unfold; we can

get a hint of it with a little trick of our own. First, let us read a portion of the description that accompanies the painting, one of the museum's most prized masterpieces:

> [Caravaggio] has literally stripped the Baptist of nearly all traditional attributes (halo, lamb and banderole inscribed Ecce Agnus Dei or Behold the Lamb of God), leaving the brooding intensity of his emotional state as the subject of the painting. Saint John's solemn pensiveness is reinforced by a Caravaggio trademark: the dramatic contrast of deep, opaque shadows, playing across the body and shrouding the sockets of the eyes, with a bright light that illuminates the Baptist from above and to his right. This stark contrast of light and darkness, the brilliant scarlet of the saint's cloak and Caravaggio's placement of him in the foreground close to our own space, all contribute to the dramatic impact of the painting.

Now, on a whim, let us revise the passage ever so slightly:

> Holl has literally stripped the building of nearly all the traditional attributes of a museum, leaving only the emotional intensity of its mute light forms. The ensemble's taut silence is reinforced by a trademark of Caravaggio: the dramatic contrast of deep, opaque shadows with bright light. This stark contrast of light and darkness staged on a draped cloak of landscape, the scattered placement of the addition's abstract forms so close to the original building, all contribute to the dramatic impact of the architecture.

3.1
Michelangelo Merisi, called Caravaggio, *Saint John the Baptist in the Wilderness*, 1604–1605. Courtesy The Nelson-Atkins Museum of Art.

3.2
Steven Holl Architects, The Nelson-Atkins Museum
expansion, Kansas City, 2007. © Andy Ryan.

How Buildings Speak to Us (A Brief Aside)

Broadly speaking and independent of aesthetic issues, architectural history has developed three distinct approaches to consider the ways in which architecture can say something about the world: intellectual, social, and phenomenological. An intellectual approach conceives of the building as an object of formal contemplation that communicates through conscious understanding and interpretation. For example, one might understand a shift or rotation in the building as completing patterns or making alignments with other features in the context. The social approach focuses on how a building communicates through its institutional role. Should an art museum resemble a temple, a palace, or a warehouse? There is no correct answer. Rather, each is an option that speaks differently about the nature of art and our relation to it, and all are at work in the Nelson-Atkins expansion.

The phenomenological approach sees the building as a knot of blended perceptions that communicate simultaneously through sensation, intuition, and comprehension to produce a place in the world. To an architect so inclined, even the echo of footfall on paving stone is important, not as pure experience, but as a contribution to place in all of its specificities. In a cathedral, it engenders meditative solitude, in a court of law, respectful obedience, on a dark and abandoned city street, fear. While every building contains aspects of all three of these approaches, architects disposed to explore new possibilities tend to bias their speculations toward one or another. In the case of Steven Holl, the architect is strongly inclined toward the phenomenological.

The term *phenomenology* is used somewhat differently in architecture than it is in philosophy, where the architectural connotation is more akin to existential phenomenology. The architectural sense of the term derives primarily from the writings of philosophers Martin Heidegger and Maurice Merleau-Ponty. Because Holl draws heavily on the latter rather than the former, a brief excursion into the differences between the two might shed some light on the architect's work in the Nelson-Atkins expansion.

In elementary terms, Heidegger distinguishes the authentic being of our world from its appearances, which he sees as fraught with inauthenticity. For example, he finds in the lure of technology an escape into inauthenticity, and seeks to return our lives to a more genuine relationship with the world of being. Merleau-Ponty rejects his colleague's position that meaning and authenticity arise from a metaphysical relationship between appearances and being, preferring to inquire how these evolve from the perceptions of a body living in a world as phenomena. To ground his discourse thoroughly in perceptions, he discusses the interplay of things, experiences, and ideas in terms of the *visible* and *invisible*, emphasizing the way these two interact with and change each other, calling attention to what he calls the "profound carnality of their doubling." In this view, meaning and the material world are inherent in each other.

Above all, Merleau-Ponty affirms the primacy of a preintellectual kinship between us and the world of perception that is more fundamental than our thinking capacities. He holds that at any point in time, the human situation is a product of both the mind and sociohistorical circumstance, implying, in contrast to Heidegger, that everyday life might collaborate with the forces of change to produce new authenticities of a different order, existential authenticities as deep-seated and timeless as "being" in its own way, yet inseparable from history and place. Because intellectual thought in and of itself can never apprehend such an authenticity, the ineluctable role of the arts in any quest to catch awareness of this elusive prize becomes evident.

Yet who is to say which aspects of life at any moment are authentic and which are not? How can one possibly tell at what point technology, commerce, media, and all of the other dizzying sources of change in our lives have given rise to a new and genuine authenticity, when they seem inexorably to lead us away from authenticity as such? Surely in the century since its invention, incandescent lighting has become for us a new kind of natural light, its 60-cycle-per-second song—B-flat two octaves below middle C—as much a part of our nature as its signature yellow. But are the social networks now proliferating on the Internet also authentic, when face-to-face social encounters were once the sine qua non of an authentic community? It is precisely the fascinating uncertainties contained in such questions that motivate the speculative design decisions of architects like Holl.

From a historical perspective, of course, a comparison of two such disparate works is mere caprice. Yet if we linger on the Caravaggio painting and an aerial view of the museum addition, we see that the conversation between the two continues well beyond the play of light and dark, reaching to the respective forms, organization, and sense of space. If we let our imagination run free, we can picture the original building as the Baptist's head, the new addition as his left arm, and the great lawn as his chest. The staid neoclassical facade seems to mirror the pensive symmetry of darkened eyes above a highlighted, aquiline nose. The shoulder hunching toward the head suggests the tense crowding of the original by the addition, while the sequence of overlit muscles in the arm becomes the new building's "lenses," the form of the last lens reiterating the bend of the arm at the elbow. Even the terraces of the great lawn reverberate in the Baptist's rib-rippled chest.

Holl names the five structures that dance across the site "lenses" to stir us from our habitual expectations of a building and to cue us to the new experiences and thoughts he wants the new addition to engender. Indelibly linked to vision, the notion of a lens calls attention to the fact that the structures we see are not—despite appearances—independent pavilions, but exaggerated clerestories of a single building that capture light and transmit it to the galleries below; in that sense, the term *lens* is perhaps not so far afield after all. The word reminds us, too, that art is never a practice of representation, but is itself a particular lens through which we see irreproducible and original views of life. Most of all, the term speaks to the building's obsession with light, which is at work in myriad subtle ways every moment of the day, in every location and at every scale, nudging us sotto voce toward the art we have come to see.

As we further explore the architecture, other conversations between the building and works of art will attract our attention. Indeed, an integral part of the architecture itself is a new artwork that graces the reflecting pool, *One Sun / 34 Moons*, by Walter De Maria in collaboration with Steven Holl. As fun as it will be to eavesdrop on these, however, they cannot be the most important of its relationships—after all, the Bloch joins not only an institution with a staff and a beautiful existing building, but a local community and a city. It joins as well the history and current practice of architecture, and in the end participates in the world at large. It enters into dialogs in each and every one of these arenas; but, since the same is true for every building, the multiplicity of its conversations is not what makes its architectural achievement so extraordinary. Rather, its special magic derives from what it has to say, and even more from how it goes about saying it.

We have already noticed that the Bloch possesses none of the symbolic trappings that architects customarily use to identify an important civic or cultural edifice, such as those so in evidence in the majestic neoclassical facade of the 1933 Nelson-Atkins Museum. With the exception of the two revolving doors at the front entry off the fountain plaza, which from a distance appear to be oversized column stubs—a nod to the great columnar entrance of its elder colleague—the new wing not only lacks a ceremonial facade but even an exterior marquee bearing its name.

Just as Caravaggio humanizes John and thus makes his spiritual struggle more palpable, Holl relaxes the formality of the museum to sponsor a more personal rapport between viewer and art. In contrast, the older building does everything in its power to engender a distanced formality between the two, in keeping with the custom of its time. In her book *The Nelson-Atkins Museum of Art*, Kristie Wolferman makes it clear that the benefactors, trustees, and architects who midwifed the museum all wanted the building be "part monument, part temple of art."[2]

Although the grand bearing and hallowed tone projected by the neoclassical architecture of the 1933 building might seem to some overly affected today, those traits were not merely custom but de rigueur for civic museums in the United States at the time. Wolferman traces this stylistic imperative to the triumph of New York's Metropolitan Museum of Art and lists some twenty-two American museums—from Boston to Cleveland to Omaha—built under its sway. Even though architecture's modern movement was by then already in full blossom as the International Style, the United States would not see a modern museum until 1939, when Edward Durell Stone's Museum of Modern Art opened in New York.

To design the original Nelson-Atkins, Thomas Wight, principal of the Kansas City firm Wight and Wight, turned to the Cleveland Museum of 1916 as a model. The resemblance between the two buildings and their settings is quite striking, except that the Cleveland is built of white marble while the Nelson-Atkins is in limestone, making the comparison an object lesson on the effects of materiality. In 1970, the Cleveland expanded with a program similar to that of the Bloch and chose Marcel Breuer, best known for his Whitney Museum of American Art in New York, to design the addition. Breuer, a staunch advocate of modern architecture's rejection of historical styles, was the preeminent practitioner in the United States of a subgenre of modern architecture named brutalism, after its predilection for austere geometry built in raw concrete or rough-hewn stone. In a tour de force of architectural one-upmanship, Breuer effectively relegated the 1916 Cleveland building to the status of picture postcard kitsch by erecting a modern monument so powerful that it confiscated the dignity of the original.

Two artists similarly discomfited by the pretensions of the original Nelson-Atkins Museum and grounds are the team Claes Oldenburg and Coosje van Bruggen, whose large-scale sculpture *Shuttlecocks* lampoons not so much the building's style as its social implications, in the great tradition of political satire. In so doing, the artists revisit a long-standing debate in the arts over whether or not a symbolic form is indelibly wed to its original content. Unwilling to dissociate the neoclassical architecture from its affiliation to the class-based society in which it originated, the artists level a mischievous critique at it. In part the sculpture's jab at wealth and power is made broadly in the name of democracy (though with some tongue in cheek, given badminton's own class associations). But more to the point, it is a jab at the mien of authority the building conveys, made in defense of the right of each of us to expect our opinion to be valued when it comes to art.

However one feels about *Shuttlecocks*, one cannot deny the economy of its critical genius. When its burlesque on scale and manners casts the art, the garden grounds, and the building as a badminton court, it unites all three of the major public components of the institution as a single target in its crosshairs. If nothing else, it reminds us that very few art institutions have so interwoven their architecture, grounds, and art into one social experience as the Nelson-Atkins, a fact that will grow in significance as we turn back to the Bloch.

If in his approach to the original building Holl identifies with Breuer's modernist bent and joins Oldenburg and van Bruggen's egalitarian advocacy, his design for the new addition does so not in the spirit of competition or critique but with tender cunning,

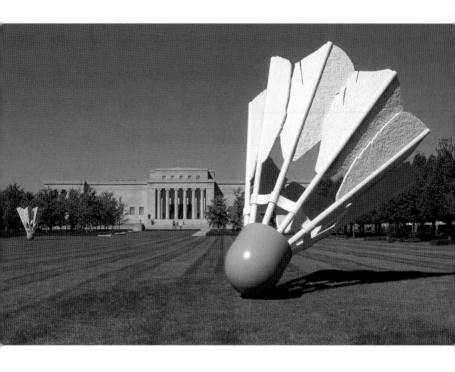

3.3
The Kansas City Sculpture Park at The Nelson-Atkins
Museum of Art, including two of four *Shuttlecocks*,
1994, by Claes Oldenburg and Coosje van Bruggen.
Courtesy The Nelson-Atkins Museum of Art. Photo:
Louis Meluso.

one of the work's hallmark achievements. The architecture uses submissiveness, flattery, and gifts to seduce the original institution into a new political posture and a more contemporary attitude in its presentation of the collection. With a few sleights of hand so brilliant-quick that they are all but impossible to catch, he turns the Wight building into both a partner and a new work of art, an unexpected "recent acquisition" for the collection.

Just consider the episode that occurs when one climbs the staircase from the gardens to the narrow gap between the first lens and the east facade of the old building. Coming from the gardens, already receptive to viewing things as sculpture, we climb toward an Ionic column of the original building framed as sculpture, with the staircase landing its pedestal. It is reminiscence in miniature of the notorious staging of the *Nike of Samothrace* on the Daru staircase in the Louvre.[3] The proximity of the old and new buildings at this point compresses the viewer close to the column, insisting on attention to the bracelet of Egyptian lotus ornament etched at the bottom of the shaft of the columns. The column has never been so lovely, particularly if one remembers that before the addition, the base of these columns stood twelve feet off the ground, landing above the entry doors to the east wing.

This difference in approach is part and parcel of the distinction between a conceptual and a phenomenological work. For *Shuttlecocks* to perform at a political level, its message must be read and understood. Holl's architecture, on the other hand, works its wiles more patiently, weaving an intricate tapestry of perceptions and intuitions with meditation and flashes of insight. Every ounce of the expansion—from the parking lot to the galleries to the grass mounds and walkways—plays an important part, as does every mood, thought, and manner of attention it solicits from a visitor. On the one hand, it assists the traditional modes of close attention associated with the institution:

the alert scrutiny of the critic, the passionate concentration of the connoisseur, or the remove of the historian. But it also supports modes of attention loosened from objectivity, to wander aimlessly in reverie and daydream. Misunderstanding, confusion, even utter distraction have their place here alongside understanding and concentration. As a result, in the expanded museum politics recedes as a distinct polemic to become instead part of a new way of being in the world, one in which the freedom from unwarranted authority is felt as much as understood.

The Gifts

About a year before joining the original building at its side, the Bloch sent tributes, a beautiful plaza and reflecting pool, Walter De Maria's *One Sun / 34 Moons*, and a new underground parking facility. In addition to their undeniable value, these shrewd gifts helped set the stage for an amiable relationship between the two.

When in 1829 Johann Wolfgang von Goethe called architecture frozen music, he inscribed one of the most enduring platitudes about any art form into our cultural consciousness. If threadbare, it still rings with truth, particularly when one thinks of classical styles in both arts—the rousing overture of facades, the rhythms of regal symmetries, the intricate counterpoint of plans, and the symphonic climaxes of spaces as superbly portrayed in Wight's rendition of the original Nelson-Atkins Museum. The plaza and reflecting pool fit easily into the neoclassical style of Wight's edifice, and begin the process of creating for it a stately forecourt that the first lens of the Bloch would complete upon arrival. As long as the first lens faces the plaza, it maintains the orthogonal rectitude appropriate to the formal setting, and its entry facade completes the east boundary of the forecourt otherwise bounded by the north facade of the Wight building and 45th Street. Only after the first lens slips past the plaza and begins the journey toward the garden does it relax.

3.4
View to the southeast of J. C. Nichols Plaza, including
One Sun / 34 Moons, 2002, by Walter De Maria. Courtesy
The Nelson-Atkins Museum of Art. Photo: Roland Halbe.

As twentieth-century architects grew more interested first in democracy and eventually in the question of individuality, a few were drawn to the energy and intimacies of bodies in motion. Their architecture assumed more the character of modern dance, as if each building froze a moment in the angular frenzy of a Merce Cunningham or William Forsythe performance.

The figure of the frozen moment is not incidental, because one desire of such architecture is to convey the sense that, like each of us, a building is never complete but always in the process of becoming. When, after taking leave from the forecourt, the forms of Holl's five lenses loosen up and jitterbug down the hill, they invoke that legacy. On the facades of the lenses, lines of metal channel appear like stringcourses on the otherwise mute exterior, the result of length limitations on the translucent glass planks. The architect breaks the continuation of those lines to suggest faults and fissures, further amplifying the impression that the forces shaping the lenses are very much still at work.

Actually, the plaza and reflecting pool take the first step of the dance when together they shift off the center axis of Wight's facade toward the Bloch. That shift refocuses attention from the original building alone to the relationship between it and its new partner, but a pivotal second step is taken when the rectangular yellow platform of De Maria's "sun" pushes the shift even more idiosyncratically toward the southeast corner of the pool. The drive of that move, directed toward the narrow gap where the Bloch and the original building meet, becomes the first strain of music that sets the forms of the lenses into motion.

If one imagines that the shifts of the pool and artwork exert a simple force on the first lens and that its walls might be able to move, one sees that the effect of that force is to push on the south end of the lens, causing it to rotate away from the orthogonal geometry established by the forecourt. Because cause and effect are so legible, an architectural purist would use a set of analytic devices, termed "diagrammatic formalism," to read these dynamics, but the metaphor of dance here serves our needs perfectly well.

Holl uses the various shifts on the plaza to connect the two buildings while allowing the public to glimpse the process, but at the same time engages his formalist colleagues in a conversation about the causal legibility they champion. After the first lens, the subsequent lenses assume such manifold eccentricity that one cannot hope to account for them adequately with the techniques of formalist reading. It is as if Holl the phenomenologist is saying to his formalist colleagues that the relevance of strict legibility ends on the plaza; beyond it, in the garden, the intuitive form of each lens evokes the untold influences that shape an individual personality.

De Maria's wise *One Sun / 34 Moons* adds its two cents to the conversation, of course. Amid the bliss of its too many moons, the sun rises from the water, bulging against the strictures of the foolish geometry imposed upon it. It consents to reason for the time being, as an adult does to a child at play, knowing full well the folly of intellect's ambition to comprehend an infinitely wondrous cosmos.

But the artwork has other important jobs to do. Belonging at once to the museum's collection and to its architecture, to the old building and the new, to the underground parking structure and to the plaza, it is key to the addition's search for a new inclusiveness. It helps produce one of the most magical of its architectural effects to that end: a new roof for the museum—not a literal roof, but a phenomenal one, every bit as real, that spans the entire site from 45th Street to Emanuel Cleaver II Boulevard. With this roof, the old Nelson-Atkins building, front lawn, and back gardens all disappear into a Nelson-Atkins Museum that one is always inside wherever one is—in the garage, on the plaza, in a gallery of one wing or another, or strolling in the gardens.

Much goes into the construction of such a fantastic roof, such as the cascade of translucent lenses south into the gardens where they become sculptures in the collection during the day and lamps in the museum space at night. The connection between the Bloch and the original building dissolves a strong sense of entering and exiting, as does the porosity of the Bloch's galleries to the grounds around them, so that one moves from the gallery to the sculpture lawns through the spaces between the lenses in the same way one moves from gallery to gallery. As we discover later, the very ground itself is transformed as part of the construction. Naturally, a new roof requires a new floor.

Parallel to softening the experience of entering and exiting, the Bloch relaxes the sharp distinction between art and architecture, and it is here that De Maria's sculpture makes another contribution. As we have seen and will see again, architecture old and new is always presented as part of the collection, even in the parking facility, where the light from the sculpture's 34 moons penetrates the sinusoidal wave form of the ceiling to reflect the plaza and liquid depths of the pool into the garage. The eccentric shift in the pool of De Maria's sculpture also secures a tie between Magdalena Abakanowicz's *Standing Figures (30 Figures)* and George Segal's *Rush Hour*, as it asks the two works to help the architecture by defining the limits of the forecourt. Finally, it foreshadows a theme that we will soon discover to be the heart and soul of the Bloch and its quest for serenity and inclusiveness: light become matter.

Having plied the original building with flattery and gifts, the architecture next makes a risky gambit—like the sacrifice of a pawn in chess to secure a positional advantage—in its effort to defer to its elder partner as a means of beguiling it into a more contemporary political posture. At a glance during the day, it would be easy to mistake the Bloch for a scattering of functional sheds, an intrusion of the ordinary into a neighborhood of

3.5
Steven Holl Architects, The Nelson-Atkins Museum
expansion, Kansas City, 2007. Parking garage.
© Roland Halbe.

beautiful homes, the rustic campus of the Kansas City Art Institute, and expressive modern and contemporary buildings, such as the Kemper Museum of Contemporary Art. In that fleeting impression, the Bloch does not belong to the local architectural context any more than Wight's monument. The difference, however, is that the extroverted 1933 building seems to come from somewhere else on a mission, as expressed in the subtitle of Wolferman's history of the museum, "Culture Comes to Kansas City." The daytime appearance of the Bloch, on the other hand, mirrors the workaday buildings of Kansas City, as if to say, "Culture has always been here, if we look for it in the right way."

To discover splendor in ever more common things, processes, and circumstances has been one of the great quests of art throughout its history, but the pursuit fairly obsesses much of modern and contemporary art. Very few works in the gallery dedicated to the collection from these periods remain untouched by it. Only that obsession can explain how a difficult work like John Chamberlain's *Huzzy*, which seems like it might well have been junk taken out of a trash can, can hang next to Tom Wesselmann's slick pop painting *Still Life No. 24*, with its hilarious pack of Tareyton cigarettes and bottle of Wish-Bone Italian dressing, as if the two artworks could be spoken of in the same breath. For some of us, coming across a work like *Huzzy* can be uncomfortable; its apparent lack of artistry can make us feel vulnerable, confused, perhaps even the butt of some joke. How are we supposed to look at it, to think about it?

In the uncertainty of that moment, the museum as a contemporary institution offers a rare gift to its guest. While making no guarantees, it assures us that it just might be worth our while to let our guard down and become acquainted with the strange thing on the wall. Most important, it promises that we can do so without fear. And so some can begin to enjoy the intense beauty and celebration of process in the rust, rough edges, and bends of the painted metal and worn fabric of *Huzzy*, and to grasp the connection it makes between the everyday stuff in the Wesselmann and the spontaneous actions that Jackson Pollock used to make his painting, as seen in the example hanging just around the corner. In essence, then, today's museum is no longer an absolute authority entitled to tell us what we should think and feel, but an institution of manifest trust that mediates a priceless intimacy between total strangers: artist and viewer.

A principal part of the job of any contemporary architecture for a museum is to set the stage for that fragile encounter. It must be able to guide and direct attention without imposing its will too insistently, be generous but have an opinion—a museum is, after all, only human—while encouraging other opinions. Like the soundtrack of a film, the architecture must also shape the dramatic arc—the moods, tempos, and rhythms of intensity and repose—for each visit by innumerable persons and personalities. Compounding the complexity, an encyclopedic museum of the stature of the Nelson-Atkins contains a vast variety of art and design. It gathers under one roof (and let us not forget that the Nelson-Atkins still has only a single roof, though its extent and location are no longer so obvious) some of the greatest achievements of old and modern masters along with less-known works and the adventurous and sometimes obscure, cross-your-finger-and-pray experiments of living artists, as well as works from other cultures, other histories, other worlds.

It can be tricky to fathom the subtleties of any work of contemporary architecture in its effort to fulfill these charges, for two reasons. First, because buildings are so insinuated in the crass realities of our day-to-day life—from getting out of the rain to going to the bathroom—we bring a well-rehearsed awareness of a building's basic functions, which shapes our reaction to it over and above all other conceits. Secondly, like the film soundtrack, architecture can best exercise its persuasions by operating for the most part beneath close attention; even in a museum as eye-grabbing as Frank Gehry's Guggenheim in Bilbao, the preponderance of the architectural measures the building uses to choreograph the experience is barely noticed. Fortunately for us, however, an extraordinary painting in the Nelson-Atkins is perfectly suited to guide our next steps into the Bloch.

Tracer

Hanging in the second of the Contemporary Art Galleries is *Tracer*, arguably the finest of Robert Rauschenberg's silkscreen paintings for which he won the coveted grand prize at the 1964 Venice Biennale. For this work, the artist plucked incongruous images from books, magazines, and newspapers, transferred them to the canvas, and then stirred. We see two helicopters over Vietnam, a bald eagle, a pair of caged lovebirds, an excerpt from a Peter Paul Rubens painting, two line drawings of boxes floating around and out of the painting, and a street scene made unsettling by, if nothing else, the red that tints it.

Unlike the biting humor of *Shuttlecocks* or the intensity of *Huzzy*, a peculiar equanimity emanates from *Tracer* despite its imagery. The space of the painting exercises no effort to lure us in, yet we and all the flotsam and jetsam in our immediate surrounds find ourselves already in it and part of it. Thus, despite first impressions, it is not a collage. Right before our very eyes and yet without our quite noticing, *Tracer's* power of inclusion gathers its miscellany into a holistic world staged on a new kind of ground and unified by a new kind of coherence. In its own way, the Bloch, like the painting, also radiates a spirited calm and possesses an uncanny power of inclusion, incorporating the underground parking facility, the art, the grounds, and the original building into a new whole with the same effortless ease that has *Tracer* joining a helicopter to a seventeenth-century painting of a goddess.

3.6
Robert Rauschenberg, *Tracer*, 1963.
Art © Robert Rauschenberg Foundation/Licensed
by VAGA, New York, NY.

Few other paintings operate so intricately at so many levels. There are the obvious slippages of meaning when, for example, aggression moves to patriotism and then on to love as symbolism passes from one bird of prey to another. But of more interest to its conversation with the Bloch are its formal and material means. Rauschenberg's painting is built around a remarkable catalog of doublings: Venus is reflected in the mirror, the "helicopters" in the upper left corner are actually the same helicopter printed twice, while the film-negative source of the helicopter image appears as an almost imperceptible apparition in the lower right corner. The lovebirds are paired, the words "Coca-Cola" appear twice, and the two figures in the foreground of the street scene stand in mirror symmetry. Even the apparently solitary American bald eagle reverberates as a latent figure in the white highlights of its own shoulder.

Because each image transfer brings its own space with it, *Tracer* hosts a dizzying array of spatial illusions: the street recedes deep into the canvas, the helicopter twice told hovers above Vietnam, while the same helicopter occupies the lower corner in a space as thin as camera film; all the while, two boxes float around in the axonometric space of geometric drawings. Yet the cacophony of irreconcilable spaces coexists harmoniously in the familiar space of a single room. From either of the bottom corners of the painting, we can trace the line where wall meets black floor to the corner of the room as it disappears from view under a taxicab. Thus, a key ingredient of the painting's firmament is borrowed from architecture, the simple power of a room to join together everything and everyone in it, if but for an instant.

While there are light sources in each of the transferred images and a brightening in the area of the box on the left, the painting itself does not have its own light source—no illusions of illumination complement its spatial perspective. Light, shadow, white, and color are material effects of the paint and ink. The quotation of Rubens's *Venus before a Mirror* has been screened on a white ground with blue ink swabbed quickly. The beveled glass of the mirror on Venus's left hovers in front of slashed brushstrokes, although one stroke overlaps the top edge of the glass, while the right side of the mirror disappears into a blue ether that curls around the goddess to stripe her back (or is it now her front, since a blue belly button appears where the small of her back should be?). Meanwhile, the slashing brushstrokes become even more pronounced as they move left from Venus toward the helicopters, mixing first with the blue and then with the black ink of the helicopters to enshroud them in a cloud.[4]

Just below the helicopters, the red line drawing of a box floats free of gravity—as an arrow tells us. Paint, continuing to thicken, washes under the box and just laps over its lower edge before encroaching on the eagle, turbulently churning up more black ink as it begins to encircle the bird in a vortex whose strokes end in heavy daubs of paint. If we scan to this same vortex starting instead from the room's floor at the lower left corner, what we see is white paint erupting from the room's wall to capture the eagle in a violent cartouche. Under the spell of the painting's alchemy, light become visceral matter has congealed into a second spatial ground.

When that second ground encounters the New York street scene screened in red, things get interesting. The largest single image in the work, it depicts a pedestrian in the foreground waiting for a taxicab to clear an intersection, a hard-hatted construction worker to his right, and the street's building fronts receding into deep perspective from the corner, where a cafeteria sign is circled in white. The heavy white strokes of paint at the bottom of the eagle spill into the top of the scene, thrusting the head of the waiting pedestrian toward us. Just to his right, a ghostly white rectangle pulls the wheel and quarter panel of the taxi out of the street scene even closer to us than the pedestrian, and makes the rectangle to its left—a chimera of body, cab, and ink—almost seem like a chest of drawers, the cab's blurred door medallions its top-drawer handles.

So *Tracer* is a magical room, and what wizardries we see it perform. Follow the left wall up from the floor and it soars beyond ideas and the disturbing events of the world into the heavens; follow the right wall up, and find a Rubens hanging on it. This is not just any room, then, but a gallery. The original Rubens painting has been cropped tightly, bringing the viewer in close. *Tracer*'s corner perspective places Venus further away on the wall of the gallery, at mid-distance. The inscrutable dashed line across her bottom has cut away the red upholstered chair upon which she sat for four centuries and replaces it with another red piece of furniture in the gallery—the buildings of the street scene, on which she now sits. The painting, then, seems to say that the whole world is an art gallery, with every person, thing, and event in it a part of its collection. Have we not already heard something like that before? "All the world's a stage, / And all the men and women merely players: / They have their exits and their entrances; / And one man in his time plays many parts." But then, whether as a stage or a gallery, architecture has always shaped our lives in ways that none of us truly comprehend.

There are three clues, then, that *Tracer* offers to its inclusiveness and edgy composure: doubling, a new kind of ground, and light as matter. We have only to check the Bloch for its versions of each of these clues to see what role in the architecture they might play.

Doubling

Since at least the late fourteenth century, painting has been likened to a view through a window. This tenacious analogy is credited, among other things, with the discovery of perspective, and some of the most sophisticated developments in architecture continue to derive from it. Holl's Y House in the Catskill Mountains, for example, replaces the predictable large picture window looking out on a spectacular view with a compound window wall consisting of eight panes of various sizes of rectangular glass, arranged to resemble a late Mondrian painting. Thus, every time the client looks out on "nature" he sees a "painting." Like much of Holl's work, the experiment straddles the conceptual and the phenomenological, suggesting that, for some at least, art has today become more authentic than nature.

This analogy thrives inside the Bloch, where the ubiquitous translucent glass and milk-white walls hold the focal length of the eye to a middle distance, quietly establishing the limits of a snug zone to amplify the presence of the art and encourage close attention. Two circumstances occasion more distant views and allow attention to relax. First, interior vistas from the lobby, along the spine, and in the ceiling reveals between galleries invite eye and mind to wander the pleasures of the voluptuous curves, folded walls, and small-scale details such as the twisted struts of the handrails. Second, intermittent zones of transparent glass capture views and frame them as borrowed art, whether they are of the neighborhood houses, the streetscape, or the sculpture garden. There are two variations on the theme that merit special mention. First, in the lower lobby we encounter the limestone wall and three doors of the old entrance to the east wing that now connect the original building to the Bloch to form one continuous museum. Though obviously not transparent glass, the abrupt presence of the wall signaled by the change in materiality produces the same transparency effect. Again, the Bloch makes its colleague both partner and art. Certainly, the depictions of Henry Wadsworth Longfellow's *Hiawatha* in the twenty-four cast bronze panels of the 1933 doors have never been so underscored.

The transparent wall that cleaves the Noguchi gallery and courtyard serves less to borrow the landscape as a painting than to join the space of the gallery to the sculpture park. It is a poignant episode; the stone-lined catch for the spill water of the fountain passes under the glass wall and continues to the courtyard. Meanwhile, the courtyard is surfaced in the same granite pavers as the gallery, though in a different pattern and texture—polished in the gallery, rough in the courtyard. Just beyond the glass, the stones bridge a small "stream" of grass before reaching the court. The play of imprecise symmetries makes the glass both window and mirror, merging the world of the garden and the world of introspection into the same reality.

Many architects of other contemporary museums have used transparency similarly to frame views, but, in one instance at least, Holl uses the window/painting relationship to a more radical end, one that brings us back to *Tracer*. If we take a second look at Rauschenberg's Venus, we notice that while her face in the glass looks straight at us, her gaze tinged with eroticism, the goddess herself appears actually to look away, as if out of a window or perhaps at the doubled image of the helicopter, but in either case in the fixed way one might contemplate a view or art. Since we know she is at her mirror simply to see herself, the circuitous pathway of her gaze in the painting draws a marvelous map of the twists through the world taken in the course of self-reflection. The Bloch Building reenacts that strange pathway almost literally, doubles it, and then goes back in time and doubles it yet again before it happened in the first place.

However you enter, whether from the old building, the parking facility, or through the forecourt doors, your first encounter with art in the new building is to see other visitors viewing paintings and sculpture as you look at them through the glass doors of the Contemporary Art Galleries, where Willem de Kooning's *Woman IV*, Chamberlain's *Huzzy*, Rauschenberg's *Tracer*, and Robert

Arneson's *Pablo Ruiz with Itch*, along with scores of other famously ill-mannered misfits, stand around and hang out. You notice your own reflection in the glass against the backdrop of art as you walk in, chuckle at the equation, then light down the stairs. After about ten minutes in the gallery, you glance back out the glass only to see another visitor looking in at you. In that split second, you realize that the lobby scene you now see framed by the glass entry might as well be an artwork hanging on the wall in the gallery, and that, come to think of it, it *is* hanging on the wall in the gallery; finally, that the gallery scene the viewer in the lobby now sees is actually the first work of art he sees, turning you into the same work of art you just now turned your counterpart into, and that the person looking at you was you ten minutes ago, and will be you again in just a few more minutes.

As you continue through the galleries, should you visit the small conference room south of the upstairs library in the first lens, or the meeting room above the contemporary gallery in the second lens, you will notice picture windows with glorious views of the streetscape and grounds. But now you will also notice that the large window in the next lens faces back at you. If perchance someone is in that window, you will again be looking at yourself through the eyes of another.

What you will not realize, until a subsequent visit finds you entering the Bloch from the fountain forecourt, is that the addition has already set this journey of self-reflection through art into motion, because the glass forecourt entry is actually the first of these paintings with you in it. Just above the two doors that rotate into the first lens, a fissure in the skin of the lens divides the lobby space visible through the long glass wall into two sections. To the left, you see a relaxed arrangement of the café and other customary accoutrements of a back lobby. To the right is something quite different. An uninterrupted wash of translucent interior glass on the rear wall thins the space of the front lobby as seen from the forecourt into a minimalist canvas, cut full-length by the diagonal of the open staircase. Just behind the staircase begins the ramp down to the galleries. So as you approach the doors, you see an oddly familiar painting of bodies ascending and descending a staircase (though not nude), and a moment later the painting includes you.

A New Ground

It is not hard to tell that something is afoot with the ground of the Holl expansion, something unusual. The original building takes command of the land with the full weight of its authority. Its giant Ionic columns, like sentries forever at attention, assert the resolve of its foothold as its temple staircases elevate the visitor from the vulgarities of the everyday to the nobility of its lofty domain. But the Bloch's lightberg lenses drift afloat, bobbing amid swells of lawn gently lapping at their sides. At the south end of the first lens just before the stairs, we catch one swell lifting the paving from beneath our feet to a crest; beneath it, a facet of the lens resurfaces. Old building and new are as "stone and feather," an epithet meant not only to suggest differences in temperament, but also to recall Galileo's demonstration that when summoned by the deeper truth of gravity, even two natures so very different become the same.

Place, ground, and land seem more or less synonymous, but for certain disciplines, like politics, law, and architecture, each of these and related concepts carry crucial distinctions. According to phenomenology, we have a native relationship to place that precedes all identities and laws we later learn, and place is rooted in the ground. Yet it is land on which we live out our lives; land names our collective and individual relations to the ground as effects of a constellation of laws and social practices. Ground and land are distinct, yet inextricable; if we think of homeland or landlord, we think of feelings of patriotism, or just being at home. While we regularly seek to transform place by changing the land, say with new names or laws, Holl's expansion seeks to transform the place of the Nelson-Atkins Museum by changing its ground.

With modern architecture's urge to democracy came perhaps its greatest experiment: to renovate profoundly the traditional relationship between building and ground. Recognizing classical architecture's participation in a bond between power and land that dates from feudal times, modern architecture sought the means to break that bond. Le Corbusier, for example, lifted his buildings into the air to return the land to free ground. If his idea today seems naïve, it and others like it set into motion a century of efforts to invent more poetic and psychological means by which architecture might truly disentangle building from land as an exercise of power.

For example, while Wight's building greets the arrival of the visitor with great aplomb, the Bloch stages no such ceremony. We do not enter the Bloch so much as find a footpath into it from here or there—from the original building, the parking facility, the south gardens, even in passing from the sidewalk along Rockhill Road. We simply cross a threshold—always on grade—into an ethereal space where vaults, cusps, and folds sculpt a ceiling that filters light like a coppice at dawn. In contrast to the interior splendor of the original building, it is easy to forget inside the Bloch that we are in an important civic institution. Its space encourages us to amble around—up, down, through the galleries, out to the sculpture park, and back in again.

The garden spaces between the lenses are so important to the architecture that it is better to consider them open-air galleries, even though, like the gallery room of *Tracer*, they lack not only a ceiling but also two walls. Doubling the interior galleries, these exterior rooms amplify the sense that the sculptures contained in them, and by extension all of the outdoor sculptures, are "in"

3.7
Steven Holl Architects, The Nelson-Atkins Museum
expansion, Kansas City, 2007. © Andy Ryan.

the museum. At the same time, linked to the interior galleries as way stations on a meandering path, they blur the distinction between floor and ground, lightening the mood and relaxing the decorum inside.

The architect's dedication to the meander reaches a literal extreme between the second and third lenses, where the paved walkway zigzags back and forth like the notorious convolutions of its namesake, the Maeander River. One suspects Holl of imagining furtive hops through the shrubs here to spice the walk with a dash of misbehavior.

Farther on, between the fourth and fifth lenses, a quieting occurs on a simple lawn floor, where two sculptures whisper about a meander of their own. Whether of great consequence or none at all, some coincidences possess such serendipity that the soul cannot accept them as chance though the mind insists otherwise—these we call fate. The appearance together here of Tony Cragg's *Ferryman* and *Turbo* is just such a happenstance. The story of the two sculptures coming to the Nelson-Atkins Museum is a parable in miniature of the best ambitions of the Bloch, not to mention incontrovertible proof that magic happens.

Conceived years apart, *Ferryman* and *Turbo* each belong to a different series by the artist, and one has little to do with the other except for a family resemblance. The two works embarked from the studio on separate journeys, but somehow found themselves together in the gallery of Cragg's New York dealer, Marian Goodman, who temporarily lent them to a public art project that placed them at one of the entrances to Central Park. There they stood, two strangers glancing awkwardly at each other, aware that in the eyes of passersby accidental proximity and family name made them appear a couple. Today, having meandered around the world, they have finally settled together as a couple made for each other. So charmingly do they twin the relationship between the addition and the original building that it is hard not to believe they were commissioned for the purpose.

Playing the role of the original building stands the opaque, topsy *Turbo*, once the very image of power and stalwart industrial will, now a lovable relic of a great history struggling valiantly but in vain to stay in motion and to resist the wear and tear of time on its body, its dignity, and its way of being in the world. Playing the Bloch is the porous and wiggly *Ferryman* who basks in change—a wisp to *Turbo's* will. Translucent during the day, *Ferryman* glows at night as the light from the Bloch spills through its pores.

But the buildings and these works reflect each other at another level. For the better part of his career and across an unbelievable assortment of sculptural experiments, Cragg has been guided by a compulsion to synthesize, in as many ways as imaginable, two great traditions of sculpture's history that by the 1960s had come to oppose one another: figure and field.[5]

Sculpture and figure were for centuries, even millennia, almost synonymous. People all over the world have fallen under the spell of the aura of solitary sculptural figures, whether representational or abstract. It is the stuff not only of art but of archaeology, history, and religion, and we need only walk for a while among the Nelson-Atkins's collection of Henry Moores to be reminded of this. The roots of sculptural fields are also ancient, as Stonehenge and the buried terra-cotta warriors in Xian, China, bring to mind. By the 1960s, however, the time-honored predisposition toward the figure had so shifted to the field that influential artists and critics considered the figural tradition to have all but exhausted its creative possibilities. Sculpture as field, it was thought, broke free from the self-orientation of the figure to engage the more complex manifold that constituted modernity's social, political, and formal space.

In his early works, Cragg started with a field, which he then drew toward a unified figure. Typically, he might gather large

3.8
The Kansas City Sculpture Park at The Nelson-Atkins Museum of Art,
including *Turbo* (foreground), 2001, and *Ferryman* (background),
1997, by Tony Cragg. Courtesy The Nelson-Atkins Museum of Art.
Photo: Roland Halbe.

numbers of familiar objects—plastic toys, combs, cups, plates—and compose these in large, easy-to-recognize two-dimensional figures, such as a crescent moon, a painter's palette, or a silhouette of a person. No matter how one paid attention to one of these works, whether looking closely at its individual elements or taking in its overall composition, one recognized something in its own right, a toy shovel or bubble blower, never a simplified part subordinated to a larger whole. The ever-whimsical quality of both the colorful elements and the overall figure also countered the leaden solemnity that sculpture had accrued over centuries, and a fresh door opened for the discipline. Works like these by Cragg and other artists gave sculpture a powerful vocabulary with which to imagine new affiliations between one and many as metaphors for connections between the individual and the collective. Eventually, Cragg's assemblies began to consolidate into denser accumulations—a stack of bottles or crockery, for example. *Turbo* and *Ferryman* may seem to return to the traditional sculptural figure, but are more intriguing when we understand them as continuations of the artist's process of compressing whimsical fields into figures.

In keeping with its strict sense of order, neoclassical architecture is the study par excellence in the subordination of the part to the whole at every conceivable level of detail, from the importance of proportions to the hierarchical ordering of the massing and the plans, to the use of ornamentation and decor. If *Turbo* is less disciplined than the Wight building, it shows strong traces of neoclassical order in its stacking of disks from small to medium to large and back in mirror symmetry. Neither *Ferryman* nor the Bloch obeys such rules, but more important, each is more concerned than its counterpart with an unassuming participation in a field than with the assertion of a figure. Perhaps the difficulty that critics have had in interpreting *Ferryman* has been caused by the fact that, still in thrall to old habits, they think the most important thing about the work is the organic metal form, when, all along, it's been about the holes.

Taking advantage of the fact that architecture not only depicts relations between one and many but actually stages them, the Bloch is able to go *Ferryman* one better in its particular proposition about fields, inclusiveness, and imagining new connections between individual and collective. But to do so, it takes a substantial architectural risk.

Because of its porosity and informality, departing from the fourth lens for the sculpture park brings no denouement, no satisfying sense of conclusion. Classical architects, keenly aware of the effect of their building's relationship to land and power, used it to craft endings with an operatic touch. With the last step off Wight's grand staircase into the sculpture park terraces, the weight of the building's protocol begins to lift from our shoulders, and a giddy feeling of liberation overtakes us as we move farther into the gardens. Palaces, villas, and their counterparts in every country around the world have developed that transition into a cornucopia of creative processionals and garden types to and from the building, and it is no accident that nineteenth-century literature is so rich with romantic trysts in manor gardens. The Bloch does not take leave, because it seeks to join us as a companion presence in our wanderings away from its interior, intrinsic to the edgeless extent of its new ground. If, by the time we leave, the building has not already shed all sense of control over us to become, in a sense, one of us or part of us, it risks orchestrating a disappointing conclusion.

The freedom sought by the Bloch, then, is not just the momentary license that obtains from the recess of embodied authority, but an abiding freedom of the spirit that we can carry with us wherever we go. Yet for the Bloch to take such a risk and aspire to such intimacy with us is not just a matter of how free it might make us feel. If the Bloch's new ground can conjure such a compelling equivalence, then something more miraculous can occur. After all, the five lenses we see are not individual pavilions but manifestations of one building that we cannot see. The new ground of the Nelson-Atkins forged by the Bloch extends the manifestations beyond the five lenses to include the original building and the garden sculptures as other kinds of lenses that join into a unity we need never see. As are we.

Light Matters

For all of the achievements of the new addition, any claim it makes for immortality will turn on the night, when the Bloch seems made of light the way other buildings are made of limestone or brick. It glows but the light does not move, arrested in such perfect stillness that it has time to acquire stiffness, tangibility, and weight, and sink into the ground. In winter, when the surrounding trees are bare, the light incorporates them as if to become a colossal gelatin-silver print or perhaps a Chinese hand scroll. As one approaches, the apparition spellbinds, intensifying rather than weakening; one begins to hear it and feel its coolness. Its appeal is so immediate and complete that it is difficult to fathom that this light-become-matter is Holl's most daring experiment with a new authenticity, and his most precarious.

The vulnerabilities are patently obvious. As an illusion of material and technology, it is subject to the all too familiar life cycle of engineered magic. Electricity is not free, and the Bloch will require long-term maintenance and cleaning. Even with the best of care, it will weather and age, while new breakthroughs will enable more spectacular trickery. So we will become inured, as we did with Gothic cathedrals, perspective, and moon landings. But these are results of the properties of matter itself, and the history of art and architecture are testimony to the power of authenticity not just to survive the exposures of matter, but also to spring from them.

"One of a kind" is the name we give to art's obstinacy against such degradations, but the construction techniques used by Holl are easy to imitate, so we will see similar buildings cropping up everywhere, all the more because of the addition's success. However certain we feel that the total achievement of its architecture is more than sufficient to elevate this work to a one-of-a-kind, in truth only time can tell.

Thanks to science and engineering, architects today know more about light and have more power to control it than ever before in history. This knowledge includes the spectral and scattering effects of various glasses, plastics, and surface finishes, computer-control shading devices, and advanced artificial lighting systems that allow the color temperature—the red or blue bias of the light—to be tuned much as one increases the treble or bass in a stereo. Less obvious but no less valuable is the ability of engineers to enable the architect to place windows, lunettes, slots, and other strategic light apertures in roofs and walls without compromising structural integrity.

But choreographing the play of light inside a museum is not a science; it is an art, and like any art, its practitioners vary in their talents and personalities, as do their results. Louis Kahn launched our golden age of museum light in 1972 with the opening of his Kimbell Art Museum in Fort Worth, Texas, not because of its extraordinary engineering or bland neutrality, but rather because of its distinct architectural character, its reserve and serenity. For all it owes the Kimbell, the Bloch is a different creature.

Indeed, despite the popular misconception of "the white box," there is no such thing as an ideal neutrality of light and form for a museum; not even architects and museum directors whose tastes lean toward white boxes believe that. Nor, for that matter, is there even such a thing as natural light. We are aware of a painter's predilection for north light, thinking rightly of the value its even luminosity pays throughout the day. We may be less aware that painters also relish the fact that north light is fickle, changing colors a little with each chance reflection and so animating the paint on the canvas with endless fidgets of hue and overtone. Which, then, is the natural light, south or north?

Long before sunlight passes through a pane of glass and glances off a facing wall, it is chosen by the building, which then colors, filters, dims, shapes, and otherwise manipulates it. A building thus recapitulates the processes Earth herself uses to calm the unbearable insults hurled at us by the Sun into warmth and daylight. And even these, without further mitigation, remain too noxious to endure full measure. It would be more accurate to say that each building uniquely stirs the brute materiality of sunlight into a poignant potion that we call Natural Light.

Of course, architecture cannot claim exclusive license to blend this infusion. Urban and landscape designers, for example, each mix their own cocktails of natural light, from wholesale and quotidian to rare and intimate. But as poets, artists and filmmakers attest, architecture can craft exquisite achievements in the stuff. From inspiring shafts to shimmering shadows to hypnotic washes, architecture's Natural Light whispers directly into our soul. We offer it no resistance as it rouses in us divine awe or abject horror, lascivious sensuality or transcendent repose at a whim.

Architecture's powers with light border on the mystical; a building can, for example, transform any profane source into a Natural Light. What else can, in the time it takes to draw a breath, detect a pair of headlights moving down a road at night, capture its beams and the tree shadows they subtend; stretch, reflect, refract and double these, blend in more ingredients—silhouettes of furniture, dancing shadows of drapes and blinds—and then project this ghostly ballet onto a bedroom wall? We have all been enthralled by these night light visitations. They last but seconds by the clock, but they stretch time into concrete substantiations of Henri Bergson's *duration*.

In this sense, a museum is a special optical instrument akin in many ways to those nineteenth-century microscopes, telescopes, and the like, whose sculptural form and impeccable crafting still earn our admiration, though their true measure rests even today on the achievements of their lenses. But where these instruments transform their light source into scientific images, buildings transform their light source into something entirely different, into moods and evocations and atmosphere.

As we abandon a naive notion of natural light, then, we should reaffirm it as a constructed phenomenon no less real, no less essential, no less transcendent. As a construction, Natural Light carries all of the histories intrinsic to any construction, histories of time and place, of course, but also of materials and technology, culture, economics, sociology, and politics. One can see this unfold as the evolution of the construction of holy light—from the phallic shaft at the Pantheon to the colored spray at Chartres, from the chthonic tones at Ronchamp to the equanimous wash of pale in Jørn Utzon's Bagsværd Church, another of the Bloch's predecessors. Thus, Natural Light itself is a topic for research into new authenticities—a topic Holl has made his life's study.

When we enter the first lens, for example, so many pleasures vie for our interest that it is unlikely we will pay much attention to the large plaster wall, though radiant sprites glint across a paler shade of light on its impenetrable surface as its lustrous finish reflects back the translucency and transparency of the exterior glass. This wall is the kind of thing we are likely to take for granted, not realizing the amount of energy expended to make it just so. To achieve the finish and large seamless expanse of area required a plastering technique called hard-troweling, which demands that the entire wall be completed in one application before the plaster dries, using a uniform stroke. To prepare, the architects and a team of some fifteen plasterers together studied the arm motion that best yielded the desired finish, and then held practice sessions on mock walls to coordinate the final application.

As in *Tracer*, light, white, paint, and wall all come to life as one fantastic protean organism, a living ephemera that haunts the galleries of the Bloch to extraordinary end. Using it, the gifted curators and installers of the Nelson-Atkins conjure their own miracles. Pink, translucent light flows like skim milk from the wall into the canvas of Agnes Martin's *White Flowers II*, soaking around its gray bands and atop its cream ones, exhibiting the artist's genius for constructing a wholly original painterly space as few museums have ever done. Yet right next to it, light recedes from the harsh white of Ellsworth Kelly's painting *White Black* to become a shadow of its light, if such a thing might be imagined. Similar effects happen many times over throughout the galleries and collections, more often than not to good end. Some may agree, though, that the LeWitt sculptures are not as well served. The multiple-source reflected light in the gallery butts into the artwork's internal play between mathematical hard-edge and op reverberation to muddy it a bit. No one singer can sing every song well, fortunately.

The stroke of ingenuity that enables so many of the Bloch's interior effects is the triple duty performed by those elements in the building the architects call the "breathing" or "fluttering" Ts. These thick masts camouflage structure, ductwork, and electrical service, unfettering the outer walls to enable the translucency, and hoist the network of light scoops that reflect the sunlight from the lenses into the galleries along manifold gradients and ray paths. The Ts intersect large areas excised from the ceilings to form luminous voids that add pictorial interest and plasticity to the space while further kneading the light. Many of the scoops assume a form that faintly echoes the vaults of Romanesque cathedrals. These add a dash of solemnity to temper the informal atmosphere produced when the other scoops distort into warps and facets, and branch into one another to weave the ceiling into a surreal garden arbor.

More than an optical instrument, then, the Bloch is a light-manufacturing factory. Whether it originated from the sun or an electric light fixture, before any single photon is allowed to leave the Bloch for someone's eye—inside the galleries or out—it has been processed and reprocessed; bounced, bent, stretched, and filtered by physics, educated by history, groomed by psychology, and scented by poetry. This new light of the Bloch is its radical claim for a new authenticity.

But the most controversial effect of the Bloch's glowing exterior is surely its complicity with a pervasive and increasingly decried feature of our contemporary cities: night lighting. Scientists despair and socialists warn of dire consequences that attend the pending extinction of night. Anyone of a phenomenological bent must be keenly aware of the depth that the dark night is ingrained in our aboriginal being. We know from the uncanny stillness of its glow and the dedication to shadow of its chiaroscuro that great care has been taken to guarantee that the Bloch does not wound the night. Nevertheless, for an architect of Holl's disposition to challenge darkness must give us pause.

Like every city these days, Kansas City is awash in typical night lighting: cars, signs, streetlights, sidewalk lamps in Art Deco lampposts, architectural spotlighting, and cosmetic highlighting. In addition, it boasts its own quirkier lights; during the winter holiday season, the entire fourteen square blocks of the Plaza shopping district is decked out in strings of multicolored Christmas lights. Nothing, however, quite compares to Frank Lloyd Wright's contribution to Kansas City's evening glory, the great steeple of light that blasts into the heavens through the roof of the Community Christian Church in midtown.[6]

3.9
Steven Holl Architects, The Nelson-Atkins Museum
expansion, Kansas City, 2007. © Andy Ryan.

The dilemma is simple to articulate and presents a classic scenario for both critical and phenomenological speculation on the potential consequences for architecture. Because of night lighting, cities are safer and more active, pleasant places to be, and buildings lit at night add drama and spectacle to skyline and streetscape alike. In some version, it is here to stay. But the escalation of urban night lighting contributes on several fronts to real ecological problems that adversely affect us all—not just astronomers.

For Holl, the general issue must stand on a conjecture that we, today's city dwellers, have become a kind of being for whom light at night is no longer just a convenience, but a basic element of our world. The specifically architectural issue derives from the unfortunate fact that, popularity notwithstanding, current practices of architectural night lighting—all of which are merely copied from stage lighting—count among the most inauthentic of architectural effects, crass dispiriting display and nothing more.

In response, the Bloch conjures a new light that belongs to architecture, speaks to the soul, and savors the night.

4 THE CUNNING OF COSMETICS (A PERSONAL REFLECTION ON THE ARCHITECTURE OF HERZOG & DE MEURON)

During the toasts celebrating the opening of "Light Construction,"
the deep-seated tension . . . broke out in a bristling exchange between
Herzog and Koolhaas.
—*El Croquis* 79

How long now—six years? eight?—since I tossed off my first snide dismissal of the work of Herzog & de Meuron? Of course, for a critic such as myself, advocate of the architectural avant-garde, intellectual apologist for the extreme, the exotic, the subversive, was it not *de rigueur* to scorn the superficial propositions of HdM? While one branch of the avant-garde proposed exotic form as a vector of architectural resistance, HdM offered flagrantly simple Cartesian volumes. While another branch cultivated event theory into seditious programming techniques, HdM indulged contentedly in expedient, reductive planning. HdM's fixation on the cosmetic, on fastidious details, eye-catching materials, and stunning facades, appeared frivolous in comparison with those other, more overtly radical experiments. Even worse, the overall cast of their work seemed complicit, if not aligned, with the taste for neomodern confections that had already begun to emerge as the hallmark of the reactionary New Right in Europe and elsewhere.

The question more to the point, then, is when exactly did my infatuation with HdM's work begin? When did I start returning to publications to gape secretly, furtively, at the Goetz Gallery, the Signal Boxes, Ricola Europe, or the sublime Greek Orthodox Church, like a schoolboy ogling soft porn? Did my longing for the work grow over time, or was I beguiled from the outset, my oafish snubs but the hackneyed disavowals of one discomforted by the throes of forbidden desire?

In any case, it was not until March 1996 that the utter cunning of HdM's project dawned on me in its full dimension. By then, I had already realized that their architecture's ability to insinuate itself into my psyche was a powerful effect that, like it or not, must be taken seriously. All the more so when it occurred to me that HdM's work did not, by virtue of any polemic, force itself on me against my will; rather, like a computer virus, it slipped into my consciousness through my will, eluding any and all resistance as it began to reprogram my architectural thoughts and feelings.

In March 1996, I encountered an *Arch+* special issue on HdM. What shocked me into a new awareness was not any particular essay in the issue, though it contained several excellent ones.[1] Rather, the agent of my epiphany was the unceremonious cover title: *Herzog et de Meuron: Minimalismus und Ornament*. As soon as I saw it, I knew something was wrong, very wrong; I could feel it, though I could not quite put my finger on it.

Thumbing through the magazine, I found that Nikolaus Kuhnert had, without comment, separated the firm's work into two sections: *Ornament* held all of the projects with printed surfaces, *Minimalism* everything else—a brute act of blunt taxonomy. The source of the uneasiness spawned by the cover title became apparent. How could such a coherent collection of works by one architectural intelligence lend itself so easily to partitioning into such antagonistic categories as minimalism and ornament?!

At first glance, the division seemed quite sensible, but, as might be expected, it did not sustain closer inspection. For example, Kuhnert placed the Signal Box—a key work in the HdM oeuvre—in the minimalist section, no doubt in respect of the simple form, the monolithic uniformity effected by the copper banding system, and the functional role attributed to it. On the other hand, does not the luxurious field of copper bands also fit any nontrivial definition of architectural ornament, even, as we shall see, if it also undermines the concept of ornament at the same time? After all, each band was painstakingly warped to engender a mesmerizing, ephemeral gesture in light, shadow, and form over a large area of the skin, one much larger than required to admit natural light to the few interior spaces. And the functional rationalization of the system as a Faraday cage is merely a smokescreen.[2] My point, however, is not to contest the details of Kuhnert's partitioning; rather, it is to admire the insidious guile of an architecture able to infiltrate so effortlessly such irreconcilable categories, and, in doing so, begin to dismantle and reform them.

Already I have touched on the most potent characteristics of HdM's architecture: an urbane, cunning intelligence and intoxicating, almost erotic allure. It is these traits that enable it to go anywhere, to go everywhere, into site and psyche alike, to appear ever fascinating yet ever harmless even as it plies its undermining subterfuges and sly deceits. And while this constellation of themes and its attendant techniques are ancient indeed,[3] the most precise placement of HdM's work in contemporary architecture is simply that it is the coolest architecture around. All that remains for us, then, is to watch it in action, to speculate a bit on its methods, and to begin an audit of its gains and losses.

Let us return to the Signal Boxes. Would it be too much to liken them to sirens, to temptresses that lure the unsuspecting into dangerous territory? The sirens of the *Odyssey*, if I remember correctly, charmed sailors into hazardous waters with the sheer beauty of their voices, voices that sang but said nothing, meant nothing, promised nothing. Do you not feel the song of

4.1
Herzog & de Meuron, Signal Box, Basel, 1994.
© Hisao Suzuki.

the Signal Boxes? Are you not enticed by it, drawn to a distant train yard to drink in its presence with your eyes? What pulls you there? And why go, when the only thing certain is that there is absolutely nothing for you there, save, perhaps, peril?

In their single-minded obsession with unspeakable beauty, the Signal Boxes are exemplary of the HdM project at its most radical. To achieve its edgy *à la mode*, HdM brushes aside the Big Questions that such a project would, today, customarily trigger. HdM ignores the fact that signal stations belong to remote networks and interurban infrastructures and, therefore, that their architecture should be conceived more in terms of flows and intensities than in terms that might be likened to the visual niceties that have come to appoint bourgeois travel. Nor does HdM give a moment's thought to the inappropriateness of High Design in the harsh, dirty reality of the site, though the shrill understatement of the Signal Boxes is as hip to its surroundings as a gangster in colors is to South Central L.A. In that regard, the Signal Boxes raise doubts about the subtly patronizing fantasy of a context so brutal, so unrelentingly utilitarian that it cannot even broach the cloying frippery of design.

Make no mistake about it, these are not just hypothetical interrogations made in the name of the infrastructuralists and dirty realists. In his published comments on HdM, Rem Koolhaas first remarks on the undeniable beauty of the firm's facades. Then, on the way to framing his final indictment as a question, "Is architecture reinforcement therapy, or does it play a role in redefining, undermining, exploding, erasing?," he begins to signal his misgivings by asking HdM, "Does every situation have a right to architecture?," no doubt with the Signal Box in mind.[4]

For the proponents of exotic form, the Signal Boxes would have been an opportunity of another ilk. Largely free from the demands of human program, unencumbered by historical or formal typology, unobligated to a prevailing contextual language of architectural merit, the signal station offered an ideal prospect to experiment with the very limits of form. Furthermore, because several would be built, the morphological research could have been extended to the fascinating question of non-prototypical serialization. That HdM should adhere so closely to the box, that they should even consider developing a prototype, was anathema. To this group of architects, the appearance in the second Signal Box of warped surfaces will surely seem a tacit admission of the futility of the original prototypical ambition and the inadequacy of the Cartesian box. As we shall see, however, nothing could be further from the truth.

In brief, the design of the Signal Boxes shows no concern whatsoever for flows or event structures, for realism or new form. Their architecture is entirely a matter of cosmetics, a hypnotic web of visual seductions that emanate entirely from the copper band system, a system, it should be said, that is in fact not the building's actual skin, which lies just beneath; it only poses as the building's skin.

The point here, however, is not to diminish the architectural import of the Signal Boxes by relegating them to the cosmetic, but to embrace their irresistible intrigue, acknowledge their vitality, and, in so doing, assert the transformative power of the cosmetic. Some care must be taken here, for the *cosmetic* is not just another member of the family of decorative architectural appurtenances collectively known as ornamentation. The field of effects of the cosmetic is quite different from those of its relatives, and it is precisely in those differences that HdM's contemporary project is born.

Ornaments attach as discreet entities to the body like jewelry, reinforcing the structure and integrity of the body as such. Cosmetics are indiscreet, with no relation to the body other than to take it for granted. Cosmetics are erotic camouflage; they relate always and only to skin, to particular regions of skin. Deeply,

4.2
Herzog & de Meuron, Signal Box, Basel, 1994.
© Hisao Suzuki.

intricately material, cosmetics nevertheless exceed materiality to become modern alchemicals as they transubstantiate skin into image, desirous or disgusting. Where ornaments retain their identity as entities, cosmetics work as fields, as blush or shadow or highlight, as aura or air. Thinness, adherence, and diffuse extent are crucial to the cosmetic effect, which is more visceral than intellectual, more atmospheric than aesthetic. Virtuosity at ornamentation requires balance, proportion, precision; virtuosity at cosmetics requires something else, something menacing: paranoid control, control gone out of control, schizo-control.

Though the cosmetic effect does not work at the level of the body, nevertheless it requires a body—or at least a face—as a vehicle. Like veal for the saucier, or the gaunt, featureless visage-of-choice recently for makeup artists, the ideal vehicle for the extreme cosmetician is a body, face, or form denuded of its own ability to engender affect. These days, the effects of form as such are just too obtuse to be cool.

If the attitude of the cosmetician toward the body is a minimalism, then it is of a very different sort than the minimalism spawned by the art world more than two decades ago. While the two share a desire to collapse the time of impact of a work to the immediate, the former pursued that goal by distilling form and material into an essence that radiated (spiritual) affect through unmediated presence. The reductions of cosmetic minimalism, on the other hand, are anorexic, a compulsion to starve the body until it dissolves into pure (erotic) affect, like a Cheshire cat in heat. Witness the necrophilic charge of the anemic Kantonsspital Pharmacy, or speculate on the rejection of HdM's dazzling Greek Orthodox Church by the bishop. Was it because he grasped the conversion of its space from the spiritual to the erotic?

Thus, Kuhnert's bipartite distribution missed the decisive achievement of HdM's work thus far, the sublimation of the antithesis between ornamentalism and minimalism into a new coherence. The most famous example of this synthesis to date is Ricola Europe, with its renowned flourish, walls patterned with translucent tiles silk-screened with leaf images. When backlit, as seen in the interior during the day, the leaf pattern takes on the empty, numbing, camp fascination of a Warholian wallpaper. On the exterior, the images are rarely visible, emerging only fleetingly as hallucinations when hit at exactly the right angle by glancing light. Photos (actually, photographers) of this building tend to exaggerate the leaf image to the point of kitsch; its presence on the exterior is actually much rarer and more ephemeral. But in any case, this slick, eye-catching device belies the range and depth of technique HdM exercised in realizing the full cosmetic sophistication of the work.

As usual, the form is starved to skin and bones and gutted of any distracting conceit in plan. The silk-screened panels tile the two long walls; starting on the underside of the cantilevered awning, the strip paneling turns to wrap down the wall. The effect of the wrap is to subvert the integrity of the two distinct formal elements of the building, the facade and the soffit, blurring them into a single field. Ironically, this leaves the thin strip of clear glass revealing the terminal truss of the roof extensions as, strictly speaking, the only actual facade.

To further distance the thin, weightless leaf field from a wall, even a curtain wall, it is edged like a draped veil. The edging causes the long, thin strips to seem to stream from the top to the ground, trickling so gently that the slight thickness of the upper track of the horizontal glass doors breaks the flow.

This streaming illusion on the panels blurs the front translucent fields into the side concrete walls. On those sides, roof water flows over the concrete, causing it to reflect like glass when wet and leaving a field of parallel vertical tracks, the residue of evaporated flow. In the same device at the wraithlike echo of Ricola

4.3
Herzog & de Meuron, Ricola Europe Production and
Storage Building, Mulhouse-Brunstatt, France, 1993.
© Hisao Suzuki.

4.4
Herzog & de Meuron, Ricola Europe Production and
Storage Building, Mulhouse-Brunstatt, France, 1993.
© Hisao Suzuki.

Europe, the Rémy Zaugg studio, iron on the roof dyes the rainwater rust-red to create a more dramatic if somewhat disconcerting effect. At Ricola Europe, these flow tracks and the pattern of widths they delimit reiterate uncannily the field of translucent tiles and seams in form and proportion.

For all of its modes of assertiveness, its blatant use of images, its indulgence in materiality, and the bluntness of its form, the genius of Ricola Europe is that the building, in itself and as such, is never there. Its promise of stark presence withdraws to leave pure allure, a tour de force of architectural cosmetics.

As with other critical treatment of HdM's work, for example as neomodernism or as applied minimal art, the question of cosmetics with all of its allusions to makeup and scents, to skins and bodies, would have only the force of analogy were it not for the matter of HdM's technique.

With form, planning, structure, and construction, even with materials, HdM's technique is architectural to the point of fanaticism. In the firm's entire body of work to date, there is not a single use of form, structure, or material that does not belong to the strictest canon of the architectonic. Every experiment is an effort to reanimate and update that canon, never to augment it with new entries: certainly not with new forms or programs, but not even with new materials. Even the stained water tracks and the algae, lichens, and molds that grow on old surfaces have belonged to the canon, albeit as nuisances, for centuries.

What makes the firm so interesting is that, unlike the avant-garde, HdM derives its critical edge from an assumption of architecture's basic adequacy and an ease with the controversial proposition that architecture has no other more profound project than to fabricate a new sensibility from its own palette. In that it pursues the new not as a matter of ideology or as a condition of marginality, but as a forthright, even aggressive assertion of the center, it is perhaps the most *au courant* practice.

4.5
Herzog & de Meuron, Studio Rémy Zaugg, Mulhouse,
France, 1996. © Hisao Suzuki.

If the notion of the cosmetic has any deeper purchase for HdM than mere analogy, it is because the firm does not apply cosmetics to architecture as theory or borrowed practice. HdM unleashes the destabilizing power of the cosmetic as a moment and a movement already residing within architecture's orthodoxy. In so doing, it often accomplishes timely effects *en passant* that other practices grounded more in applied theory have pursued with less success.

By working steadfastly within the protocols of architectural materiality, HdM achieves a far more convincing realization of architectural dematerialization than Peter Eisenman, who has pursued that idea in his architecture for over two decades. Eisenman, steeped in a poststructural account of architecture as an endless system of references by immaterial signs, theorized that the tradition of materiality in architecture was a perversion manifest either as fetishism or nostalgia. Accordingly, he sought to render his forms as pure signs by constructing them as empty shades in indifferent materials, for example EIFS or gyp board. As a result, more often than not his buildings fail to insist on themselves and are easily dismissed as irreal, like stage sets or amusements parks.[5]

By beginning with more traditional and tactile materials such as glass, wood, or concrete and then manipulating them in nontraditional ways, HdM is able to insist on the reality of the building while never allowing it to settle as a reliable and persistent presence. In other words, HdM does not dematerialize a concrete form by replacing the concrete; it dematerializes the concrete itself.

The unbuilt Kunstkiste Museum for the Grothe Collection provides an acute study in this aspect of HdM's work. As published, the project promised to be nothing short of an essay in extreme concrete, one whose rude materiality would make Tadao Ando's renowned use of the material seem hopelessly genteel, as the building would certainly have done to the saccharine confections by Axel Schultes and Gustav Peichl nearby.

The top-heavy proportions of the vertical slab make the form of the Kunstkiste seem poised to topple, the threat further intensifying the insistent weight of the materiality. But the roof water, destined to stain every surface with its vertical striations of rust and algae, would transform the appearance of the concrete box into that of a viscous liquid in an aquarium, the image confirmed by the blackened windows floating at random like objects at neutral buoyancy. Heavy or light? Solid or liquid? Essential presence or imagistic illusion?

But as intriguing as the project is in its published form, Jacques Herzog reveals that HdM entertained an even more astonishing thought for the project. At one point they considered printing exactly positioned, full-scale photo images of the interior of the galleries on the concrete. The photo-printing surfaces would, in effect, make the concrete appear transparent! As if the phenomenal dislocation were not enough, the idea also carried a deconstructive implication, perhaps its downfall. The photographer would have been a young artist of note from Berlin, whose presence on the surfaces would have marked his absence from the collection and raised questions about the collection itself. For whatever reason, the idea seems to have been abandoned. Nevertheless, it was a brilliant thought, and one that indicates just how aware HdM is of the eruptive force of its cosmetic techniques.

5 RECENT KOOLHAAS

I've seen the future and it works.
—Prince, "The Future"

It's absolutely fascinating, but utter nonsense. You say he talks about it. Where? [He opens a copy of S,M,L,XL.*] Look, the words* freedom *and* liberty *don't even appear in his dictionary, or anywhere else in these 2,000 pages that I can remember. Koolhaas is like any other architect, all he does is try to make things beautiful. He has a tougher, grittier eye than most, but he's great at it, probably the best in the world. That's why the kids loved him before anyone else, and that's why he has finally become so fashionable for the rest of us old farts. If you really want to take a chance, try writing that. But then, your articles will be too short and no one will think you are brilliant.*
—Philip Johnson

Who is that tall guy sitting next to Willy Lim?
—Tao Ho, Hong Kong architect (pointing to Rem Koolhaas
at the Anywise conference in Seoul, 1995)

Over the last few years, Rem Koolhaas's work has attracted interpretation from the standpoints of such vogue sophistications as the economic theory of flexible accumulation, complexity theory, and new biology. As art historian Jonathan Crary writes,

"By now it is customary to engage the work of Rem Koolhaas in terms of its active alignment with processes of cultural transformation, its planned instabilities and flexible components—an architecture designed as a dynamic ingredient of perpetual social flux and reorganization."[1]

Though rarely probing any OMA project in detail, these abstruse approaches have yielded compelling insights into the general case of Koolhaas's work, consistently outwitting more customary techniques of architectural analysis. The latter have been conspicuous in their inability to probe the work's architectural features, its handling of site, program, form, construction, and materials, in correlation with a convincing account of why certain of the architect's projects have come to exercise such sway over the discipline.

Thus far, traditional architecture criticism tends to conclude any study of an OMA project with generic praise either for the work's wit, its renewed attention to the city, its perceived reanimation of dormant social responsibilities, or its neomodern avoidance of formal excess, its cartoonishly reductive diagrams, or its cheap, even ugly, construction. Each of these judgments can be confirmed in one or another of OMA's projects, but none grasps why Koolhaas's architecture has today become the most debated and influential in the world.[2] One frustrated critic, retreating to mythic platitudes, writes, "There is no other way to put it; Koolhaas is the Le Corbusier of our times."[3]

This outbreak of critical ineptitude is all the more interesting when one considers that of his confederates—Peter Eisenman, Zaha Hadid, Daniel Libeskind, Bernard Tschumi, etc.[4]—Koolhaas has been the most single-minded in deriving his trajectory and techniques from a frank meditation on architecture rather than from contemporary philosophy or cultural theory. "For four hundred years, architectural values have arisen from the same humanist wellspring. Today, these must change," Eisenman argues, "because of fundamental new insights achieved by philosophy." "Today, these are fundamentally changed," Koolhaas argues, "because of the elevator."

One might speculate that traditional criticism's less than convincing engagement with Koolhaas's architecture arises from the fact that his designs are subtle or that he pursues an unusual cultural project. Nothing could be further from the truth. Almost without exception, Koolhaas's designs are blatantly straightforward. More importantly, one, and only one, cultural aim drives the work, from the writings to the projects and buildings, coloring each decision at every scale, from domestic to urban, from diagram to detail. That aim focuses the work into such an acute convergence that as a body it begins to constitute a treatise on the topic. That aim, so brazen that almost no one but Koolhaas ever mentions it in other than occult terms, is simply this: to discover what real, instrumental collaboration can be effected between architecture and freedom.

The failure of modern architecture to fulfill its promise as a tool able to implement democratic political form or egalitarian social theory would from the outset seem to cast a pall over such an ambition, as would the reflection by some twentieth-century thinkers such as Georges Bataille on a fundamental conflict between architecture and liberty.[5] Other doubts nag the notion of freedom itself: that it is a goal perpetually compromised by the conflict between the individual and the collective, that it is an abstraction debatable beyond resolution by competing political and philosophical theories, that it is a naïveté unable to cope with the clandestine forces of determination deployed by global techno-corporate-military economies, that it is a delusion of consumerism mobilized by masters of the mechanisms of desire, etc.

Koolhaas's work stipulates many of these doubts. His architecture offers little resistance, for instance, to the intoxications of consumer culture. But he sidesteps flagrant entanglement with those complications by avoiding any a priori, universal definition of Freedom. For Koolhaas, architecture is able, but only able, to engender provisional freedoms in a definite situation, freedoms as the experiences, as the sensations, as the effects—pleasurable, threatening, and otherwise—of undermining select patterns of regulation and authority. He goes to some lengths to demonstrate that tangible, liberating experiences supported by architecture can be engendered in restrictive contexts. His celebration of shopping in Singapore is perhaps the most notorious example, but *Delirious New York* and his design for the Panopticon prison are also poignant case studies.

Thus, there can be no Koolhaas manifesto on Architecture and Freedom, no axioms of comprehensive emancipation through architecture, not even a consistent catalog of liberating techniques. At any point in time, his treatise consists of the collected successes and failures of his efforts to use architecture to license as far as possible a situation's real constituencies, proper and marginal.

For similar reasons, a convincing critical engagement with a Koolhaas project depends more on an assessment of the particular sensations it posits and attempts to realize than a judgment of the work against a received set of expectations and values, that is, against a prior standard, though such judgments cannot be simply abandoned. The problem that confounds architectural criticism is that at many levels—formal, material, and contextual—Koolhaas embraces traditional architectural standards perfected by the modernists. In each project, he adjusts and suspends select aspects of these standards piecemeal to accomplish his goals, rather than attempting a total reinvention of the discipline. Koolhaas's work never resists authority; it sabotages authority from within. Thus, though his practice is thoroughly radical, it is removed from the tradition of the avant-garde, with its ceaselessly exuberant efforts to overthrow the Old and assert

5.1
OMA, Kunsthal, Rotterdam, 1992. Exterior ramp.
Photo: Hans Werlemann / © OMA.

the New. On the other hand, in its rejection of the renewed call for the supremacy of beauty in architecture,[6] it is equally removed from the aestheticisms, such as new minimalism, that have of late gained such momentum.

Consider the precocious Kunsthal in Rotterdam, a building of striking complexity that nevertheless remains virtually unapproached, not to mention unappreciated, by criticism. An adequate treatment of this definitive work is beyond the scope of this essay, but a few remarks about it may help portray some of the issues raised. Like many of Koolhaas's works,[7] the Kunsthal is a coherent synthesis—not a collage—of several familiar modern precedents, the most conspicuous being Mies van der Rohe's National Gallery in Berlin. As is well known, Mies uses the processional at the National Gallery to extraordinary effect to situate the fragile but exalted state of art in the modern city. The visitor leaves the street by climbing a staircase and landing on a great, empty concrete plinth overlooking the whole of the cultural district. Such rising to a second datum is an elaboration of the curtain-rising entry sequence of the Renaissance church, where the staircase elevates the parishioner from the profane to the sacred. Isolated at the center of the plinth is a platonic, glass-and-steel pavilion, at first impression the arrival point. Soon, though, the visitor discovers that the pavilion, too, is empty save another staircase that descends into the plinth, now a bunker/crypt for the art. Continuing through the underground galleries, the visitor's journey ends as he exits to a sunken sculpture garden, a sanctum sanctorum carving out a profound retreat from the destituting forces of the city.

There are several distinct entries to the Kunsthal—already a significant contrast. A major sequence begins in the park and spirals up to the galleries in a parodic organizational reversal of Mies's National Gallery. You walk up the ramp toward the deferred entry to the galleries, all the while glimpsing the galleries and lecture halls through glass. Your first encounter with the art thus occurs from a service space, and forces the art into comparison with the banal furnishings and fixtures that punctuate the ramp and the lecture halls. After entering and proceeding through the galleries, you end up outside the building on a plinth of sorts, though one markedly different from that of Mies. A steel-grate platform steals the ground from under you, jutting out from the building at street level far enough to seem as if it connects to the street's surface. At the end of your journey through the Kunsthal, you find yourself in the exciting but somewhat precarious position of being slightly dizzy while standing in traffic!

At the Kunsthal art is a major performer, but one among many in the profane, animating theater of the city, not the last, beleaguered embodiment of the sacred. What then is the measure of the Kunsthal? Its perversion of a modern masterpiece? Its impertinent treatment of art? Or the refreshment it achieves through its meticulous disestablishment of an institution laboring under the weight of an increasingly irrelevant orthodoxy of experiences?

But assessing Koolhaas's experiments is rarely that simple. Take Congrexpo in Lille, often dismissed as poorly built, an attack extrapolated by some critics to suggest that the architect cannot build. An examination of the Kunsthal or the exquisite rendering of Villa dall'Ava easily demonstrates that the generalization does not hold. Nevertheless, it does pertain at Congrexpo. Already, low-grade concrete crumbles and large corrugated plastic panels at best look tacky when they are not detaching from the wall! Whether the accusation of inadequate attention to construction stands as sufficient criticism, however, is not so clear.

Koolhaas generally disdains designs that are unusually costly, especially where money is spent on exotic form or expensive material. In part, he sees such tactics as senseless extravagances, whatever other claims are made for them. Mostly, however, his

5.2
OMA, Kunsthal, Rotterdam, 1992. Auditorium.
Photo: Hans Werlemann / © OMA.

contempt unfolds from self-interest. When the exorbitant costs of a building make headlines or bankrupt the client, it is the celebrities of the profession that suffer the backlash.

At Lille, frugality, but not modesty, became a theme. The town was poor and low-grade concrete readily available. All the better, because in any case Koolhaas wanted to try a huge, raw, inexpensive construction, a building, as he puts it, from "the wrong side of the tracks." The architect hoped the success of Congrexpo would be measured by the degree to which it intensified the buzz of activities, coarse and genteel—rock concerts, auto and boat shows, bathroom fixture expos, political gatherings—rather than by the quality of its construction. Why should architecture always rise above vulgarity?

Perhaps the experiment was a failure. Rather than feeling unpretentious, perhaps the cheap construction just feels shoddy to the users, confronting them with the crassness of their own activities. It is not possible to tell from the extant criticism, however, since none is based on the performance of the building in use. Notwithstanding the question of whether still photography is adequate to represent such an architectural endeavor, almost every published photograph of Congrexpo since its completion is of its exterior, or its interior—empty! In the end, of what relevance is a rote application of the standard of fine materials and tasteful appointments to Congrexpo's architectural proposition that cheap construction is not always at best a compromise but might in and of itself be a radical architectural attribute?

Though Koolhaas's architectural notion of freedom never strays far from the realm of politics, its emphasis on experience and its preference for demonstrable instrumental effect over abstract ideality situates it as much in the realm of erotics. The work often contradicts conventional wisdom on socially responsible architecture. In his influential entry for the Bibliothèque Nationale de France competition in Paris, for example, the architect proposed the extensive use of mechanical circulation, isolated reading rooms, and visual opacity to eradicate the weight of institutional presence, and to allow the building to engulf the visitor in that sometimes euphoric, sometimes menacing isolation peculiar to the city, an experience of freedom not often celebrated by social urbanists. In his project for the university libraries at Jussieu, the architect revisits Corbusian themes to generate a social setting organized less by the program than by the erotic fantasies of the voyeur.

Jussieu initiates many of the major tendencies of Koolhaas's more recent work, such as the projects for the Miami Performing Arts Center, the new Tate Modern, and the Cardiff Opera House. The library can be understood as a hybrid of Le Corbusier's Dom-ino diagram and a diagram of a commonplace automobile parking structure. Le Corbusier's Dom-ino scheme, of course, was a prototype for social housing mostly concerned with repeatable concrete construction techniques. However, it came to inhabit contemporary architecture far more powerfully as a conceptual diagram. Its implication of endlessly extendable and stackable free-plan plates skinned by a curtain wall suggested certain themes through which architecture might support an egalitarian political ideal, all more or less in disfavor today. Mass production, generic form and organization, the erasure of poché, and the evocation of an infinitely removed horizon line placed the detached inhabitant in a radically denatured slab of volume floating in an undifferentiated space.

At Jussieu, Koolhaas invaginates Dom-ino, mobilizing it from a static diagram of infinite, equalizing solitude into a finite, fluid field of interactions, benign and otherwise. To insure adequate activity in the facility, he disobeys the brief, reducing the two distinct thematic libraries originally required into a single, generic construction, one barely recognizable as a library from a semiotic or typological standpoint.

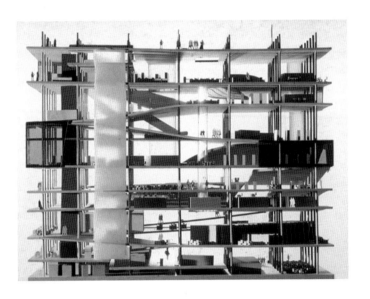

5.3
OMA, Jussieu—Two Libraries, Paris, 1992.
Photo: Hans Werlemann / © OMA.

Such radical reduction of the expectations of a given brief is characteristic of Koolhaas's recent approach to a project. More like a sadist than a surgeon, he has begun to knife the brief, hacking away its fat, even its flesh, until he has exposed its nerve. The focus of these reductions is always on *disestablishment*, that is, always on excising the residues in the project of unwarranted authority, unnecessary governance, and tired convention.

Reductive disestablishment provides the crucial stratagem in each of Koolhaas's recent projects, the intellectual modus operandi by which the architect begins to transform the design into an instrument of freedom. What is a university library today but a surface on which to locate books and computers and a path to bring the public to them? What is an art museum but a version of the same organization, a surface to display the art and a path for the public to reach it? Why use two pieces of land when you can use one; why design a sculpture when all you need is a box? What is an opera house but a facility for the company to manufacture performances and a place for the public to assemble and watch them? Such reductions can nail a project with agonizing clarity, and the results can be astonishing. Jussieu is such a case, the Cardiff Opera House even more so. Occasionally, though, he cuts the nerve and kills a project, such as at the Tate.

In Jussieu, the architect stacks the libraries in a unified structure formed by using a ramping system typical of parking structures to connect the isolated floor plates of Dom-ino into a single-surface concourse. Program elements erupt on the slab/ concourse like kiosks on a city street, and the interstitial and residual spaces delimited by the ramps are left untreated. The plates are cut and the rims warped, allowing visitors to gaze surreptitiously at others above and below. The effect shatters the ideal horizon line of Dom-ino and folds the fragments back into the space as an eroticized web of partial horizons.

The disestablishing design of Jussieu severs the library from a history in which the institution has sedimented into an unyielding building type. In this alternative, library functions are loosely inserted as provisional program in an infrastructural setting whose event structure[8] is not only incongruent with the library's program but exceeds it to the point of interference. Liberty is staged at Jussieu as a permissiveness attained by lifting the burdens of convention—institutional, historic, even moral. A "Quiet, Please" sign would seem merely comic as one searched in vain for a proper place to hang it.

The Miami Performing Arts Center, the Tate Modern, and the Cardiff Opera House projects draw upon the basic tactics of reductive *disestablishment* developed at Jussieu: the aggregation of program to generate an event structure incongruent with program, the reliance on generic form to suppress historical or typological reference, the use of infrastructure-like organizations to liquefy rigid programming into nonspecific flows and events, and the erasure of poché to weave together exterior, interior, vestigial, and primary spaces into a frank differential matrix that rids the building of the hackneyed, bourgeois niceties of cosmetic hierarchies.[9]

The OMA Entry to a Limited Competition for the Miami Performing Arts Center

Over the last two decades, the population of Miami, Florida, has experienced an explosion in human diversity to rival any other city in the world. Cubans, Puerto Ricans, Haitians, and other Caribbeans live—not quite side by side—with African-Americans, Jews, WASPs, rednecks, gays, lesbians, the elderly, tourists, and seemingly innumerable other ethnic, racial, cultural, demographic, and lifestyle groups. Most observers of the American scene agree that Miami is the test case of the viability of the urban melting pot model of tolerance and assimilation that the

United States prides itself upon, but that has been under such pressure of late.

To design such flamboyant symbols of traditional class and culture as an opera house and concert hall in this situation would be challenging at best, even for an architect with no political interests. For Koolhaas, it must have seemed at once an impossible task and an irresistible test. Go too far toward a disestablishment of the institutions and OMA would surely lose. Do not go far enough, and sacrifice OMA's polemical reputation.

The OMA scheme unfolds with the quiet cunning of a John Le Carré novel, a taut, tightrope walk back and forth across the chasm between the clients' revanchist fantasies and the architect's deterritorializing realism. It does not reach a conclusion as much as a settlement, shrewdly negotiated with more than a few touches of brilliance.

The curtain rises on the drama in the first line of the text introducing OMA's entry to the limited competition, signaling the aggregation of program that launches the design: "In physics, the notion of *critical mass* indicates the point whereby accumulating mass, an object passes from one condition into another, more dynamic one." A brief calling for two distinct buildings on catercornered sites is set aside in favor of a consolidated organization massed on one city block. Koolhaas achieves practical advantages by combining the two facilities into a single complex, eliminating functional redundancies and freeing one of the sites to become open public space. The project's full-block massing and crystalline forms have a benign '50s flavor, a clean retro-modern response to the florid neo-nouveau of the city's recent wave of ocean-front development. But his deeper motive is also announced by the text in expedient disguise. A critical mass is not just the point where radioactive matter becomes more dynamic; it is the point where its internal interactions soar beyond control. An apt metaphor, for Koolhaas would like to amplify the

5.4
OMA, Miami Performing Arts Center, Miami, 1994.
© OMA.

event structure of the performance complex to the point where it, too, risks spiraling out of control.

In political terms, intensifying the event structure amounts to unaligned activism, to a profligate operation that does not selectively enfranchise so much as it diminishes restriction. When achieved, it muffles a badgering program and distracts the visitor with frissons of danger and excitement as it magnifies the possibility of the unexpected. It should, in principle, stage a richer range of all events—including none. It is a minor point of vulnerability in the work, because, in fact, public projects such as this one always feel dedicated to busyness, with no place for the pleasures of repose.

In the name of acoustics but with other implications, the sponsors commissioned consultants to execute a basic design of the concert hall and opera house auditoria. The brief required participating architects to accept the predesigned halls without exception. Now, theaters, with their rituals, their collective audiences, and their dialectic relationship between performer and listener, have been a favorite subject of architects for revisionist experiments of a political bent. Given a freer hand at Cardiff, Koolhaas builds upon that legacy with marvelous results. Unfortunately, the full potential for such experimentation in Miami ended as soon as the auditoria became set pieces. All that remained for OMA to work with was the public areas of the two theaters and the interior design.

To make room for the entire complex on the larger of the two sites, Koolhaas proposed razing an old but negligible building and retaining another of more architectural merit to be incorporated in the new construction. (He had already declared at La Défense his willingness to propose tabula rasa erasure and reaffirmed his intention to discriminate in matters of preservation. An ethic of historical preservation born in a reaction against the wanton erasures of modernism had, over a generation, metastasized like church doctrine into a pack-rat mindset that traumatized architects into inaction. Koolhaas's La Défense master plan reminded architects not only of their right but of their responsibility to exercise qualitative judgment when confronting previous work, even at the risk of being wrong.)

Koolhaas placed the given concert hall and opera house envelopes as naked forms on the site and bridged them with a transparent, multistoried structure suggestively called the mixing chamber containing the collected public areas and functions. He fleshed out the remainder of the city block with ancillary facilities. A clever automobile circulation scheme plucked from an airport shunted traffic off the main highway to the drop-offs for the two theaters, on to the parking facilities, then back to the highway.

Automobile circulation was not merely a functional matter in the scheme, because the complex was situated in a transitional commercial area of Miami near lower-income communities whose classical music and opera buffs were unlikely to be able to afford tickets. Probable users of the complex would come by car from remote neighborhoods and, like any colonialists, would not be completely comfortable walking the streets at night. Koolhaas's unceremonious, infrastructural approach did not solve the social distortions—a task beyond architecture—but it did deal with them without a whitewash.

The thematic centerpiece of the project, the mixing chamber, was a revised and reproportioned Jussieu stripped of its sensuous warps, its ramps stiffened into escalators. The total area of box office, foyers, and lobbies of the two theaters was too little to fill a structure large enough to make adequate visual impact on the facade. Thus, the architect added almost four floors of "foyer" space, bolstered by vague references to additional program such as banqueting, fund raising, and so forth.

Restricted entries and the lack of broad attractor programming on the upper levels made the mixing chamber at Miami generally less convincing as an event structure than Jussieu. The more aggressive decision was to add broad civic programming to attract locals into the large spaces in the plinth beneath the overhangs of the auditoria, adjacent to the automobile drop-off and the mixing chamber's major entry street. The actual intensities and incongruities implicit in the idea of the mixing chamber would occur in this area.

OMA's presentation perspectives of the entry to the mixing chamber were cropped so as to make the people standing on the top of the plinth appear at first glance as if they were on the city street. It was a gimmick, a seduction, of course, but also a hint of the more radical dimension of the design, its canny duplicities of representation. However compromised the mixing chamber may be as an event structure, it is an extraordinary optical instrument, a giant proscenium stage/projection screen displaying the performances of the concert-goers for all to see. The ceiling of the opera house, where one has grown accustomed to great works of mythical painting by the likes of Marc Chagall, is clad in enormous Cindy Sherman photographs, and the backdrop of the concert hall stage is wrapped in an exquisite gold link curtain. Each of these devices gratifies without cynicism the bona fide desires of self-aggrandizement and ostentatious display that are inseparable from the experiences proffered by such institutions, and at the same time reflects the excesses of those desires back on the participants critically. As a formally attired couple stands at the glass wall of the mixing chamber enjoying the magnificent view of the Atlantic Ocean, they cannot mistake the unsettling certainty that they too are characters in a continuous opera buffa performed for an entirely difference audience.

Sherman's photographs are works of contemporary art equal in stature in today's art world to Chagall's paintings during his lifetime. These contemporary masterworks perform their doubling, their critical mirroring of events below, as soon as one recognizes that the photographs depict the artist herself in scenes of exaggerated performance. And could anyone miss the reflection on institutionalized excess—critical and indulgent—as one gawks, mesmerized by the flowing gold link curtain ringing the stage?

The power of these extraordinary devices emanates from their ability to both maintain and yet subvert the institution they mirror. As such, they demonstrate a key difference between essentialist reduction and disestablishing reduction. An essentialist reduction attempts to assert what the essential nature of an institution should be and organizes experiences according to that ideal. Inevitably, it is trapped by the habits of history, whether those retain any relevance or not. A disestablishing reduction explores what, if anything, remains of a relevant, contemporary experience in an institution. The former, wittingly or not, guided the acousticians, the latter the architect.

OMA lost the competition.

The OMA Entry to a Limited Competition for a Renovation of London's Bankside Power Station into the New Tate Modern Museum

A new period of equalities must begin.
—OMA New Tate Modern project report

On the one hand, the OMA entry to the Tate/Bankside competition is the most aggressive, most meticulously disestablishing design ever to emerge from the practice. On the other hand, as a work of architecture it is disappointing, even desperate. It must be said that the design might well have led to a sensational situation for experiencing art, but if it had, it would have been an achievement that hurried the extinction not only of the museum but of the discipline of architecture. Perhaps that was the point . . .

Koolhaas lifted his epithet for the scheme, *Danger: 66,000 volts*, from a sign found at the abandoned power station and

5.5
OMA, Tate Modern, London, 1994. © OMA.

used it to announce his now-familiar intention to turn up the voltage on the museum's event structure at all costs. With a twist here and there, Jussieuian tactics are in evidence in the extreme. Form is suppressed, program is augmented, nonspecific flows and events are encouraged, vestigial spaces are deployed, and poché is erased. The problem is that the disestablishing reductions are carried so far that nothing substantial remains of the museum as such. Koolhaas dissolves the Tate/Bankside into pure organization.

There are, of course, strokes of genius in the project, not least of which is its focused assault on the mechanisms by which the museum customarily exercises expertise over its contents and authority over its constituencies. Perfecting a tendency that began at the Kunsthal, the design denies the art any mystifying aura obtained from its architectural setting. As required by the program, the three stacked blocks of galleries present each of the various periods of twentieth-century art in appropriate settings in terms of space, scale, lighting, etc. What the mercilessly generic scheme withholds is the possibility of any cosmetic staging of the art. There are rooms of different sorts for art of different sorts, but no house; the rooms just sit on the street.

Even the institution's right to maintain an atmosphere of simple dignity by choreographing a stately circulation is challenged. Koolhaas makes a point of giving rapid, inattentive visits a status equal to their more somber counterparts by elevating every mode of sectional movement—stairs, ramps, escalators, and elevators—to equal status, even collaging them together on occasion into a walk-run interchange. Like most of the architect's inventions, it is a gesture that optimistically embraces the reality of an institution's current use. Today, visits to the art museum already assume the form of quick courantes as often as solemn sarabandes. Koolhaas's scheme underwrites these movements, even inviting the occasional crash dance and rave.

Other twentieth-century art museums are famed for their subversions of one or another tradition of the institution. The Pompidou Center's open-space apron, theme-park image and circulation, and unceremonious loft spaces are renowned for democratizing the institution and engendering an event structure far exceeding its program. The Guggenheim's extraordinary section generates excitements, sublime and voyeuristic that simply overwhelm the art. Indeed, Frank Lloyd Wright's museum is a key antecedent to all of Koolhaas's Jussieuian works. What each of these buildings possesses that Koolhaas's Tate project lacks is an affirmative architectural presence intrinsic to the design.

OMA's scheme is rife with efforts to correct this lack. A bizarre perspective and urban section places the scheme in direct comparison to Christopher Wren's St. Paul's cathedral. OMA's design expressly formulates the Tate/Bankside as the next (tourist) stop after St. Paul's, the theme of the drawing. But the isolated presence of Wren's masterpiece only serves to caricature the impotence of the one element that would mark the OMA scheme's presence in London's urban space, a chimney left over from the power station, whose retention was required by the brief. At least OMA skins the bricks off the cloying souvenir to reveal the raw skeleton of its structural tower, a blatant symbol of the similar operation it performs on the institution beneath.[10] To give the south facade formal interest and an identifiable entrance, OMA appropriates the enormous cloverleaf of oil tanks left over from the station. On the interior, each of the three, stacked blocks of galleries is rendered in ascendance in a different material, from stone to wood to aluminum, perhaps to signify the denaturing of art or its movement toward dematerialization.

Compared to the irreducible role played by form and material in most of OMA's projects, these devices seem clumsy afterthoughts to the internal logic of the scheme, half-hearted efforts to find a place in the project for contextual relations, historical quotations, interesting shapes, and fine material. But the OMA scheme has as little to do with architecture as with the museum. It is a work of urban infrastructure whose core strategy is organization, whose techniques belong to engineering, and whose fundamental measure is not aesthetic quality but performance over time at maximum use. These factors may have contributed to a singularly interesting proposal, but they also led inexorably to a losing effort in an important architecture competition.

The Cardiff Opera House

To liberate Opera from its bourgeois associations . . .
—OMA Cardiff Bay Opera House project report

A curiosity of Koolhaas's career is the unusual number of unpremiated competition entries it has produced that have come to assume the status of paradigmatic projects, even contemporary masterworks. La Villette, Agadir, the Très Grande Bibliothèque, Melun-Sénart, Yokohama, and others continue to exercise profound influence on experimental architecture long after they have been forgotten by the juries and the press. It is a circumstance worthy of its own study, related, no doubt, to the difficulties that the architect's work presents to traditional criticism.

OMA's extraordinary entry for the Cardiff Bay Opera House competition will almost certainly join this group. It went virtually unnoticed at the competition, perhaps because at first impression the design appears inelegant. After some study, however, one realizes that the scheme stands out not just among Koolhaas's projects but among the strongest projects by any architect in the last decade.

Cardiff brakes Koolhaas's acceleration away from Architecture toward pure organization that we have tracked from Jussieu to the Tate. Compared to those projects, the scheme appears tame, a throwback to an earlier period when the architect's work abounded in playfulness and irony, though that appearance is misleading. Though the urge to license and liberty are unabated at Cardiff, its institutional reductions are less strident and are accomplished in a richer palette of architectural effects.

The genius of the scheme begins with its graceless massing. A pavilion crashes into a large box and scrolls into an aneurysm at the point of collision. Yet, the awkwardness of the massing is compelling, etching instantly into memory. No architect who has seen the scheme could ever fail to sketch it later.

Each of the massing elements is clad in an architecture fitted to its role in the program, form and tectonics as simple as possible, but not so simple as to erode architectural presence. The pavilion, attaching the lobby and foyer to the theater, enjoys a sophisticated architectural rendering in Miesian strokes, though not without its iconoclasm.

Koolhaas fills the slab of space beneath the main floor of the pavilion with entry program. Elevating a slab over a wafer-thin void was a persistent feature of Mies's spatial signature, found again and again in his work, from the Barcelona daybed to the Farnsworth House. It can be argued that the most important difference that distinguished the diagrams of modern architectural space by Wright, Mies, and Le Corbusier was in the height each raised the building off the ground: Wright none, Mies a little, Corb a lot. Koolhaas's saturation of the Miesian void with program is a knowing perversion with a by-now-familiar theme.

The scroll, the crucial source of visual interest of the massing, contains the auditorium. Constructed as a continuous concrete plate, it is reinforced with a diagonal grid of ribs of varying width that corrugate the ceiling, contributing to the hall's acoustics. A full-width truss supports the terminal loop, insuring that no columns obstruct the entry. The form, construction, and function of the scroll reach a rarely achieved degree of contingent interdependence, making it a remarkable work of architecture in its own right.

5.6
OMA, Cardiff Bay Opera House, Cardiff, 1994.
Photo: Hans Werlemann / © OMA.

The large, white box holds administrative offices, production facilities, the performance stage, and other working spaces of the two resident opera companies. Accordingly, it is designed prosaically, like a factory, says OMA's report. Almost, but not quite. After all, exigencies of function guarantee that a factory never assumes so uninflected a form.

Careful study of the plans and sections confirms what the pocks and mottles in the box suggest, that OMA went to considerable effort to maintain the rigid, rectangular outline. Far from mere expediency, the form's rectitude performs subtle architectural functions. It reinforces emphatically the massing as an ad hoc necklace of different elements, a point that increases in importance when one turns to the sections. Secondly, it subsumes the fly tower, the functional requirement of theaters whose endlessly repeated profile has accreted into an irritating architectural tic, a tell well on its way to becoming a nostalgic sign, like chimney stacks for power stations. Finally, it performs one of the scheme's few aggressive reductions, though few would know it. The building houses two companies, the Welsh National Opera and the Cardiff Bay Opera House, and the brief required the design to express distinctly the headquarters of the two. A continuous section washes through the pavilion and scroll into the box, transforming the discordant elements into zones knit into a new, coherent spatial unity. Here Koolhaas achieves a breakthrough on a problem that design theory has grappled with for some time: how to bring differences into larger coherent organizations without subordinating those differences to overarching unities. The coherence of Cardiff has nothing to do with the intricate formal relationships of compositional notions such as Robert Venturi's *difficult whole*. Nor does it rely on exotic techniques such as morphing or weak form that have dominated research in this area, though the scroll clearly draws upon this work.

At the level of form, the elements remain unreconciled. The new coherence occurs in the sectional space, in the domain of

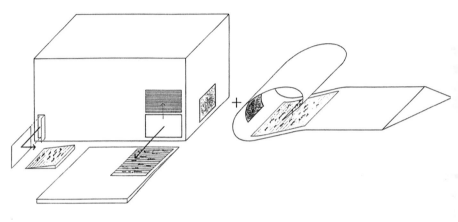

5.7
OMA, Cardiff Bay Opera House, Cardiff, 1994.
© OMA.

the event structure, rather than in the sculptural or narrative domains of the architecture, where other architects interested in this problem have tended to concentrate. Even the functional zones of the sectional space—the lobby, the auditorium, and the stage—remain distinct; there is no layering, no overlapping. At first, the complex unity is achieved entirely as a visual effect. Upon entering the lobby, one encounters a vast, unimpeded vista through the auditorium to the stage. As soon as the eye recognizes the cues of the discreet functional zoning filtered through the memory of the tripartite massing, the new coherence is consummated. However, as one proceeds into the auditorium, a stunning bifurcation of the space occurs and elevates the unity from the realm of the visual to the realm of the political. In a brilliant development of the single-surface technique used in Jussieu, the floor of the lobby descends to become the main floor of the auditorium, rolls up, conceptually incorporating the stage window and proscenium, and scrolls back to become the balcony. The activity of the surface splits the space into a branch that continues into the stage and one that folds back into the audience. The single-surface/bifurcated space unites the disparate social sectors of a performance—the performers, those on the main floor, and those in the balcony—into an experience of coherence that does not suppress the differences but depends on them.

Cardiff is the most effective work of political optimism to be seen in architecture for a generation. It is no surprise that it came from Koolhaas and his colleagues at OMA, who have mounted the most liberating, optimistic practice of our time.

Epilogue

The Miesian pavilion and block of production facilities in the Cardiff scheme remind us of Koolhaas's fondness for the modern. It is an attachment that has placed him in a curious relationship with other architects who have spearheaded various manners of modernist revival. The most interesting of these latter today are the new minimalists and neomodernists. Similarities that would seem to join Koolhaas's work to the objectives of these other architects mask an irreconcilable tension between the two bodies of work, one that promises to be the dominant organizing debate in contemporary architecture in the near future. This tension turns on perhaps the single most significant issue of disestablishment that Koolhaas and others of his ilk have championed, the proposition that the architecture of a building be biased toward its performance in full use. Let us name the proposition the *infrastructural tenet*.

Given the attention that architecture claims to pay to program, how can the infrastructural tenet ever be considered disestablishing? The answer is simply this: without exception, every criteria of conventional architectural judgment remains dedicated to a conception of architecture as being at its best when a building is empty—that is, to a garden principle. Whatever the criterion—fineness of material and joinery, brilliance of structure and construction, elegance of shape and proportion, drama of light and shadow, intricacy of formal relationship, sensitivity to context, profundity of space—one fact prevails. Acute architectural connoisseurship requires a quiet contemplation whose exercise is only possible while undistracted. The architectural concept of program is entirely complicit with the garden principle. Pre-scripting activity with efficiency and functional specificity limits use and moves people quickly to and from their destinations, reducing distraction.

Circumstantial evidence mounts to support this conjecture. An excursion through a century of published architectural photography finds an overwhelming preference for empty buildings. The canonic drawings of architectural design and representation—plan, section, elevation, axonometric, and perspective—all are denuded of activity. In fact, there is no canonic representation of activity in the building other than the adjacency and circulation diagrams; none whatsoever exists for the more complex issue of event structure. The only class of drawing that attempts to undertake such a representation is collage, a prevalent but far from canonic technique. And is it an accident that the media best suited to represent activity, such as film and video, still have found no intrinsic role in architectural design technique or criticism? When they are employed at all, they are used to create serialized perspectives that depict buildings according to the garden principle values perfectly embodied in still photography.

It may be argued that perspective is an exception; not only do perspectives often show people, but they represent a person's viewpoint. But the garden principle saturates the perspective. People in perspectives serve as accents to the primary assets of the architecture, its form, detailing, or space, adding a sense of scale or a wash of use. More importantly, the single-person viewpoint of the perspective is the very essence of connoisseurship.

A garden or a building is never so poignant as it is with one person walking through it. And nothing is so irritating as trying to appreciate a garden or a building full of people.

The disestablishing mechanisms of the infrastructural tenet are a profound threat to the discipline of architecture as we know it. As we glimpsed at the Tate, the infrastructural tenet is, at its limit, a prediction of the extinction of architecture. The garden principle, on the other hand, is the central dogma of architecture as art, and the new minimalists and neomodernists reaffirm it without apology. Every decision in their design process is meant to achieve exquisite visual refinement, and extreme effort is spent to maintain the integrity of those decisions in the work's materialization. Program is no exception; these architects have formulated brilliant strategies to anesthetize a building's use and users. Cunning lighting allies with translucent materials to dematerialize people into surface shadows and silhouettes. If necessary, core function is sacrificed. It is sad that at some of the fashion boutiques in London, as little as twenty percent of the clothing line can be displayed in the arresting new minimalist showrooms.

The difference between the infrastructuralists and the garden-variety new minimalists is fundamental: while the former strive to maximize the event structure of the architecture, the latter must minimize it for best effect. Accordingly, Koolhaas commands the attention of the new left (the old left hates architecture, period), while the new right has begun dumping the neohistoricists for the new minimalists with shocking alacrity.

In his provocative exhibition "Light Construction," Museum of Modern Art curator Terence Riley attempted to set aside such categorical differences to examine the emergent architectural commonality underlying these various practices. He makes a good case that, from an architectonic point of view, such brute, dialectic categories as left and right, infrastructuralism and new minimalism ride roughshod over the crossover concerns that lock these architectures together in a macabre minuet of conflict and collusion.

On the other hand, during the toasts celebrating the opening of "Light Construction," the deep-seated tension between the two positions broke out in an understated but bristling exchange between Jacques Herzog and Koolhaas. Herzog toasted the show for suggesting that perhaps the most radical architects of the day were those who abstained from intellectualism and dared just to be beautifully boring. Koolhaas applauded Riley's effort to bring dissenting architectures into contact with one another in the same space. He finished by asking himself aloud if, when we look back at the show five years hence, it will seem to have been prophetic or naïve. Will its tensions simply have dissipated into a prevailing aesthetic or escalated until the uneasy détente exploded into open conflict? What he hoped the answer would be was obvious to all.

6 MONEO'S ANXIETY

Rich with thoughtful deliberation on eight practices that have shaped late-modern and contemporary speculative architecture, Rafael Moneo's *Theoretical Anxieties and Design Strategies in the Work of Eight Contemporary Architects* provides a valuable anthology in the sheer number and significance of the works it documents. Of course, the book's merit as a primer is not what is at stake when one such as Moneo addresses the likes of Rem Koolhaas, Peter Eisenman, Jacques Herzog & Pierre de Meuron, Robert Venturi and Denise Scott Brown, Frank Gehry, Álvaro Siza, James Stirling, and Aldo Rossi, particularly when that address is christened *Theoretical Anxiety*.

Moneo is the epitome in architecture of the figure crucial to any praxis in which speculation and experimentation are essential: the forthright, learned practitioner who speaks with conviction for the persistent worth of established values and methods. Alert to the necessity of change but wary of it, such a voice holds speculation accountable to a sober measure of its consequences, damping novelty's penchant to intoxicate and quicken into exoticism.

The major attraction of the book for me derives from the prospects of such a figure undertaking to confront the considered work on theoretical grounds. Inevitably, therefore, the discussion must turn to the question of theory, though I have no interest whatsoever in wrangling over the meaning of the word *theory*. More important to ask is what the discipline can and should expect from work whose speculations and experiments pretend to the theoretical.

In his preface, Moneo accounts for his title by distinguishing a systematic *theory* from *critique* motivated by disquiet, terming the latter a theoretical anxiety and thus situating it in the domain of the polemic, the refutation, or the reflection. He offers the opinion that insofar as the practices he considers have produced written tracts, these operate more in the latter category than the former, and, whether they have tracts or not, the work of each practice is best understood in these terms. That Venturi and Koolhaas both styled their first books manifestos supports the author's point.

Though I concur with his portrayal of such theorizing, I take issue with the inference that the results of critique fall short of theory. While this view may hold for the hard sciences and classical models of theory in the arts and humanities, these latter two have embraced critique and its discursive relatives as a recognized and in some cases preferred approach to theorizing. To be sure, such methods no longer engender systematic theories like those of Jean-Nicolas-Louis Durand or structuralist semiotics, but today the very comprehensiveness of such systems is itself a source of deep suspicion.

Theorizing by critique can do much more than express disquiet and catalog oppositional tactics. At its best, sustained critique unveils something larger, slowly, through the accumulated weight of its discontents and alternative proposals, something that, even if it is more provisional, rises to the order of theory if not to its traditional form.

Moneo approaches these practices not as a scholar or critic but as a peer. Of the eight, seven join the author as Pritzker laureates, and at this moment the single omission casts doubt less on the one passed over than on the credibility of the prize itself.

The imprimatur of the author's position is not incidental; he relies on it to underwrite the sufficiency of his opinion and to absolve himself of any responsibility to engage the considerable commentary that these practices have accumulated, though they have enjoyed disproportionate attention from the field's best minds for over a generation. Moneo enlists very little other than each architect's own projects, buildings, and writings.

Whether strident in his rebuke or lavish in his praise, the author never strays from disciplinary high ground, but his neglect of the literature is at times unfortunate, if for no other reason than accuracy. In one instance, for example, he credits Eisenman with the Museum of Modern Art "Deconstructivist Architecture" exhibition in its entirety—its conception, the selection of the exhibited architects, the title—as if Mark Wigley and Philip Johnson were mere pawns.[1] The puppet master caricature of Eisenman is perhaps forgivable as one of architecture's favorite urban myths. On the other hand, in these pages it belongs to a more insidious problem, a tacit perpetuation of the fountainhead trope reflected in the dedication of each chapter to a digested history of a practice in which the biographical development of the lead architect largely shapes the account of the work.[2]

Influential frontline practices such as these warrant a more discerning exegesis than can be achieved by the genius narrative or the tradition of art as embodied biography. To his credit, Moneo rejects the idea now in vogue that theoretical architecture refers only to the work of architects who write theory; instead he locates the decisive consequence of an architecture in its buildings' effects. But the book's monographic organization all but forces the author to measure these effects piecemeal, severally, and thus ultimately against the presumption that his own values are absolute.

That reservation notwithstanding, my favorite chapters in the book are on Gehry and on Siza, the architect closest to the author's own disposition. Moneo's affection for Siza resonates in the commentary, which passes to the buildings through the writings of Fernando Pessoa, the singular Portuguese poet. In nuanced recitations of the Beires House and the house for Siza's brother, the author, "overcome [by] the impression of tangibility," extols the architect's courage to find a place for sentiment in his work. It is not that Siza makes no missteps, but that in the author's eyes his course is so true that a reader might forget the theme of theoretical anxiety entirely. In Gehry's architecture, Moneo sees an obsessive quest for immediacy, and he emphasizes the phenomenological tilt that results, a point that will bear further discussion.

The readings of Stirling and Rossi weave together fact, interpretation, and lore in the way only reminiscence can, but, though poignant, these readings add little to standard views. The chapter on Herzog & de Meuron favors the work up to and including the Dominus Winery. Moneo revels in the originality of the handling of materials under the restraint of the box, chafing as the practice strays toward skin effects and other frivolous excursions. Above all, he is drawn to an intimation of what he terms the "archaic" in Herzog & de Meuron: "Let us say that the prize awaiting those who take such intricate paths is a reencounter with a reality that expresses the desire for permanence present in much of primitive architecture: the logic of construction is so evident that any temptation to let aesthetic parameters come into play is forgotten."[3] While it is not difficult to detect those aspects of Herzog & de Meuron's work that lend themselves to such elegant meditation, insofar as it sidesteps a great deal of invention in the work it reveals more about the author than it does about the practice's theoretical achievements.

Addressing those five practices, the author takes care to distinguish his summary of the architect's theoretical objectives from his own observations and opinions. But when he turns to Venturi, Eisenman, and Koolhaas, that care dissolves, to the point that it sometimes becomes difficult to discern whether he simply misapprehends the work or refuses on principle to accept its fundamental conjecture. Of the columns in Eisenman's Wexner Center for the Visual Arts he writes, for example, "Some suspended prisms never reach the ground. A superficial reading of the construction might well have taken them as columns."[4] Now, Eisenman's entire critique starts from the premise that architecture as a cultural discourse is never founded on structure but on the significations of structure. For Eisenman, the material or load-bearing differences between column and *pilotis* are of little import; on the other hand, the idea that a column signifies the metaphysical hierarchy that relates sky to ground while the *pilotis* signifies the erasure of that hierarchy is all-important. If an architectural element must bear a load to be a column a priori, the discussion is over before it begins.

The Wexner Center column-signs join the other speculative design devices in the building as part and parcel of the architect's contention that the building conducts a radical rethinking of the relationships between contemporary architecture and contemporary art, its institutions, audiences, and contexts. Certainly, at the core of much contemporary art is a skeptical critique of the so-called self-evidence of what stands as the signified and what stands as the signifier, the very self-evidence that permits Moneo to distinguish prism from column without hesitation. Of course, in this case as elsewhere, I do not mean to suggest that just because an architecture attempted an experiment, the experiment succeeded. There are substantial grounds to debate both Eisenman's premise and the effectiveness of the design strategies he used at the Wexner Center to pursue it. But even if the author doubts the merit of the premise, should he not at least acknowledge it?

Similar difficulties arise in the chapter on Venturi and reach a discomforting pitch with Koolhaas. If we collate a few dispersed observations, the issue becomes clearer. On Venturi's Vanna Venturi House: "Deliberately ambiguous, the house ignores both its social and its physical environment. Just look at the site plan. The front facade makes no reference to context whatsoever."[5] On Eisenman's House II: "The result is pure form that ignores all the circumstances surrounding it . . . with no references whatsoever, either to the topography, to building techniques or to tough climatic conditions that would in theory call for a foundation."[6] On Rem Koolhaas's Villa dall'Ava: "Koolhaas ignored context. With no regard for the bourgeois surroundings . . . The house is a whole reflection on suburban life. . . . It's a house designed to be consumed visually, to speak of how its owner wishes to be perceived."[7]

In his reading of the Vanna Venturi House, Moneo draws attention to the strategic use of the generic double-square organization and the floor plans to frame the "autonomy and independence of individual elements" while binding them together. Thus does he call attention to the parallel work done by an ingenious plan and the more famous front facade. The plan coordinates its disparate elements as the facade does its similarly incongruous collection of stuff. That something is askew in the author's reading, however, first becomes apparent when he addresses the absence of the expected on-axis front entry and the ninety-degree turn that the actual placement of the front door requires after one passes under the cornice. He writes, "The porch, key to an understanding of the house's public facade, does not frame a central entrance. Venturi reckons that the door, as in old fortifications, must be handled only by the owners."[8] A bizarre rationale, it seems, for a formal device whose thwarting of expectations sets up the plan effects the author has already enumerated. The explanation becomes all the more curious when one later reads the analysis of a similar formal effect by Siza a decade later. In the Beires House, Moneo describes the eccentric diagonal entry as necessary to establish the effect of autonomy in the house that comes to a climax in the living room and its relationship to the garden.

The author concludes his discussion of the Vanna Venturi House with the assertion, quoted above, of a patently obvious lapse: "Just look at the site plan . . ." Rather than debate his assessment of Venturi's siting, let us stipulate its accuracy. Why might an approach to site detached from a traditional appreciation of the amenities of the setting not be just as necessary to the architectural conjecture as the other design devices, the generic double square and floor plans? As the author has argued, everything about the house is devoted to the appreciation of isolated episodes that lack any organic intimacy. Not only does Venturi's design make of the house a commentary on the political and social context of the suburb, but might it not also propose a formal distinction between a suburban house and those domestic architectural typologies long perfected to the setting such as the garden folly, the villa, or the vacation home?

Might not a similar line of thought apply, too, to Eisenman's House II? In the chapter on Herzog & de Meuron, the author asserts that the key element of the bourgeois house is the room. Why, then, does the replacement of rooms in House II with a syntactic field of forms not constitute a critique of the bourgeois? Not until Koolhaas's Villa dall'Ava does the author allow for the possibility that a calculated disregard of setting, locale, or other conventions might be part of a larger architectural proposition. That such a proposition, even where admitted, might have an affirmative ambition is not considered. Though he notes that the house creates an atmosphere in which modernity is based on "tolerance and nonexclusivity," in the end the author pronounces Villa dall'Ava to be Le Corbusier's Villa Savoye "manipulated in a personal and malevolent way" merely to serve base vanities of the client.

As a fellow critic of architecture, I dispute his interpretation. But as a reader of the book, I simply ask again: If the author seeks to engage these architectures in terms of their theoretical anxieties, how can sympathy for the site, or any established value for that matter, be immune to questioning? While the eight practices bicker among themselves about which values to challenge and which to maintain, each is included in the book ostensibly because it sets out to conduct such a challenge.

Not only is Moneo entitled to firm convictions, they are expected of him in such a critical exercise—not as dicta, however, but as positions open to debate. Throughout his career, Moneo has consistently championed certain values: that the primary responsibility of the architect qua architect is to resist the banalization of building culture; that, while it is necessary to be vigilant against simulacra, clichés, and platitudes, the history of architecture nevertheless provides the best resource from which to mount that resistance; that the ultimate encompassment of architectural knowledge is the building and, therefore, that the just measure of architectural achievement is found in a building's qualities; and finally, that architecture finds its cultural apotheosis when it serves not merely a constituency or a public but a community, understood both in social and contextual terms. As venerable as these principles may be, they are each confronted several times over with astounding variety and invention by these practices. In that light, the author's pervasive *comme il faut* response, particularly to Venturi, Eisenman, and Koolhaas, is disappointing.

Moneo's skilled, discerning eye rarely misses a deviation from a prevailing norm. But when the deviation reaches a certain limit, rarely does his criticism allow that a changing circumstance in a broader disciplinary or cultural context might conceivably vindicate it. Though the three architects mentioned provoke the reaction at its extreme, it is not confined to them. Recognizing the influence of Andy Warhol on Herzog & de Meuron's experiments with skin printing, he nevertheless dismisses that body of work. Of the library at Eberswalde, he writes, "Despite the radicality, the underlying structure of the building is conventional. I hesitate to approve of an architecture that is only in control of the skin."[9] Might not Warhol, whose work above all took advantage of a conventional underlying structure to achieve an inestimable force of cultural argument, have augured the possibility that a building could achieve similar cultural force with just its skin, an experiment whose hypothesis may well have required a conventional underlying structure in the remainder of the building?

By the time Moneo discusses a specific building or project, his evaluations retreat to predictable terms. For example, in his introductory pages on Venturi he goes to some length to discuss the design strategies proposed by his *Complexity and Contradiction in Architecture*, and, as his interpretation of the work proceeds, he recognizes in general the commitment of the practice to a synthesis of those strategies with the symbol-oriented populism expressed in *Learning from Las Vegas*. Thus does he set out the terms of Venturi and Scott Brown's theoretical anxiety. But when he comes to the Sainsbury Wing in London, regarded as the quintessential test of that anxiety, that is, of the ability of the practice's experimental design techniques to materialize that populism in an institutional, architectural, urban, and political context inherently resistant to it, that test barely colors the discussion. His exhaustive analysis is a brilliant lesson in formal analysis, but not a single detail of it is brought to bear on the larger question. Among other critics, a lively debate surrounds the controversial third-floor plan, where the transition between the original Wilkins building and the new wing occurs. Some see the linear array of the galleries, entered from the old wing incongruously and ignobly along a haphazard diagonal cut, as an ideal way architecturally to chip away at the majestic crust accrued by the collection in

Wilkins's ceremonial plans, a gentle iconoclasm capped by the droll placement of the great Cima da Conegliano painting as the climax of the entry's dead end. Others see it as a trite slap in the face of a venerated collection made all the more regrettable by the pressing of a masterpiece into the service of a bad joke. Both views, however, grasp what is at stake. Though Moneo's is an extraordinarily keen analysis of the formal effects of the plan, all he sees in it is an obstinate interest in introducing contradictions for the sake of the exercise.

To go so far as to so interpret the deviation would still fall short of the full potential of a criticism that compared and evaluated the variety of responses by different practices to changing circumstances. One cannot help but notice, for example, the recurring themes of autonomy and isolation identified by the author in suburban houses across all eight practices over more than 40 years. To what force are these projects responding, and toward what end is the response directed—an alienation to be forestalled or a new way of being in the world? Strictly in terms of design strategy, one does not fail to notice throughout the book various debates among the practices about plan, section, materiality, and context. Moneo does little to tease out the discussion the works have with one another and with others about such fundamental issues.[10] Occasionally, he contrasts work in passing, but without elaboration. He mentions, for example, a provocative relationship between Gehry and Koolhaas: "For among the eight taken up in this book, only Koolhaas and Gehry consider that program lies at the origins of architecture," opposing Gehry's treatment of program as a given constraint to Koolhaas's view of program as "more diffuse and much less directly related to the architecture that is to be built."[11] Yet nowhere does the distinction guide the analyses of specific works by either architect in such a way as would indicate how the particulars of their design strategies contest program.

To follow further the question of the respective treatment of program and see where it leads, consider Gehry's Guggenheim Bilbao vis-à-vis Koolhaas's proposal for the Bibliothèque Nationale de France competition. Moneo's appreciation of Bilbao unfolds its architect's use of layered gestures and scale shifts, symbolic allusion, material effects, and a cunning urbanism to revitalize the possibility of the monumental just when some in the field had begun to argue for an end to monumentality as such. By the time we read that the building's "continuous changes of scale, leaps, breaks, interruptions, spans, etc., bombard our senses and transform our visit into a chain of surprises that leaves no time for reflection,"[12] we have gained insights about the possibility of a new monumentality. Those so inclined, meanwhile, are better prepared to mount a discriminating interrogation of the building, for it is reasonable to ask whether immersion in architectural sensation is an adept surround for art.

Gehry's theoretical anxiety concerns a vanishing immediacy and authenticity of experience. He sees in most conventional architecture what William H. Gass calls a courteous kitsch, a riskless use of familiar forms that at best reminds us of but does not produce a breathtaking urban vista or the edgy pleasures of the sublime. Much as the ultimate task of the writer, the composer, or the filmmaker who hopes to arouse basic emotions is to shed the medium's accumulated clichés of those emotions, so too should that be the first task of the architect.

That is why Gehry's architecture adheres so closely to the program as a given and why his plans are so traditional. Not mere expediency, the narrative backbone of a familiar, uncontested functional program is necessary to secure Gehry's architecture in the here and now. The sequenced perspective plan is exquisitely tailored to the goals of the architecture; perfected since the baroque, that planning strategy provides an effective instrument with which to unfold individual architectural experience in time and space. As you approach from any direction in the city, the building performs a dazzling fanfare, transforming from flower to sail to mountain-scape with almost every step. You enter . . . only to land, disappointed, in a mean foyer. A sharp turn, a short narrowing walk, one last twist, and suddenly the hysteria of the great hall's open section drowns you in the sublime. What staging of the sublime could be more cinematic, more contemporary? And what dispute with Koolhaas could be more rancorous?

On OMA's Bibliothèque de France project, Moneo musters little more than admiration of the "extraordinarily expressive" drawings and models, and the "plastic mastery" evidenced in the facade, with its use of translucency, its "note of color," and the "uncommon dexterity" of the figures he uses to "liven up" its four planes. A feeble appreciation at best for a signal project that reverberates in an extraordinary range of speculative work to this day.[13] But then, Koolhaas is altogether the architect whose theoretical import Moneo most fails to grasp.

Moneo does ascribe to Koolhaas an important innovation: the free section. At first the provenance seems capricious, given the spate of section-driven projects that proliferated in the '80s, coalescing into the box-in-box investigations that continue to develop. Yet there is merit to the author's attribution, I think. Although, oddly, Moneo ignores the Miesian vector in OMA's work, he is keenly attentive to its Corbusian trajectory. Much as the free plan in Le Corbusier's work simply cannot be equated to a generic open plan, neither can OMA's free section be equated to a generic excess of volume enveloping formal activity in the section; moreover, it is the distinction between the two in each case that transforms the former (open plan, open section) from an elemental design device into a specific theoretical design strategy (free plan, free section).

Only when an open platform works in concert with ribbon windows, rooftop garden, and *pilotis* does it become the free plan. Together, they consummate the effect that, in theoretical terms, is the goal of Le Corbusier's design strategy as a whole: to transform the land from ground into an equipotential datum, one among others. That effect critiques the discipline's history of complicity in the metaphysics of land's groundedness with all that that entails, from *holy land* to *fatherland* to *my land*, and, more importantly, broaches an architectural realignment.

Le Corbusier's use of the open platform to create free plan is utterly different from Mies van der Rohe's use of the open platform. Both remove the platform from the ground, but the distance of the remove, coordinated with the other building elements and devices, is crucial. To free the ground as datum, Le Corbusier removes the platform a large distance. Thus must he always cloak the door, which works against the architecture by reestablishing the priority of the ground. In Mies's architecture, the overt use of entryway, stairs, and door, in concert with the comparatively small distance the platform is lifted off the ground, transforms it into a theatrical stage. But then, Mies is less interested in reconstituting a political ground than in creating a retreat from it. Similarly, the specificity of OMA's free section can only be distinguished from other open-section design strategies in its coordination with plan, building form, and other architectural devices.

No practice has made more cunning use of the differences between Corb's free plan and Mies's stage plan than OMA, which has synthesized the two into an architecture that, in its critique of the two, posits a fundamental shift in the liberal project from the modernist pursuit of democracy as a collective ideal (in the future) to a contemporary desire to instantiate individual freedom (in the present). In that revision, the metropolis is reconceived not as artifice or traditional city, but as an ur-zone uniquely capable of staging being as emancipation, the delirium of New York. Koolhaas's architecture infuses the political dimension of Corb's free plan with the performance qualities of Mies's stage plan. The free section, then, is the necessary invention, a recasting of the metropolis's vertical infrastructure into a building device to achieve the unregulated anonymities—and thus to stage the unfettered behaviors—that are not possible in free plan. Free section is at best indifferent to the sublime, to awe-inspiring vistas and panoptic perspectives; if it has an optical character at all, it is that of inexorable voyeurism.

Most of all, free section cannot be reduced to a solid-void relationship; it can be an open section, as in the Zentrum für Kunst und Medientechnologie Karlsruhe (ZKM) or the Seattle Public Library, or a solid, as in the Bibliothèque. Like free plan, it is rather a set of characteristic effects achieved by a close coordination of sectional effects with a revision of other devices of a building, such as the elevator—recall Koolhaas's analysis of the Downtown Athletic Club, in which he narrates the violence visited by that mechanical vulgarity upon the genteel entry ballet, once choreographed so elegantly by plan, section, and staircase. For more than two decades, mechanical circulation has played a pivotal role in OMA's experiments.[14] But among the more contentious of these revisions is OMA's treatment of *plan as diagram*.

May 31. We begin to "think" the plans. There is nothing to think.
—"Weird Science: Excerpts from a Diary," *S,M,L,XL*[15]

Plan-as-diagram, in brief, is a design strategy that uses the plan (in concert with other devices) to detach the subjects in a building from the regime of immediate experience, with its emphasis on satisfied expectations and phenomenological, haptic, aesthetic, and symbolic pleasures, in order to place them elsewhere as subjects of a different spatial regime, one with other pleasures, other expectations, other politics. Where "elsewhere" could or should be is a matter of discussion; it may be in the intellect

(Eisenman) or in the metropolis (Koolhaas) or in the clouds (Prix), but in any case, plan-as-diagram can help get there.

A map offers a useful analogy. Driving through the streets, you are immersed in immediate experiences and expectations until you turn your attention to a map. At that point, you are removed to elsewhere, to an abstract space of information. In an Eisenman building such as the Wexner Center, the plan-as-diagram works to transport you to a space of conceptual abstraction and keep you there, even when you look back out the window.

OMA's use of plan-as-diagram works more like a subway map, an uninflected instrument to get you from one activity to another. More abstracted than a street map, a subway map is pure diagram; it works on the basis of relations, conveying no actual information about distance, route, or location in the geosection underground. Moreover, a subway map diagrams the blunt quotidian life of the contemporary metropolis. According to the premise of the plan-as-diagram, for the Parisian, the New Yorker, the Londoner, or the Tokyoite, the day-to-day drag and thrall of the city is not a matter of strolling sights, views, vistas, and boulevards, as it is for Gehry, but of traversing a diagram, dropping into a hole, moving to another hole, then popping back out again. And the hole need not be a subway entrance; the contemporary urbanite moves in that space while driving, even while walking, as every New Yorker who has bumped into an oblivious tourist gawking on the sidewalks of Fifth Avenue will readily attest. Thus, in order to produce their intended effects in a building, that is, to transport one from comfort and accommodation to metropolitan intensity, the plan-as-diagram and free section must together erase the given institutional program and its accreted architectural tropes.

The Bibliothèque de France project is a tour de force of free section and plan-as-diagram knit together by their inseparable companion, the elevator, in which program is completely concealed as massive poché, which in turn structures the free section. The abstract figures and translucency of the facades that Moneo admires distance the building from its surrounds and detach it from the city. Arriving by car, subway, or foot—the differences do not matter—visitors pour into an enormous glass-walled plaza, a horizontal cut separating bottom floors from the great mass hovering above. From there, elevators shuttle through the solid mass of books and services to be off-loaded somewhere, in one alien, cavernous void or another. From agoraphobia to claustrophobia, without respite, one could never know where one was in the building. To some, it would be perverse, dehumanizing, unbearable. To others, however, such as those who grow vexed the moment they set foot in a pastoral setting, it would materialize the nascent, immanent pleasures of the metropolis, that is, what Koolhaas posits as a new and authentic mode of being in the world.

Despite these long digressions on Bilbao and the Bibliothèque, the issue here is not at all to hold Moneo's book hostage to a reading of the two buildings, but to trace their respective anxieties and the resulting contest that lurks beneath the author's casual remark about their common consideration "that program lies at the origins of architecture." The two employ opposite uses of program because the speculative goal of their architectures are opposite. In my opinion, to the extent that projects and buildings are ever theoretical at all, they will never differ merely about program, plan, or section.

For all that I admire in the book, its failure to rise to the promise of its title must give pause, particularly because it is not a matter of Moneo's lack of skill or intelligence, but of his will. Permit me, then, to conclude by noticing one last feature of the book. Each chapter, without exception, tells a story of an architectural practice that eventually loses its way, including that of the luminary Siza. That narrative arc suggests to me a kinship between Moneo and Martin Heidegger. I am not saying that Moneo is a Heideggerian; he mentions the philosopher in the book only once in passing and with short shrift. Nevertheless, both hold that authenticity and meaning in life flow from groundedness, which in turn flows from place. And both despair of the capacity of sophistication, artifice, and technology to set us adrift, if not the inevitability. Perhaps, in that sense, the book was never about the theoretical anxieties of its subject architects, but about the anxieties of the author as an architect searching for authenticity in a world that feels to him more interested in novelty. In his Gropius Lecture at Harvard in 1990, Moneo said, "It is not possible today to put forward a single definition of architecture. Today's understanding of the concept of architecture . . . includes what architecture was before, but embraces also many other marginal and not-so-marginal attempts to react architecturally to different circumstances."[16] After reading the book, I began to feel that, although the author may believe that statement intellectually, he does not believe it emotionally.

7 THROWING STONES—THE INCIDENTAL EFFECTS OF A GLASS HOUSE

Whatever other debates it may engender, one fact is indisputable. No other episode in the history of twentieth-century architecture can compare with the one staged in New Canaan, Connecticut, by Philip Johnson, America's most renowned and controversial architect. For over forty years, Johnson's Glass House and the additions he has made to its surrounds have continuously demanded the attention of scholars, critics, and the popular press alike, making it one of the most widely publicized works of modern architecture in the world.

However the Johnson estate is understood—as a collection of buildings, pavilions, and follies assembled by Philip Johnson the Curator, as a working sketchbook drawn by Philip Johnson the Architect, as an evolving microcosm designed by Philip Johnson the Landscape Architect, as a diary reflecting upon developments in architecture written by Philip Johnson the Critic-Historian, or as a publicity event of remarkable longevity choreographed by Philip Johnson the Media Star—one cannot deny the sway this elusive enterprise has held and continues to hold.

Each of these characterizations belongs to a different critical perspective; indeed, over the years, the Glass House has become a signpost for the vicissitudes of architectural thought.[1] As new ideas have arisen, critics have often used the occasion of a reconsideration of the Johnson estate to elaborate their consequences.

Thus, critics have not visited the Glass House as much as they have revisited it.

The urge to return again and again to New Canaan has been fueled, in part, by Johnson's periodic additions to the original design, such as the pond, the pavilion, the galleries, the study, and so on. As one surveys the history of these, one cannot help but sense an exquisite timing in their execution and a provocateur's hand in their design. It is as if, aside from whatever other role each addition was to perform, they were always also intended to spark new interest. Whether cultivated intentionally or not, the effect has been dramatic; over four decades, almost every mention of Johnson in the press makes reference to the Glass House.

Like a restless child bored with his toys, Johnson incessantly sought justifications for adding elements to the complex, often experimenting with a stylistic innovation that caught his eye at the time. In the periods between these additions, he fiddled compulsively with the details of landscape, cutting trees, installing and removing works of art, and so on. This process continues today; at the time of this writing, the architect is in the midst of designing at least two more projects for the site.

Each new construction fundamentally transformed the context and reset the character of the previously existing buildings, rendering prior interpretations vulnerable and opening the door to critical reassessment. To make matters more complicated, Johnson frequently endorsed the new interpretive perspective, incorporating its themes into his own ongoing account. Virtually from its inception, the Glass House, the architect, and its many interpreters have woven an unending and intricate conversational network that resembles nothing so much as a spider's web. Thus, perhaps more than any other architectural masterpiece preceding it, the Glass House is in a process of evolution inseparable from its evolving commentary. No experience of it, no retelling of its story, no rethinking of its content nor reestimation of its merits can disentangle itself from this web.

Throughout his career, the otherwise mercurial Johnson has remained steadfastly faithful to one principle alone, that architecture is first, foremost, and finally a visual art. In Johnson, architecture-as-art found a formidable champion. When some argued that in architecture, art must always serve function, Johnson placed function in the service of art; when others argued that architecture was more a matter of history than art, Johnson made art out of history. The ancient dispute of priorities between form as the source of beauty and form as the bearer of meaning has animated the development of the Glass House, setting the stage for some of the most vigorously contested debates in architecture to occur during the past two decades.

In fact, the first and most influential critical revisiting of the Glass House was by Johnson himself in his 1950 *Architectural Review* essay "House at New Canaan, Connecticut," published almost immediately after construction of the original scheme was completed. In the essay, Johnson sets out a comprehensive account of the various sources for his design. His list mixes such estimable antecedents as Claude-Nicolas Ledoux, Karl Friedrich Schinkel, Auguste Choisy, Kazimir Malevich, Le Corbusier, and Mies van der Rohe with such oddities as a reference to Count Pückler's estate at Muskau in Silesia, a stock steel-and-glass construction detail, and an anecdotal memory of a burnt wooden village.

The importance of this essay both to contemporary architectural design and discourse cannot be overstated. Of course it shaped the scholarly treatment of the Glass House. Beyond that, however, it established the Glass House as a watershed for much of the architecture to follow, for its irreverent recombination of incongruent materials provided a cornerstone strategy for postmodernism. Finally, the essay demonstrated the instrumental value of a tool that would eventually come to be commonplace in the discipline: the critical essay written by the architect about his own project.

Many other architects before Johnson had written on their own work, describing the effects they hoped to achieve or setting out their polemic vision. Like a parenthetical thought, however, these writings always occupied a secondary position vis-à-vis the design, respecting if not valorizing the primacy of the actual building. Johnson's text on the Glass House, on the other hand, quickly assumed a status equal to that of the Glass House itself. Soon one was unthinkable without the other; they became, and remain, inseparable.

Eventually, Johnson would witness the coequivalence between theory and design that he achieved with "House at New Canaan" underwrite a new form of practice—as purveyed by such diverse architect-theorists as Robert Venturi, Leon Krier, and Rem Koolhaas, and then carried to an extreme by Bernard Tschumi and Peter Eisenman. These latter systematically attached theoretical texts to their designs on the principle that the project itself existed only as the two taken together. Viewing such proposals as an overintellectualization of the art of architecture, Johnson came to disdain the very practice that his own work foreshadowed. In characteristic fashion, however, he supported the design activities of these architects because, as he put it, he liked the sculptural quality of their forms.

Johnson's fundamental ambivalence, his equivocation between the intellectual and visual sides of architecture, ever engaging in the former while ever extolling the latter, operates throughout his career as a designer. Perhaps for these reasons, he never repeated his critical undertaking at the Glass House. Though he often writes about his subsequent work in New Canaan and elsewhere, citing sources and so on, in these later remarks he always follows a more traditional form of explanation and emphasizes the aesthetics of the work.

Johnson's own graphic design for "House at New Canaan," as well as his rhetorical style in its capsule descriptions, gave the essay its decisive tone. There is little doubt, moreover, that one can readily find in his original design the presence of the references he cites. But is this essay truly the encyclopedic catalog of sources it claims to be?

Today, those who know Johnson would be less enthralled by the authoritative demeanor of the essay. These confidants would know well the architect's uncanny ability to put forward a cogent and uncompromising position, only to reverse himself a few minutes later with complete confidence and persuasive force. In his work as well as his personal life, Johnson is always the consummate purveyor of effects. His agile mind suffers none of Ralph Waldo Emerson's hobgoblins and has little patience for the pedantries of truth. To Johann Wolfgang von Goethe's charge that the pilaster was a lie, Johnson adjusted his tie and replied, "Yes, but what a delightfully useful one."

Yet there are many other reasons to question the limitations of Johnson's original list of sources. As the estate grew and transformed, Johnson amended the list and, on occasion, even suggested a different genealogy. For example, by the time he is discussing his thoughts on the property with art critic Rosamond Bernier in 1986, his story focuses on his landscaping intentions, ideas only vaguely suggested in his 1950 essay. Also, there is the evidence of the dozens of developmental sketches leading up to the final design, sketches that come to play a central role in discussions of the Glass House in the late '70s and indicate other influences not previously mentioned.

But perhaps the most glaring omission was the essay's understatement of the history of the idea of a glass house, whose allure had developed, along different trajectories, for over three hundred years. With conspicuous restraint, Johnson writes that "the idea of a glass house comes from Mies van der Rohe."[2] No doubt it is true enough that the specific stimulus that launched the architect on his three-year obsession to build a glass house for himself was Mies's 1947 sketch for the Farnsworth House. But hidden within this simple attribution to Mies was a complex and powerful idea.

Johnson knew from the very moment he saw Mies's sketches that there was much more at issue than the material, tectonic, and formal problem of constructing a house whose walls were entirely of glass. He knew that his glass house would exercise an extraordinary power over the imagination of professional and layperson alike. More than most, Johnson the architectural curator and historian knew that history almost guaranteed the effect.

He knew of Hardwick Hall, whose facade, "more glass than wall," fascinated English society at the beginning of the seventeenth century. Perhaps the poet and moralist George Herbert had already envisioned the long-term implications of Hardwick when he immortalized the trend to transparency two decades after its completion in his aphorism, "Whose house is of glass, must not throw stones at another."

Johnson knew the history of the glass house conservatory, such as the Great Conservatory at Chatsworth built by the gardener and architect Joseph Paxton with Decimus Burton for the sixth Duke of Devonshire, a descendant of Bess of Hardwick. Burton went on to collaborate with Richard Turner in such famed glass houses as the Palm House at Kew Gardens, but when Paxton's Crystal Palace of 1851 stunned the world, the mesmerizing power of glass architecture became evident in full measure.

Johnson knew the fascination that glass held for the German architectural avant-garde of 1910 to 1920. Besides his familiarity with Mies's visionary projects for glass skyscrapers from the period, he would have known of Paul Scheerbart's *Glasarchitektur*, a polemic tract glorifying glass as the material par excellence of modernism. He also would have known of the architectural group

Die Gläserne Kette (the Glass Chain) and, in particular, of the stir generated by its most renowned member, Bruno Taut, and his Glass House for the Werkbund exhibition in Cologne in 1914.

He knew all this and much more—from the dizzying ecstasy of reflections in the Hall of Mirrors at Versailles to the ephemeral transparency of Walter Gropius's glass walls at the Bauhaus. In short, the architect knew that for over three centuries the history of architecture was, as Le Corbusier put it, "the history of the struggle for the window," and that his house would rivet attention as it brought that history to its most daring conclusion.

And, as was to become his habit, Johnson was dead right. Before construction was finished, the *New York Times* was already reporting that throngs of uninvited visitors were creating traffic jams on Ponus Ridge as they looked upon his "ultramodern residence" with "awe, wonder and indignation."[3]

As might be expected, the initial popular reaction to the house was preoccupied more with its material vulnerability and its unscreening of private life than with the intricacies of modern design. On the other hand, more learned studies of the work pay little attention to the voyeuristic implications of the Glass House, debating instead the formal, spatial, tectonic, and cultural themes of the work. When the issue of the glass walls arises in these writings, it is in terms of the reflections, vistas, and framed views that these afford the occupant. This is, of course, as it should be, for however delighted the architect may have been with the popular effect of the house, he struggled over the design for three years in order to produce a rigorous work of architectural art, one that would substantially rethink the problem of modernism.

Yet at least one bit of evidence suggests that the exhibitionist motif of the house was never far from the mind of this master of the architectural exhibition. In his 1950 essay, the image that Johnson chose to introduce the Glass House was the remarkable Arnold Newman photograph, which captures the building's richest visual effects, from its panoramic views to the vertiginous collage of its multiple reflections. But what gives this photograph its edge, what makes it so unnerving even today, is that it casts the viewer as a Peeping Tom. With more than a hint of prurient pleasure, we steal a glance across the bedroom to catch Johnson sitting at his desk with his back to us, reading. We know he is unaware of our staring at him—that is, unless he happens to catch our furtive reflection in the pane of glass he faces.

Though each of the other elements of the original scheme was eventually revised—the interior of the Brick Guest House redesigned, the Jacques Lipchitz sculpture sold, and the driveway relocated—the Glass House itself remains today exactly as it was upon completion in 1950 in every detail except two. The Johnson candelabra and the Alberto Giacometti sculpture *Night*, both of which figure prominently in early photographs of the interior, are absent. Not much more can be made of the disappearance of the odd, medieval candelabra than simply to point out that Johnson's considerable talent for architecture and interior design has never extended to the design of furnishings. Within weeks after finishing the interior, the architect removed the clumsy fixture.

The disappearance of the Giacometti, however, was entirely accidental. The sculpture began to shed plaster and was returned to the artist to be repaired. Giacometti stripped off all of the plaster down to the wire frame, but died before he had a chance to reconstitute the work. The sculpture was lost and never replaced; nevertheless, its situation in the original interior is worth further consideration.

The genius of the Glass House obtains from the fact that, although it derives its style from modernism, the discrete, ordered space it engenders belongs more to classical architecture. There is little disagreement among critics on this point, though the argument persists as to whether this is a contribution to or a detraction from the development of modern architecture. The

7.1
Arnold Newman, *Portrait of Philip Johnson*, 1950.
© Getty Images.

quarrel is most frequently staged in terms of a comparison between the Glass House and the Farnsworth House. Though the
Farnsworth House is the immediate predecessor of the Glass
House, Mies's design is directed toward the exact opposite effect.
In the Farnsworth House, Mies redeploys all of the components
of a neoclassical house in order to achieve the characteristic
flowing, continuous space of canonic modern architecture.

In contrast, every detail, every nuance of Johnson's design operates to merge the modern into the classical, and in his interior
the architect brings the effect to a climax. Within the confines of an
1,800-square-foot box, Johnson uses the Miesian furniture, the
modern fixtures and cabinets, the works of art, and the fireplace
to zone the open space into an intricate organization containing as
much differentiation and hierarchy as a Georgian mansion, complete with wainscoted walls. In order to accomplish this extraordinary condensation of the modern and the classical, the architect
multiplies the tasks performed by each interior element.

Thus, for example, the Nicolas Poussin painting serves as a
work of art, as a wall delimiting the room within which the living room sits, as a door to the bedroom, as an object floating in
the intermediate register of the section, layering the space into
three floors, and as an edge of the modeled residual space outlined in remainder by the fireplace, the closet wall, and the edge
of the carpet. The significance of this leftover space and the others like it punctuating the scheme should not be discounted, for
nooks and other residual spaces are signatures of the classical
plan while anathema to the modern plan. As Venturi observed in
Complexity and Contradiction in Architecture, often the most interesting spaces in architecture are residual.

Since Johnson has never shown the slightest hesitation to revise his work in New Canaan, we must conclude that he has left
the interior of the Glass House unchanged because to his eye and
mind it is perfect. Yet in this context of precise and meticulous

7.2
Philip Johnson, The Glass House, New Canaan,
Connecticut, 1949. Ezra Stoller © Esto.

overdetermination, what are we to make of the accidental disappearance of the Giacometti? Did fate wrest a pivotal detail from the space?

Giacometti's eerily elongated figures have stimulated endless interpretations; many have seen them as meditations upon the existential isolation of modern man. But for an architect, the most enviable quality of these sculptures is their uncanny ability to articulate a vast, almost infinite space, the very space that Mies, Le Corbusier, and others sought for modern architecture. Thus, to find a Giacometti as a centerpiece in the most explicitly bound area of the Glass House, poised precariously at the edge of the coffee table so as to emphasize the limitlessness of the space it commands, is to encounter a stunning spatial counterpoint. It is as though the purpose of the sculpture was to render the finite, domestic space of the living room once again infinite, to merge, that is, the modern and the classical.

The duality of the modern and the classical contained within the Glass House may account, in part, for the cool reception of its counterpart in the original scheme, the Brick Guest House. Most critics gloss over the original design of the Brick Guest House, focusing instead on its role in the site, but Arthur Drexler, whose 1949 review was the only major treatment of the Glass House to be published before Johnson's *Architectural Review* essay took control of the discourse, is brutal in his dismissal of it. In an essay marked by brilliant insights as well as stunning boners, Drexler sums up the virtue of the Brick Guest House with rapier in cheek, writing that "under certain circumstances, the attractiveness of a house can be gauged according to its resemblance to a prison."[4] Five years after the publication of this essay, Johnson chose Drexler to succeed him as architectural curator of the Museum of Modern Art.

In fact, the Brick House serves its primary functions in the site design very well: it frames the arrival and fixes one of the vertices of the triangular organization of the three elements of the original scheme: the Glass House, the Brick House, and the sculpture. Finally, with the Glass House, it set up the parallel sheering essential to the dynamics of the site. But the form and materiality of the Brick House suggested a certain equivalency in opposition to the Glass House—two rectangular prisms, one solid, one void. The apparent equivalency created an expectation about the interior of the Brick House that it did not fulfill. If the two were truly equal but opposite, the interior space of the Brick House should have been as complex and textured as that of the Glass House, with contrary themes. Not only did the restricted scale of the Brick House make such an achievement unlikely, but more importantly the Glass House interior already contained its own spatial oppositions.

Thus it was that in 1952 Johnson undertook his first major revision of the original scheme, converting the interior of the Brick House into his master bedroom. Lifting vaults from the Sir John Soane House in London, Johnson set these within the Brick House floating in front of walls resurfaced with textured Fortuny fabric.

Finally, he backlit the arches, creating the romantic illusion of a sunset. When he wrote of the renovation eleven years later, he did not mention the obvious historical reference; instead, he focused on the feeling of the space. "The domes in my guest room . . . have a calming, quieting effect on the guests—most enjoyable." Here, then, another conversion is complete, for now Johnson is strictly the artist of visual experience and no longer the scholar-architect.

With the renovation of the Brick House, the architect began a pattern that would be repeated in many of the additions to come, one that confirmed Drexler's early intuition that the entire complex was best understood as a single house. Again and again, Johnson would take one part of the functional program already contained within the original scheme—for example, the painting gallery or the study—split it off, and elaborate it into a new and independent construction on the site. In keeping with that pattern, Johnson worked for several years on the design of a dining pavilion to be located north of the Glass House before abandoning the idea. Thus, each addition was like a new wing enlarging the complex-as-house. The partitioning of functions into individual forms was, of course, a residue of modernism; hence, as the estate grew larger and moved away from a modernist aesthetic, ironically, it moved closer to its principles of space planning.

After the initial five years of activity, the Glass House slipped into relative quietude. Johnson turned most of his attention elsewhere, to his collaboration with Mies van der Rohe on the Seagram Building and to his own designs for museums in Utica, New York, and Fort Worth, Texas. In New Canaan, he slowly started to acquire additional land, beginning with the parcel north of the Glass House, the site of the unrealized dining pavilion.

Initially, Johnson was reluctant to purchase more property and had to be goaded into buying the house that overlooked the Glass House from the southeast on Ponus Ridge Road. While visiting the architect in 1956, Libby Holman, the actress and torch singer, noticed the house. When she learned that it was occupied, she chided the architect in no uncertain terms for compromising his (and her) privacy in such a way. He bought the property, dividing the house into an apartment for his butler and a summer home for his sister; later, it was occupied by the caretaker and his family.

When Johnson finally decided to rouse the Glass House from its eight-year repose, he did it with a splash. In 1962, he completed construction of the pond, complete with a one-hundred-foot jet fountain, as well as the notorious Lake Pavilion, his obscene gesture to the puritanical functionalists dominating architecture at the time. The indignant response to the pavilion was immediate. Kenneth Frampton wrote: "Although it is passed off by the architect as a 'folly' by virtue of its entirely false scale, it is, nonetheless, in its trivial historicism, quite typical of Johnson's recent work. . . . It is indeed hard to believe that this is the same man who once designed and built the . . . famous Glass House in which he still lives, or that a former admirer and collaborator of Mies can, in a few years, come to conceive such feeble forms as these."[5] Writing as technical editor, Frampton published his comments in England's *Architectural Design* without a byline, an omission he would go to some pains to correct nearly two decades later.

Johnson reveled in the attack, responding to Frampton's commentary "that we need more of this pointed, beautifully written criticism in this country!" Undeterred and completely in his element, he went on the warpath in the name of architecture as art. In a series of articles and lectures, he attacked the prevailing tendency toward bland, utilitarian architecture, frequently using the pavilion as his opening volley. As usual, he laid out the historical references for the design, but a noticeable shift occurred from his earlier, academic appeal to antecedents. Historical material was borrowed for the sake of its intrinsic beauty, and from that point on, beauty and experiential delight became the hallmarks of Johnson's approach to design and criticism.

Though anticipated by the Brick House renovation, the flippant, classical style of the pavilion seemed jarring to many, as if a noisy alien had landed uninvited upon the serene, modern field established by the original scheme. However, its roots may be found in the developmental sketches for the Glass House itself. In addition to the well-rehearsed features of the pavilion—its illusionistic, reduced scale and its overt classicism—other aspects of its design are of particular interest to the evolution of the Glass House.

During the course of its design, Johnson had experimented with over two dozen distinct versions of the Glass House. Most studied different massing or organizational relationships between the Glass House and Brick Guest House. A few others attempted to unify the two houses into a single scheme, with one of these clearly suggesting the pinwheel arrangement of the pavilion. But the most blatant evidence that the stylistic issues of the pavilion were on Johnson's mind as early as 1948 can be found in the so-called Syrian arch scheme. These sketches, like the pavilion itself, seemed to come out of nowhere and show the architect flirting with the idea of configuring one of the walls of the Glass House as a series of three arches. The enigmatic scheme disappeared almost as quickly as it arrived.

From the perspective of these sketches, the pavilion appears to be something of a repository of ideas developed for the Glass House that the architect did not use and yet did not want to discard. Johnson went so far as to treat the pavilion like an alter ego of the Glass House. As if to supplement its missing rooms, he named the pavilion's four spaces the entrance hall, the library, the living room, and the boudoir.

The design of the pavilion shows the architect for the first time explicitly using the estate, as Frampton suggests, to work out ideas for major commissions elsewhere. Also, in both its historical postmodernism and its reflection upon the column designs of Minoru Yamasaki, the pavilion is a clear commentary on prevailing architectural issues of the time. Thus, it sets into motion two of the interpretations of the Johnson estate which others would develop, and which Johnson himself would adopt: that it is a sketchbook for his own work and a diary of his thoughts on the work of other architects.

Johnson remained a staunch devotee of the pavilion from the beginning. As late as 1977, in a discussion with Calvin Tomkins, art critic for the *New Yorker*, Johnson said he had devoted more time to the pavilion than to any other work in New Canaan. Yet the folly has never earned the respect Johnson felt it deserved, and did not find an unequivocal admirer in the critical community until 1986, when historian and critic Vincent Scully revisited the Glass House. Even Robert Stern, the architect's best student at Yale and, later, the most ardent advocate of Johnson's historicist postmodernism, did not find the design quite satisfying. For Stern, however, the problem with the pavilion was not that it was frivolous, but that it was not frivolous enough!

The furor over the pavilion preempted recognition of the more fundamental mutation of the complex effected by the pond and, to a lesser extent, the fountain. The pond expanded the original scheme from a complex into an estate, and transformed the space of the Glass House from a tightly knit relationship among forms to one between the forms and the landscape. From then on, all of Johnson's work in New Canaan was affected by landscaping issues. Though he had been discussing the estate in terms of English landscape design since he completed the pond and pavilion, it was not until 1970, when *Time* magazine's art critic, Robert Hughes, described the Glass House as belonging to the tradition of eighteenth-century ducal estates, that the issue came to the fore in criticism.

Another change occurred in 1960 that had as profound an effect on the further evolution of the Glass House as any architectural event, for it was then that Philip Johnson met and began a relationship with David Whitney. Whitney's most palpable influence at the Glass House is on the art collection. For years, Johnson purchased art, and his most publicized acquisitions were those advised by the legendary Alfred Barr, founder of the MoMA—Johnson's first employer and best friend. But it was Whitney who molded Johnson into a collector. Under his curatorial guidance, Johnson assembled a coherent collection of contemporary American art of astonishing quality, containing important works by such artists as Jasper Johns, Warhol, Frank Stella, Michael Heizer, David Salle, Julian Schnabel, and Eric Fischl.

The collection Johnson and Whitney assembled ultimately stimulated the architect to add two major buildings to the estate, the Painting Gallery in 1965 and the Sculpture Gallery in 1970. It would be a misrepresentation, however, to restrict Whitney's influence on the Glass House to issues surrounding the art. An avid gardener in his spare time, Whitney also advised Johnson on many of his landscaping decisions. As Johnson tells it, "David and I sit outside The Glass House and argue for hours over which trees to cut and which to keep." Of course, such decisions do not appear in any journal; nevertheless, the ineffable refinement of the space of the estate today is a result of their cumulative effect.

Johnson once invited a landscape architect to offer his recommendations for the estate. Over lunch in the Glass House, the expert suggested familiar ideas about paths and terracing. As he was departing, he stepped out of the Glass House, turned to the two and asked, "By the way, where is the main house?" The anecdote is all that remains. Johnson hired many consultants, but, fortunately, he listened to very few.

The period from 1960 to 1973 was a time of enormous energy and activity at the Glass House—architectural, intellectual, and social. During this period, Johnson completed his remaining land acquisitions and made major changes to the estate. He purchased an additional parcel to the north, site of the painting and sculpture galleries, and another to the south, where the new driveway, study, and chain-link Ghost House are located. Finally, he acquired a last parcel still farther south, on which Whitney's turn-of-the-century, shingle-style house sits. Later, Whitney added to this house a square, granite-walled heather garden designed by the architect. After Johnson decided to donate the estate to the National Trust, his neighbor, Audrey Phipps Holden, gave the Trust an additional eight acres to the far northwest, bringing the total to forty acres.

The final revision to the original scheme occurred in 1964, when Johnson moved the S-curve driveway to its current location.

Moving the driveway sacrificed an unintended formal feature of the original design, but better fulfilled the experiential program Johnson initially hoped to achieve. In the first version, as you drove down the driveway, you caught a momentary glimpse of the east facade of the Brick House through an opening in the trees. The virtual axis created by this frontal presentation of the brick wall articulated by three round windows was more akin to Roman than Greek planning. Afterward, you proceeded round a tree quite near the Brick House and then into the car park, where the Glass House unfolded on the oblique.

In the current version, you proceed down the longer, more picturesque driveway, through trees that screen both Glass House and Brick House until the last moment. Then, as you pass the trees, the curtain rises on the complex, presenting first the Brick House and then, at a distance and partly screened by a wall, the Glass House. Now both houses are obliquely revealed, in better accord with the principles of Choisy so admired by Johnson.

Soon after the driveway revision, the architect codified his ideas about arrival and procession in his 1965 essay "Whence and Whither: The Processional Element in Architecture."[6] Many architectural theorists consider this reintroduction of processional considerations to modern architecture to be among his most significant contributions. While such ideas may seem appropriate and even commonplace today, they were in fact quite subversive in the intellectual climate of modern planning that still prevailed at the time.

In order to achieve a more neutral, objective space and to shift the political focus of architecture from the individual to the collective, modernist architects rejected planning ideas that took advantage of single-viewpoint effects, such as perspective or oblique screening. Not only were such effects illusionistic and dishonest, they reasoned, but they unduly celebrated the individual, particularly the few privileged enough to enjoy them.

Thus, for Johnson to subordinate modernism's loftier goals to discredited experiences was nothing short of heresy to the apostles of modernism's political project. To Johnson, for whom such political arguments were nonsense, it was merely a matter of designing the most pleasurable visual experience. Since 1965, the architect's ideas have gained wide acceptance, but the controversy surrounding them remains unsettled.

The formal and spatial changes of the estate in the '60s were paralleled by transformations in its social life. During the late '50s, social activity at the Glass House consisted primarily of architectural discussions Johnson held for students. Over time, these discussions gave way to luncheons and lawn parties for friends and distinguished guests. The increasing pitch of social activities during the '60s brought a semipublic atmosphere to the Glass House, which came to be embodied in the two institution-like buildings Johnson added to the estate during this period, the Painting Gallery and the Sculpture Gallery.

The Painting Gallery was announced as a paraphrase of the ancient Treasury of Atreus at Mycenae, but such architectural allusions had by then lost their coin for many critics, who found other aspects of the gallery more to their liking. The exception to the rule was Scully, a critic whose greatest joy derives from his unparalleled ability to see something ancient in almost everything. Not content with the relatively recent vintage of the Treasury, purportedly built in the fourteenth century B.C., Scully preferred to detect in the gallery shades of the earth goddess as drawn in the plans of the Neolithic temples of Malta.

In any case, such blatant allusions may have lost some of their luster for Johnson as well. After the Painting Gallery, there would be no more overt quotations of historical precedents in New Canaan. Instead, the subsequent work drew its energies more and more from developments in contemporary architecture.

Of greater interest to writers at the time were the gallery's display system and its siting. Johnson mounted the paintings on screens hung from circular tracks in the ceiling of the round bays that served as storage wells. This system enabled the architect to re-hang the gallery space at liberty by rotating desired paintings to the front. Such hanging techniques were well known, but Johnson integrated them into the overall design concept with notable precision. Each circular bay is of a different diameter, accommodating paintings of different sizes, and the radial screens can be aligned to create a rectangular gallery within the orbital plan.

Though it is often described as such, the Painting Gallery, nicknamed the *Kunstbunker*, is not underground. It sits above ground, though covered in sod so as to appear a chthonic mound emerging from the landscape. For Johnson, who loved artifacts, the design of the *Kunstbunker* was a concession to his developing conception of the Glass House as a garden estate. He amplified the impression with two devices borrowed from landscape architecture: a footbridge, to take one out of the formalist space of the original complex and into nature, and a moon-viewing platform, which was sited opposite the entry corridor to the gallery.

The hyperkinetic decade at the Glass House came to a climax with the 1970 opening of the spectacular Sculpture Gallery, which may be not only Johnson's best work of architecture in New Canaan, eclipsing even the Glass House itself, but the architect's best non-high-rise building, period. Moreover, the Sculpture Gallery served as a sketch-study for Johnson's pinnacle achievement in high-rise architecture, Pennzoil Place.

Informed but unfettered by direct reference either to historical or contemporary sources, the gallery is a wholly original work. In this étude of acute angles and sectional circulation, Johnson created a space so vast that it appears unable to be filled, whether occupied by one person or a hundred people; it is neither public nor entirely private.

7.3
Philip Johnson, Sculpture Gallery, New Canaan,
Connecticut, 1970. Photo: Wikimedia Commons.

As one descends through the gallery's five levels staged over two floors, one's sense of existential isolation in the space causes each ad hoc encounter with the sculpture to be at once intimate and empty. The effect is intensified by a collection that consists largely of pop and minimalism, that is, of works exploring anonymity, mass production, and the banal. No collaboration between architecture and art could more thoroughly erase both the humanist and the modernist subject to such dazzling effect. In those terms, Johnson's Sculpture Gallery achieves results that deconstructivist architecture would pursue a decade later—though, unlike the deconstructivists, Johnson achieved his ends through a detailed study of the architectures of humanism and modernism.

The recession of the early '70s brought Johnson's activities in New Canaan—social and architectural—to another halt. The estate entered into a second dormancy; when at the end of the decade it became active again, it did so as a different place, one more private and introspective.

A false restart occurred in 1977 with the publication in *Quest* of Johnson's design for a new house for Whitney. Dubbed the Red House, it was planned for a site below the one now occupied by the architect's study. Johnson presented the project as an ecological-mythological nest, discussing it as an odd mixture of mandalas, mysticism, and energy efficiency. Its stucco walls, painted barn-red, were to enclose a cloistered space, with a living area fourteen feet wide by thirty feet high. The intriguing design was never seen again, though its monastic leanings reemerged in Johnson's design for the study when the architect returned to work in New Canaan in earnest in 1980.

In a sense, however, 1977 was a banner year for the Glass House. Two essays appearing in *Oppositions* that year, one by Stern and the other by Eisenman, each reconsidered the design of the Glass House. *Oppositions* was the critical organ of the Institute for Architecture and Urban Studies (IAUS), an architectural think tank devoted to contemporary architecture. Two years later, soon after Johnson turned up on the cover of *Time* magazine holding a model of his AT&T Building, the IAUS hosted an exhibition covering that project and Johnson's Glass House; among the scholarly treatments of Johnson's work in the accompanying catalog was Frampton's "The Glass House Revisited."

Taken together, these three essays placed the origins of the Glass House at the center of a crucial debate in the late '70s over architecture's cultural role, a debate that sought to dictate architecture's immediate future. Eisenman, Stern, and Frampton used the Glass House to stake out three different positions that came to underpin most of the various trajectories followed by architecture in the United States in the 1980s.

Robert Stern, arch-postmodernist, disinterred Johnson's design sketches from the MoMA archives and discovered the aforementioned Syrian arch scheme. Using it as the centerpiece of his concise "The Evolution of Philip Johnson's Glass House, 1947–1948,"[7] Stern celebrated the eclecticism evident in the sketches in order to establish the central tenet of architectural postmodernism in the United States: that architectural design is a matter of style, not ideology. To make sure that the point was not lost, Stern repeated it three times in his six-paragraph essay.

Eisenman, on the other hand, was keen to establish another position in his essay, "Behind the Mirror: On the Writings of Philip Johnson":[8] that architecture is not only always ideological but also irreducibly textual, that is, like a language, a source of rhetorical figures and metaphors. For Eisenman, the central issue for contemporary architecture is to take advantage of architecture's textuality to "write" alternatives to both humanism and modernism. In an extended meditation on Johnson's writings, Eisenman used Johnson's own words to argue that the architect cannot extricate his work from his words, that he cannot separate literary metaphors from architectural metaphors, and that he cannot isolate form, beauty, or experience from its cultural and political context, despite his heroic efforts to the contrary.

In the essay's climactic moment, Eisenman turns his attention toward the brick floor and fireplace of the Glass House, two elements that deviate markedly from Mies's Farnsworth House. Using Johnson's own explanation of the elements in his 1950 essay, Eisenman interprets them in a new light. Johnson had written, "The cylinder, made of the same brick as the platform from which it springs, forming the main motif of the house, was not derived from Mies, but rather from a burnt wooden village I saw once where nothing was left but foundations and chimneys of brick."[9] From this statement, Eisenman suggests that the Glass House is nothing less than a monument to the horrors of war.

This elegant interpretation was a bit of a stretch, and Johnson pooh-poohed it immediately. But it could not be denied that the architect's odd wording called attention to itself. Throughout the United States, many had seen the remains of burnt houses where only a brick chimney was left standing. Indeed, such a ruin had existed near Johnson's New Canaan property at least since the 1950s. Why, then, did he refer to a "burnt wooden village"?

Frampton entered the fray as the critic most committed to deriving a project for contemporary architecture from the formal, tectonic, and ideological principles of modernism, albeit one that would correct the movement's previous shortcomings. Since among modernism's conspicuous errors was its effort to erase architectural history, Frampton had to recuperate the status of architectural history within the modernist project. At the same time, he had to rebut Stern's reduction of that history to a question of style.

Frampton also had to counter Eisenman on at least one essential point. Eisenman's discussion of architecture as text and his consequent endorsement of Johnson's eclecticism ultimately threatened to deliver architectural design over to undisciplined play, and to undermine its role as a decisive vehicle for political action. Though Eisenman argued that architecture was always ideological, he did not argue that it irrevocably installed one stable ideology, the necessary condition for Frampton's project to succeed. To the contrary, Eisenman's argument implied that such a goal for architecture was impossible to achieve. Thus, as Frampton turned his attention to the Glass House, it was inevitable that it would take the form of a comparison with Mies's Farnsworth House, a canonic work of modernism. Within the context of a debate on the Glass House, only by dint of that comparative study could the critic refute Stern and Eisenman and set in motion his project for a kinder, gentler modernism.

To establish his long-held doubts about the course of Johnson's digression from Mies, Frampton took this opportunity to reveal himself as the anonymous author of an assault on the pavilion published sixteen years earlier in *Architectural Design*. Having set the record straight, he then undertook the most rigorous and learned consideration of the Glass House ever written.

He began his detailed study by tracing the formal transformations of the loggia and the belvedere from Schinkel through the early works of Mies to the Farnsworth House. He chose this strategy for several reasons. First of all, he convincingly demonstrated the historical development of the form of one of the most respected works of modernism. Thus he recovered the essential role of such studies to contemporary architecture without lapsing into the use of history as a source of stylistic quotation.

Second, he shifted the attention in the comparison between the two houses from the simple question of glass-walled architecture to the more complex question of the formal typology of transparency. Loggia and belvedere were two distinct devices, developed over centuries, by which architects introduced views of the exterior into a building. In these terms, a "glass house," whether by Mies or Johnson, is not a modern leap to something

7.4
Mies van der Rohe, Farnsworth House, Plano, Illinois,
1945–1951. Jon Miller © Hedrich Blessing.

new, but an advanced stage in the development of a venerable formal problem.

In Frampton's view, Schinkel, one of the architects Johnson cites as an influence for the Glass House, initiated an effort to synthesize the loggia and the belvedere. Frampton then showed that Mies took up that same synthetic project in his own work. Because glass can enclose while maintaining transparency, Mies was able to use the material to complete the synthesis. Beginning with the Barcelona pavilion, proceeding through the Tugendhat and Resor houses, Mies arrived at the final condensation in the Farnsworth House.

Moreover, by virtue of his coordinated use of material and construction methods—his tectonics—Mies was able to use that synthesis to achieve other effects and advance other agendas. The tectonic expression of the Farnsworth House makes the formal synthesis clear while also frankly and honestly displaying the structure of the house, an effect devoutly desired by the modernists on moral grounds. Also, the formal organization and tectonics of the Farnsworth House rendered its space continuous.

Taking the formal and tectonic history of the Farnsworth House as his basis, Frampton compared it to the Glass House. The developmental comparison is slightly askew, in that he treats the changes in the design of the Glass House evidenced in the MoMA sketches as equivalent to the changes in Mies's work over twenty years and through many completed projects.

Frampton arrived at three related conclusions. First, "where Mies is always tectonic, Johnson is invariably scenographic." One of the key examples here is a comparison between Johnson's chair rail, the so-called wainscot, and a similar element in Mies's Tugendhat House. While the former is painted black, and thus blends into the structural system even though it is not a structural element, the latter is rendered materially distinct from the structure. Though Frampton saw the stylistic advantage of Johnson's decision and commended it as such, it is, nevertheless, an impugning observation, at least in terms of the tectonic morality of modernism.

Second, Frampton found the Glass House developmentally naïve when compared to the evolution leading to the Farnsworth House. Of course, it is only naïve if the formal issues that arise in Mies's work, such as the loggia/belvedere synthesis, are taken as the standard of sophistication. As Robert Dell Vuyosevich argued in his 1992 comparison of the two houses, if the standard is taken to be Gottfried Semper's archetype of the domestic house, it is the Farnsworth House that falls short.[10]

Finally, Frampton argued that the phenomenological impact of the Glass House—that is, its finite, domestic space—derived from its suppression of the structural system. Johnson terminated the roof plane at the corner column, turning the house into a beautifully detailed, but closed, box. The effect was amplified when he painted the structural system black and set it flush with the glass walls. To the contrary, Mies cantilevered the roof beyond the columns and expressed the structural system by painting it white and detaching it from the glass walls. Thus Mies's space, sandwiched between roof and floor, flows past the glass, through the structure and beyond. Moreover, in the Farnsworth House, one sees the shadow of the structure on the glass, a confirmation of its distinct presence.

From these three points, Frampton judged that the Glass House was a bourgeois work, "a solipsism raised to unparalleled elegance." In sum, his brilliant erudition simply confirmed what Johnson had claimed he was doing all along. In fact, in a 1976 television interview with Rosamond Bernier, Johnson made many of the same points as Frampton, though in somewhat more accessible terms. The only difference, in the end, was Frampton's political interpretation, which Johnson rejected but never contested.

Concerned that the political implications of his formal and tectonic analysis might not carry the same persuasive force for others as it did for himself, Frampton abandoned his scholarly rigor at the last moment and resorted to Eisenman's metaphorical reading of the brick chimney. But in an act of critical desperation, Frampton turned Eisenman's suggestion into an assumed historical fact, writing that the "ruin in question was almost certainly the blitzkrieged remains of a village." Given his difficulty here in putting forward a convincing statement of the project in its own terms, perhaps it is not altogether surprising that, in the next decade, Stern's and Eisenman's theoretical projects flourished while Frampton's neomodernist project struggled to survive.

Though he began sketching new additions to the estate in 1977, Johnson did not actually build there again until he erected his study in 1980. Then, in short order, he began work on the Ghost House and the Lincoln Kirstein Tower, finishing both in 1985. As of this writing, still on the drawing board is an entry tower, to be used as a visitors' center when the estate is taken over by the National Trust. Designed but as yet unbuilt is a garden slat house, to be located across Ponus Ridge Road, next to a second home owned by Whitney. Though the slat house, like the heather garden, is not part of the estate proper, its proximity to the Glass House and its design character make it worthy of consideration.

In siting, form, and program, this group is quite different from Johnson's previous work in New Canaan, more intimate and more contemplative. In them, one sees most clearly Johnson the collector and Johnson the diarist, for in each, one finds a personal meditation on issues arising in contemporary architecture. The stark, white study sits alone in a field far south of the Glass House, unconnected by any path; to get to it, Johnson must walk through the grass. Its object-in-a-park siting recalls a Corbusian theme, while its form reflects both on Le Corbusier's elemental geometries and, more particularly, on

Aldo Rossi's reassembly of those elements into icons of architectural memory.

For years, Johnson used the Sculpture Gallery as his office; the study is his retreat from the relentless vastness of that space. In it, the architect surrenders to his desire for a womblike, monastic enclosure. Within the thickened walls, lit by an overhead oculus and a single rectangular window, he reads and works on his designs, surrounded by shelves of books tabbed with hundreds of yellow slips, mostly marking his favorite architectural images.

The completion of the study led to a visit to the estate by the noted Italian architectural critic and historian Francesco Dal Co, who was the first to view Johnson as essentially a collector and the estate as an extension of his collecting activities, more obviously expressed through the art. In his essay for *Lotus*, Dal Co traces the philosophical and autobiographical implications of Johnson's collecting.[11] His dense but beautifully wrought argument turns on the study. Had the critic visited a year earlier, it is unlikely that his thoughts would have moved in the same direction.

On the other hand, when Scully revisited the Glass House in 1986, after the Ghost House and Lincoln Kirstein Tower were finished, the work he liked least was the study. Writing in *Architectural Digest*, he dismissed the white specter, finding it adrift, even sinister. No doubt this was due in large part to the fact that the mythophilic critic could not find any hint of prehistory in its form, which he could only manage to trace through Rossi back to Étienne-Louis Boullée. If Scully had taken a second look, he might have seen a *trullo*, a whitewashed, cone-roofed building type unique to the Puglia region of Italy, thought to have originated during the Stone Age. Perhaps then he would have found more solace in these ancient roots.[12]

Scully was also cool toward the chain-link Ghost House, finding it somewhat morbid. Not far from the study, and built to protect the lily gardens from ravenous deer, the garden folly was

Johnson's marriage of Venturi to Frank Gehry. In a scheme for Franklin Park in Philadelphia, Venturi raised a ghost of Benjamin Franklin's house, drawing it in three dimensions with steel I-beams painted white. Likewise, with the chain-link house, Johnson raised a ghost over the exposed foundations of a frame building long gone. Unlike Venturi, however, Johnson rendered the structure in chain-link and split it down the middle, à la Gehry. Although the house lacks the wit of Venturi and the clash of Gehry, it is far more elegant than the work of either architect. "That," Johnson quips, only half-jokingly, "is why mine is so much better than theirs."

Because of its operating cost, Johnson removed the fountain from the pond in 1977. In so doing, however, he lost a key landscaping device, a vertical element delimiting the extension of the space from the Glass House across the valley. The architect finally replaced that important element with the concrete-block Lincoln Kirstein Tower, named after the cofounder of the New York City Ballet with whom Johnson formed a close friendship while designing the New York State Theater at Lincoln Center, home of the New York City Ballet. Because of its spatial function and its relationship to the pond and pavilion, the tower's location is less improvisational than that of the study and the chain-link house. However, it is an equally personal work, as different from the public ostentation of the fountain as the study is from the Sculpture Gallery. Only one person at a time can mount the tower to enjoy its dramatic view; that is, if one is willing to dare the precarious climb, with Johnson's tongue-in-cheek grudge against handrails.

Scully was particularly attracted to the Lincoln Kirstein Tower, seeing in it Gothic ruins and M. C. Escher's staircases; as well, the tower appears a fragmented and reflected collage of the New York City skyline. Such an interpretation not only connects its design to architectural themes current at the time, but also lends another meaning to the difficult climb to the top.

Though the entry tower/visitors' center and slat house are not yet built, the issues at work in their design are clear. In the entry tower, Johnson experiments with design themes that came to his attention during his work on the "Deconstructivist Architecture" exhibition at MoMA in 1988. In its current version, a brick L-shaped wall, a copper-clad, wing-shaped wall, and a tilted roof are sewn together by a staircase into an incommensurate assembly. Though the visitor center's program makes the entry tower the most public of the late works, Johnson stacks the functions and scales down the tower to reduce as much as possible the institutionality of its space.

With the slat house, Johnson turns his mind toward the complex geometric solids that have recently replaced angles, shards, and fragments in contemporary design. In it, the architect subtends one-eighth of a sphere with a right-angled wall. The graceful form is constructed out of slats of wooden lath, aligned vertically on the right-angled wall and horizontally on the curve to produce intricate interference patterns on the exterior and similar light-and-shadow effects in the interior.

Though these late works greatly expand the space of the estate, even carrying past its proper boundaries, they do so in an ad hoc fashion. For the most part, they are local affairs whose connections to the major works on the property are informal, incidental, or even nonexistent. They do not serve any overarching concept; nevertheless, they knit a new cohesion.

To grasp that cohesion, we must return almost to the beginning one last time, to pick up the threads of a pattern. After Johnson finished the original scheme, many critics declared its triangular plan decisive and final. The claim of finality was repeated, though in different terms, after the pond group transformed the Glass House into an English garden estate. When Hughes visited, he announced that the Sculpture Gallery was the finishing touch. Even Dal Co, who saw Johnson's property as an open-ended collection, could not resist the feeling that the most recent addition—in his case, the study—completed the collection. Over the course of the estate's transformation, critics have treated each new addition as the consummate final touch.

In truth, though the Glass House has never been complete, neither has it ever been incomplete! Like an American city, it has expanded, not according to a master plan but by annexation and diverse development. Each addition of land and building has transformed it from one whole to another. For that reason, despite the multiplicity of its organization and the variety of its forms, styles, and materials, there is nothing eclectic about the Johnson estate. Like the Glass House itself, it is an amalgam of disjoint components in a remarkable organic unity, endlessly capable of growth that at the same time celebrates the differences among its parts.

In the current cultural context, to unfold the possibility of an organization whose coherence evolves more from its components' distinctions than from their similarities would seem to be among the most absorbing reasons to visit New Canaan. Yet, as for any great work of art, as the context changes, so, too, do the meanings the work engenders. Thus, although we conclude this particular exploration, let us resist the impression that we have seen the final development or written the final word on the architect's estate. After all, for over forty years, Philip Johnson's clearest message has been simply this: we can add to but never complete the catalog of the incidental effects of a glass house.

8 A TIME FOR FREEDOM

Being There, a Prologue

Blunt, thickset, elemental—these are your first impressions, having turned through the close neighborhood streets of Firminy and come upon the church in the widening expanse of its suburban setting. Contradictory impressions, however, soon follow. First, the outline of the rooftop divulges an awkward eccentricity, holding the conic form at arm's length from what at a distance seemed to be pure geometry. Then, as you approach, you learn that you have been further deceived: the massive, rounded pyramid does not rest staunchly on the ground like the mountains in the background, but alights on a fragile base of glass and thin concrete wall. What should have been devout bedrock turns out to be the lazy hemline of a skirt.

Alerted by that surprise, you soon notice others, such as the odd appurtenances attached incongruously to the volume like so many bad jokes—one thing that looks like a nose, another like a mouth, something else like an eye popping out, and positively the tiniest crucifix ever to grace a Catholic church. The inelegance of these subsequent impressions seems calculated to undermine any sense of gravitas that the first impression might have evoked.

Entering the grounds of the church, you ascend a knoll along a stone path and reach a bridge, the architecture's gentle invitation to shed your petty tribulations as you cross into the hallowed realm that awaits you. You begin to slip into a weightless calm. But

as you enter the portico, the building forces you to turn abruptly and confront the door. Its flat color panels and cold frontality slap away any spiritual reverie that might have begun to descend. Is it art? A flag? Although you cannot know what the door means or represents, you cannot help thinking about it. The door yanks you back from the realm of the sacred for a moment and places you in the secular, intellectual space of conceptual abstraction.

Shaking off that rude arrest, you proceed into a cavernous concrete nave resonating with echoes and awash in concrete's peculiar drab shadow. Once inside, you are mesmerized by a constellation of white pencils of sunlight streaming into the thick air through the perforated east wall.

Eventually, you loosen yourself from the astral display and look around to get your bearings, noticing next the shallow niches that ring the space with dashes of reflected color, offsetting the sensational constellation wall with a bit of decorative irreverence: red, blue, yellow, green—are these not the colors of the door? Finally, as you move to find a seat, you glance up to the shadow-thick ceiling, where a red rectangle and a yellow circle beckon in the celestial distance. Sun and moon? Good and evil? You do not give them too much thought, because this last, evocative incarnation of geometry and color does not insist on it. But

8.1
Le Corbusier, Saint-Pierre church, Firminy, France, 1960–2006. Realization, José Oubrerie. © Luis Burriel Bielza.

8.2–8.3
Le Corbusier, Saint-Pierre church, Firminy, France,
1960–2006. Realization, José Oubrerie. © Luis
Burriel Bielza.

then, if these mysteries are divine light, should there not, in a Catholic church, be only one?

And what, for God's sake, is that hole beneath the altar?

Whatever your reaction to the church as such—and, depending on your religious and aesthetic sensibilities, it is as likely to be consternation as wonder—you cannot deny that you are in the presence of a flagrant architectural opus, one that can only be appreciated by being there. Yet, as you depart and think back on just how many times the architecture has transported you to the brink of the spiritual, only to drag you back to the worldly, you might find yourself wondering if the church isn't somehow locked in a schizophrenic struggle with itself. As it turns out, that may be an important question.

By now, the backstory is well known. An eminent architect working with a trusted assistant accepts a commission. Together, they develop the design as far as an advanced draft, when difficulties arise and the project is put on hold; before it can start again, the superior dies. The assistant continues to work on the scheme, and after some years of prodding, manages to induce construction to start. Eventually, though, work stops, the building site is abandoned, and the project goes dormant—presumed dead. Decades pass. Suddenly, as if by miracle, the project stirs from its coma, finds new life, and becomes flesh, or at least concrete, nearly a half-century after it began.

In our case, the eminent architect is one Charles-Édouard Jeanneret, known today only by his nom de guerre, Le Corbusier, the assistant is José Oubrerie, and the commission is the Église Saint-Pierre de Firminy-Vert, a small church in Firminy, France. The two began design in 1961, but, as so often happens, the necessary support for the project dwindled, and by 1963 work in the studio had stopped; two years later, Le Corbusier died. Oubrerie continued to try to realize the church, but met tepid response. Nevertheless, by 1971 he managed to secure some funding and a sporadic construction got under way, proceeding as far as the square base of the building and the first ring of the shell. But, without the support of the religious authorities and Firminy's new civic administration, construction ground to a final standstill in 1979. In 1996, the abandoned building site was declared a historic landmark by the French Ministry of Culture, opening the door, with some restrictions, to public funding. Oubrerie began work again in 2001, and five years later delivered the finished building.

With a few minor changes, the scenario could apply to any number of renowned churches and cathedrals from the early Renaissance to the present day, from Santa Maria del Fiore in Florence to Sagrada Família in Barcelona to St. John the Divine in New York. For that matter, the story need not be limited to churches.[1] After the death of Andrea Palladio, his protégé Vincenzo Scamozzi completed two of the late-Renaissance master's most important buildings, the Teatro Olimpico and Villa Rotonda. And the infamous case of the Sydney Opera House also surely comes to mind; its architect, Jørn Utzon, walked away from the building mid-construction, unable to bear the onslaught of criticism and political maneuvering that sprang from his idiosyncratic scheme. Even Frank Gehry's Disney Concert Hall in Los Angeles ground to a halt, its massive construction site silent for nearly a decade until it, too, reawakened. Yet we must not forget that countless projects come to an end as drawings and models on the architect's desk without ever approaching construction, including many of the most influential works in the history of the discipline. Few of these premature terminations have ever earned the attention of a wider audience. Which does say something about "... Interruptus," for when it comes to risks of the imagination, there is a difference between acts begun but left unfinished and acts never begun at all.

Despite their appeal, such stories do not necessarily generate architectural content. For better or worse, a fountainhead ethos ensures that the only issue arising from the delayed completion of the likes of Utzon's Sydney Opera House and Antoni Gaudí's Sagrada Família is the extent to which an original work of genius is sheltered from insidious corruption. And, to be sure, the bulk of interest arising from the completion of the Firminy church rightly derives from the relation of the finished building to Le Corbusier's original ideas, which Oubrerie protected with some passion. But when we find new intellectual traction in the final rendition of Firminy, it is not because of the belated advent of a historic masterwork. Rather, it is because certain modifications that Oubrerie introduces nudge the spirit of the original proposal toward a new providence, one that implicates the architecture in an escalating tension between democracy and freedom.

The basis for that tension is all too familiar. Democracy is a genre of political thought that strives to achieve a more egalitarian society by conceiving new forms of governance. If it seeks to overturn one form whose exercise of authority has become an intolerable cliché, it does so to establish another. Freedom, on the other hand, is not an idea with political form but a feeling, a loose confederacy of sensations experienced as the absence of perceived restraint. In political life, freedom is gauged as permissiveness and gained through acts of disestablishment, repeal, or annulment. Freedom chafes at authority as such, warranted or not, even when the goal of that authority is to serve an ideal of democracy. The risk that democracy sees inherent in the pursuit of freedom through political, legal, or moral disestablishment, untempered by new responsibilities, is that the process as such cannot know in and of itself how to stop before it crosses the line into license.

Why that tension arises in a discussion of architecture, particularly when the work of Le Corbusier is concerned, is also not so hard to grasp. The ease with which architecture conjures obedience to authority versus the difficulty it has in staging a more liberating ambience has not gone unnoticed by its critics, from the French surrealist philosopher Georges Bataille to architecture's own Rem Koolhaas. Bataille asserts that architecture's definitive social role is to reinforce established authority. According to him, the silence conjured by a cathedral may feel like reverence for God, but it is in actuality nothing other than evidence of the covert suppression of dissent against the authority of the Church. Koolhaas says as much, if in less strident terms: "Where there is nothing, everything is possible. Where there is architecture, nothing (else) is possible."[2]

"Architecture or Revolution!" wrote Le Corbusier to announce his intention to wrest architecture from its traditional relationship to oppressive authority and use it, reconceived, to establish a more democratic space. He viewed the decorative facades, pitched roofs, hierarchical plans, and classical columns of traditional architecture as intolerable clichés that continued to perpetuate the feudal authority of landed gentry. Famously (at least in architecture) his "five points" called for flat roofs with rooftop gardens; long, horizontal windows; and free plans—all devices to insure that everyone who stood anywhere in his new architecture, on the roof, the floor, or the ground, was as equal as the manifest space was uniform.[3]

But despite the dissemination of modern architecture, those people and institutions in power pretty much stayed in power, while the monotony of the architecture itself began to feel oppressive. Le Corbusier fell into disfavor, his ideas discredited. After the work in Firminy ground to a halt, the relic of the abandoned construction site marked for a loyal few not only the indecorous end of a building project, but the disillusioned conclusion of the visionary social, political, and intellectual project that Le Corbusier had embodied.

With the collapse of modern architecture's *coup d'établissement*, new generations of architects still committed to defying collaboration had to become more cunning. Unable simply to divorce the establishment, they explored means to cheat on it. One tactic that has proven fruitful is subtly to dissolve the means by which architecture sustains one mode of authority without installing another, shifting architecture's goal from installing ideas of democracy to increasing sensations of freedom.

Notwithstanding Oubrerie's indelible formation as an architectural modern and his loyalty to Le Corbusier, his instincts and proclivities belong to this school of architectural thought. Asked by a journalist to comment on Firminy's worthiness as a church, Oubrerie declined. "In any case," he added, "I am an atheist." To find evidence in his own architecture, one need go no farther than his celebrated Miller House in Kentucky.[4]

For enthusiasts of Le Corbusier, the resemblance between the Miller House and Le Corbusier's Mill Owners' Association Building is unmistakable, though the impulsive personality of the house in Lexington could not be more removed from the solemnity of its predecessor in Ahmedabad, India. Beyond the dizzying pleasures provided by the Miller House's play of form and space, it mounts a pointed critique of traditional domestic architecture's collaboration with the institution of the nuclear family. In it, each member of the family possesses a separately accessed apartment embedded within its cubic concrete lattice, as if the house itself were a city. Mother, father, son, daughter come and go independently, meeting one another in passing as they move through the complex interior circulation of the house more often than in a formal dining room or around a central hearth. Thus, with a touch as light as the lifestyle it encourages, the Miller House affirms the freedom and litheness of spirit inherent in the oft-bemoaned dissolution of the nuclear family wrought by contemporary urban life.

1582: Vincenzo Scamozzi undertakes to complete the Teatro Olimpico, the final opus of his recently deceased teacher, Andrea Palladio. Although dutiful in his execution of the master's scheme, Scamozzi makes some few revisions in response to the client's acquisition of more land for the site. These changes, though relatively minor and grounded in Palladio's original ideas, fundamentally transform the experience of the audience.

In keeping with the classical ideals of Renaissance architecture, Palladio planned to recreate a Roman theater as specified by the writings of Vitruvius. In accordance with the ancient text, the proscenium at the back of the stage contained five portals. To draw attention to the stage, Palladio thought to spice it with a bit of trendy spectacle. Using an ingenious illusion to be created with painted screens set in a recess behind the central portal, he intended to allow the audience to look through and beyond the proscenium to a "city street"—part ancient, part modern. Scamozzi took the idea to a theatrical extreme, building recessed street perspectives behind each of the five portals and fleshing out the realism of the painted screens with sculpture and three-dimensional relief.

As historian Alice Jarrard sees it, "Palladio's initial scheme presented a perspective unified around a single vanishing point . . . [whereas] Scamozzi's three-dimensional forms diverge through five portals along five separate axes, flaunting a taste for more dramatic perspectival manipulations."[5] More likely than not, even more mundane motives provided the immediate incentive for the change in the stage plan. Most members of Palladio's audience would actually have had obstructed views of the effect once seated. Scamozzi's revised plan and more vivid scenery produced many more good seats.

But the shift did more than indulge spectacle and perhaps raise ticket prices. The single vanishing point unifies the audience into a cohesive ideality with one point of view focused on the stage. The multiple vanishing points splinter the coherence of the audience into discrete sections, each with a differing point of view. As it nudges the priority from the concept of the collective to the experience of its factions, Scamozzi's plan adds a dram of fuel to the historical processes that led eventually to the individualism of the romantics and to modernity's fragmented solipsism as portrayed by Sigmund Freud, Pablo Picasso, and Eugene O'Neill.

Oubrerie's alterations to the Firminy church, like Scamozzi's to Teatro Olimpico, are modest and arise out of exigency: a few key areas of the design, such as the entryway, remained imprecisely determined by Le Corbusier, and of course much had changed in the situation of the project over four decades, from construction technology to air conditioning to safety codes. Even the program had changed: French law prohibits the use of public funds to build or otherwise support religious institutions. So, when the town of Firminy decided to complete the building, to qualify for government funding it was redefined as a civic chapel available for any spiritual use, and a museum replaced the offices, Sunday school rooms, and priests' quarters originally located in its base.

To most visitors, Oubrerie's interventions in Firminy will be all but imperceptible, certainly too piecemeal to mount a sustained critique of authority. Yet to others inclined to exaggerate out of proportion the consequences of trifling architectural maneuvers, the building teems with Oubrerie's talent for recruiting even the most mundane design issues to his urge to pester authority in the name of freedom.

Religious architecture posed Le Corbusier a small dilemma: though a spiritual person well attuned to its devices, he saw his place in history secured by his new socially oriented, secular architecture.[6] He tried to avoid the Firminy commission, accepting it only because it came at the behest of his close friend, Eugène Claudius-Petit. As mayor of Firminy, Claudius-Petit, who believed Le Corbusier's architecture to be integral to his own progressive vision for the town, had already commissioned three other buildings from him. Capitulating in the end, Le Corbusier wrote to his friend, "I shall do it for the workers."

In 1929—the same year that his Villa Savoye delivered a compelling realization of the power of his five points—Le Corbusier began to consider the questions posed for modernism by religious architecture. Initial sketches from that year for his first church commission, at Le Tremblay, indicate an inclination to synthesize religious architecture's traditional processional, which seeks to transport a worshipper from the profane to the sacred, with the circulation established by the five points, which lift the minion from servility to equality. The sketch shows an ascending ramp spiraling around the outside of a church built in the form of a geometric solid. The path recapitulates the venerated cathedral entry but also carries the worshipper aloft in infinite space, shoulder to shoulder with the church as rational object.

Le Tremblay's processional raised basic questions: Should the worshipper have unfettered views to the outside world over the entire ascent? Should the path be wide, or narrow so as to isolate the worshipper in pious solitude? And how to compose the climax, the crucial event where ascent ends, path and church intersect, and one enters the house of God? But the commission soon evaporated and the sketches lay dormant, buried deep in his stacks of notebooks. These questions would have to wait thirty years to receive the attention they deserved, and another forty for the answer.

By the time two other commissions for religious institutions followed in the early 1950s, Le Corbusier had long expanded his formulary beyond the strictures of the five points. In the convent of Sainte-Marie de La Tourette (1953–1960) and the pilgrimage chapel of Notre-Dame-du-Haut in Ronchamp (1950–1955), he pursued other preoccupations, such as the uses of raw concrete and excursions from geometry into gestural abstraction. The aim of the five points to change the building's traditional relationship, meanwhile, relaxed. With a church, it seems, the ground belonged more to the timeless ac-

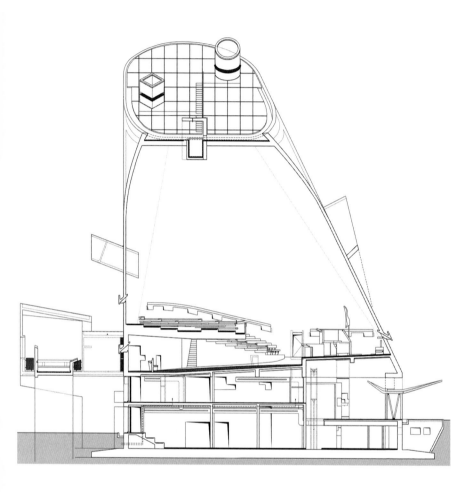

8.4
Le Corbusier, Saint-Pierre church, Firminy, France,
1960–2006. Realization, José Oubrerie. Section.

cord of God, Man, Heaven, and Earth than it did to the history of land, lord, and serf.

La Tourette and Ronchamp stand today among the most admired of Le Corbusier's buildings. Over time, the Firminy project has come in the discipline to be seen as the finale to an unfinished trilogy of religious architecture begun by its two predecessors, not only because of the proximity of the three, but because of Le Corbusier's terse remark in his *Oeuvre complète:* "[The Firminy church] consists of an hyperbolic-paraboloid shell, and, after Ronchamp and La Tourette, represents a third, new type of church."[7]

In its claim to provide a model for the future work of others, the declaration of a new type is among the most audacious in architecture, though typical of Le Corbusier. He does not, however, elaborate on what aspect of Firminy makes it a new type of church. Presumably, he relates the accomplishment to the hyperbolic paraboloid (hypar)—a three-dimensional curved surface seen in the hourglass shape of power station cooling towers. At the time, the hypar was somewhat in vogue among architects and engineers because its lyrical geometry is intrinsically structural, making it one of the rare instances when Beauty can hold itself up, unassisted. But he had already employed the hypar in previous works, most notably in the Assembly Hall of the Capitol Complex in Chandigarh, India (1953–1963), the church's immediate formal predecessor. Moreover, the advance in architectural form achieved in the church derives from the departure from the pure geometry of the hypar, compelled by the architect's desire to have the form morph smoothly into the square base. Joining such irreconcilable geometries is like wanting a round peg to fit into a square hole, but with no gaps at the corners, and it harkens to the classical architectural problem of connecting a round cupola to a square base. In the end, one way or another, the hypar must distort, and the beguiling eccentricity of the church's form is the result. The problem gave Oubrerie fits, though he solved it brilliantly. For those curious to know his trick, here is a hint: look through his computer drawings for those that show four upside-down, tilted cones. But beware; it is a bit of a spoiler. Once one sees what he did, the building never looks the same.

Firminy may not have launched a new type of church, but it did conclude Le Corbusier's trilogy in spiritual expression. Drawing on his approach to secular housing, the overall form of the convent at La Tourette is a powerful square block, formed by monastic cells on three sides and the long axis of a cruciform chapel on the fourth. The north transept of the chapel nestles invisibly inside the square, but the south transept protrudes out and is wrapped in a gestural form that supplements the rational block with an episode of expressive spirituality. Ronchamp retains the trace of La Tourette's square plan but becomes organic, with free forms billowing out of it, an expression of spiritual passion unregulated by geometry and transcending reason. Yet the abandon of Ronchamp, however affecting, stands out of character for Le Corbusier as a regression from a modern to a romantic worldview.

At Firminy, we find La Tourette's square base beneath Ronchamp's lyrical sanctuary, both now thoroughly disciplined by geometry, the synthesis consummated. But, then, how shall the worshippers ascend and enter the sanctuary? It is, of course, the same question raised by Le Tremblay, and Le Corbusier exhumes the 1929 sketches as the basis for the Église Saint-Pierre. Thus, the drafts of Firminy from 1961 to 1963 show Le Corbusier and Oubrerie wrestling with the questions first posed by the entry procession, and to the end it remained the least resolved aspect of the design. After numerous variations—just compare the models from November 1961, October 1962, and December 1963—Le Corbusier gives up. The final draft retreats from a developed solution into an outline of three elements awaiting design: a landscape climb, a bridge, and a portico.

Enter Oubrerie at his wiliest. His final design for the processional preserves the three elements and honors their intent, but
does not quite obey. As soon as the coarse-paved path climbs to
the bridge, Oubrerie erects a solid outer wall, cutting off outward
views from the bridge for its full length to focus attention inward
on the church-object. But just as the bridge joins to the portico,
Oubrerie punctures the wall—and the mood—with a large opening that presents one last view of the secular world, as if to ask
whether the decision to leave it behind is final. The moment recalls a similar choice presented in the Bible. "Remember Lot's
wife," Jesus said, in his sternest of warnings. But, pillar of salt
notwithstanding, the allure of the view seems to ask if, by looking
back, she might not in fact have chosen well, if not wisely. A delicious instance of tactical annulment, the architectural episode
raises questions but does not answer them, though one guesses
where Oubrerie's own sentiments lie.

The climax gains momentum inside the portico, where the
worshipper must turn sharply to enter the sanctuary. The unsettling surprise inherent in such a turn threatens the quieting just
when the ascent should come gently to a coda at the threshold.
Rather than mitigate the turn, Oubrerie aggravates it, dead-end-
ing the bridge into the portico's back wall. The darkened, com-
pressed enclosure will amplify by contrast the dramatic expanse
of space and play of light to follow, but at the moment it produces
hesitation and perhaps a last pluck of the individuality about to
be relinquished. And then, with the turn—BLAM!—you encounter the front door.

Where one expects a warm, woodsy enticement to cross the
threshold into God's realm stands instead aggressive sensation:
three bold horizontal metal panels of pure color—red, blue, and
yellow. The door might easily be an Ellsworth Kelly painting:
more intellectual than contemplative, more critical than rev-
erent, more self-aware than selfless.[8] Its immediate, arresting

frontality asserts the worth of this world, and because of that, one does not meekly pass into the house of God but rips into it, with a slight smile.

The effect of the door is amplified by the communication its color panels establish with the large red metal door, another minimalist color field, which Oubrerie installs on the opposite side of the building as the ceremonial entrance to the museum in the base. Though traditional museums and temples once shared an institutional interest in an atmosphere of reverence, the two have parted company. Partly a result of the evolution of the museum into an intellectual archive and partly at the behest of modern art's drive to deconsecrate its objects, the atmosphere of today's museum is more clinical, its decoration retreating into blank walls, its ornamentation become didactics. Thus, the two doors set up less an equivalence than an equivocation in the aura of one institution by the other.

Once inside the chapel, the bracing effect of the painting/door lingers. Entering the sanctuary, the constellation of point lights in the opposite wall dazzles the eye. At first, Le Corbusier had planned a traditional rose window for that wall, but structural problems prevented it. Reminders of the rose window, however, are still to be seen. As the eye relinquishes the spectacle of the constellation, it becomes aware of colored light—red, yellow, blue, green—everywhere: around the walls, in the ceiling. Like stained glass, the colors start to induce a meditative state, but the immediate recollection of those same colors at the door fends off the spell. As at the Miller House and with as light and lighthearted a touch, Oubrerie takes every opportunity to annoy just a little the architectural endorsement of sacred pretensions.

In keeping with the distinction between freedom as a feeling and democracy as an idea, Oubrerie's riffs are more witticisms that lighten the mood than intellections that challenge the bona fides of the institution. Even the altar is not left unscathed.

Viewed from the pews, a well of light beneath sets the white altar aglow. But standing at the altar, one sees that the light comes from a large hole cut into the floor beneath it, and through the hole, the museum below is visible. Nor is the museum left in peace. If, after passing through its doors, just before reaching the greeting desk, one happens to look up, one will stare through a hole in the ceiling at the bottom of the altar. Then, upon entering the museum area itself, the first and largest thing you will see is the metal air-conditioning duct hung at the nexus of ceiling and wall, a black, tubular solid positioned as if it were contemporary sculpture.

If Oubrerie's sleights of hand are particularly evident and lend themselves to interpretation in the entry sequence and museum, it is because both areas play leading roles in the drama of the church, yet neither was developed in the original scheme. But his incongruous nicks, niches, cuts, and holes are to be found wherever the architecture's monolithic tendency might lend itself to a feeling of overbearing weight or sanctimony. Most are about composition rather than narrative, and resist the type of paraphrase we have imposed upon the doors. Notice, for example, the inexplicable holes—five odd rectangles bracketed by two round periods—punched into the apron that joins the shell to the base on the west side facing the park. Everywhere else, this apron remains inviolate, in keeping with Le Corbusier's original sense of mass and his intention that the shell join to the base in a monolithic unity. Why are they there?

Yet other forces outside Oubrerie's control also helped loosen the building from the grip of Le Corbusier's original intent. We have, for example, already touched on the effect of the fortuitous addition of the museum to the program, necessitated by finance and the current legal policies in France that keep church separate from state. Such forces afford the building a chance to participate in the current discourse not just as a manifestation of history, but as a contemporary work. Though complex, the machinations of one set of such forces are worth our attention.

In 1999, Oubrerie published an essay addressing how the church has come to enjoy the benefits of developments in the field that he and Le Corbusier could never have anticipated in 1963. Applauding three fundamental changes in the field that have occurred since the time work on the church began—the advent of the computer, a sudden obsolescence of aesthetic and functional rules, and the supersession of the human scale by a more psychological and intellectual basis for architectural judgment—he goes on to identify those aspects of the church that have maintained a dialog with the architecture that follows from those changes: "Firminy proposes two features of contemporary interest: the shell and its geometrical definition and the continuous floor (influential perhaps in Rem Koolhaas's library project in Paris), the spiral that guides and activates the inner transformation from horizontality to verticality."[9] Though he calls attention to the significance of the spiraling floor, he does so only in passing. The balance of the essay uses the evolution of the shell in the atelier to proffer a small caution regarding the impact of the computer, which he otherwise celebrates. Vis-à-vis an account of the improvisational character of Le Corbusier's working process, he suggests that the power of form making the computer conveys carries with it a potential loss of freedom. Its seductions could transform the architect from an expert at responding creatively to changing situations to an expert at imagining and realizing fantastic forms.[10]

Although Oubrerie barely mentioned it, his intuition about the relevance today of the Firminy church's spiral floor is at point. His oblique reference to "Rem Koolhaas's library project in Paris" is to the Dutch architect's entry for the Jussieu University Libraries competition of 1992. Though the university is in Paris, the library strictly speaking is not, since it is yet another of architecture's landmark but unbuilt projects. The scheme's

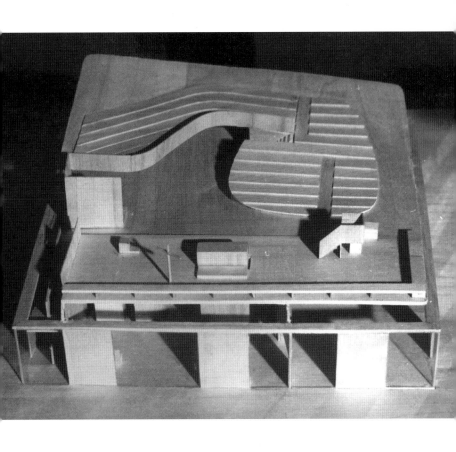

8.5
Le Corbusier, Saint-Pierre church, Firminy, France,
1960–2006. Realization, José Oubrerie. Model of the
chapel floor and lower levels. © R. P. Jean Capellades.

six stories of continuous, warped spiraling floor helped spur a line of architectural design research, termed ribbon- or single-surface, that continues today unabated. Interestingly, though the single-surface concept now appears in scores of influential projects that span more than a decade, it has yet to generate a single important built example.

In part, the goal of Koolhaas's Jussieu and subsequent single-surface projects is to join ground to floor to wall to ceiling as one performance stage whose vectors flow from the street into and through the building. Rather than replacing land with a new universal neutral datum emanating from the building, the single-surface project destabilized the traditional building/land relationship by appropriating a local zone of the ground into a field of forces and events.

The debt Jussieu owes to Frank Lloyd Wright's Guggenheim Museum is obvious, but some critics call attention also to its relationship to the circulation in Le Corbusier's project for the Palais des Congrès, an unbuilt convention center for Strasbourg. Koolhaas had already made the Palais the basis of a convention center proposal in Agadir (also unbuilt). Peter Eisenman, for example, used the connection between the Palais and Jussieu to locate the former as the signpost marking the transition between two basic diagrams of modern architecture. He proposes that the first of these is a centrifugal organization characteristic of early modernism in which the design conceptually spins forces out from the building toward the context, for example the neutral datum. The second is a centripetal organization in which forces condense from the context into the building.

Oubrerie's observation identifies the spiral floor of the church, which immediately precedes Strasbourg in the chronology of Le Corbusier's work, as a notable antecedent in the emergence of today's single-surface concept. Moreover, by calling attention to the little-known 1929 Le Tremblay sketches, he reveals them as the likely source of the Palais des Congrès! The Palais's innovative use of an external ramp as an intrinsic part of the building's circulation amounts to a furthering of the relationship between the external ramp and the internal spiral floor at Firminy. It seems more than likely, then, that the church at Firminy stimulated Le Corbusier to revisit Le Tremblay, and then his renewed interest in that early idea spurred its continued development in the Palais des Congrès. While supporting Eisenman's proposition of the centrifugal and centripetal diagrams, the early date of Le Tremblay throws a wrinkle into his simple division of modernism's history into two parts.

But things start to get even more interesting, and even more complicated, when one branch of the line of research initiated by Jussieu yields Koolhaas's Seattle Public Library, a building that opened in 2004. A tour de force of architectural guile, the Seattle library uses unrestrained surface decoration to recruit the street and every floor, escalator, and wall into a vortex that streams into, around, over, through, and on top of the building's three floating interior volumes. Seattle atomizes the literal single-surface spiral of Le Tremblay, Firminy, Strasbourg, the Guggenheim, and Jussieu into a centripetal field. Though critical, even intellectual, the architecture of the Seattle library is anything but discursive; rather, the palpable buoyancy it generates is liberating. With it and in it, one feels a little like Marilyn Monroe in *The Seven Year Itch*, dress lofted by a gust from the subway grates: sexy, free, and smart to boot.

To effect a new relation to the ground in the manner of a single-surface, the Seattle Public Library's field must break down the traditional hierarchies established by the streetscape by drawing the local energy of the street up into the vortex of the building. To do so, Koolhaas turns to a formal device. Taking advantage of the steep grade in the site, he wedges a square base containing administrative offices beneath the inflected form of

8.6
OMA, Seattle Central Library, Seattle, 2004. © OMA.

the public space of the library. Because of the base, the library connects to the street on one side, where the architect uses gardens that move from outside to inside (where they mutate into rugs) to bring the streetscape into the building as part of its vortex. But on the side opposite, the library floats above the street, sitting on the "ground" established by the base acting as a pedestal. Thus, the library's inflected form on its square base and its two-tier programming duplicate the relationship between the expressive chapel and the base in the Firminy project.

By virtue of their genealogical entanglement, the Firminy project stands as a precursor to the Seattle Public Library. But because Koolhaas's work has for decades led the effort to undercut architecture's reinforcement of institutional authority by means that attract Oubrerie's allegiance, because the Seattle Public Library makes a major contribution to that effort, and because the current generation of architects knows the library far better than the church (not to mention that the library opened before the church), it is difficult today not to consider Firminy in terms of Seattle.

All of the effects of the Firminy building that nudge it from the original concept seem to move it toward the political/conceptual discourse of the Seattle library. In addition to those we have mentioned, consider the four corners of the church. All the drawings from 1961 to 1963 and 1970–1974 demonstrate Le Corbusier's conceptual intention for the shell to join to the base smoothly as a monolith. While the models and drawings show the solid concrete of the base cut away at the corners to become glass, the line of the glass corner is brought flush with the corner of the shell in every instance. In the actual building, however, whether by Oubrerie's design or technical necessity, the glass corners of the base are recessed, leaving the skirt of the shell to blouse over them. While the dimension of the cantilever is minimal, the effect is unmistakable: the shell appears to alight weightless atop the base. Whether that difference between the drawings and the building would have been as important without the influence of Seattle we cannot know, but in light of the library, it cannot be underestimated. And then, there are those holes in the apron on the west side . . .

Of course, the Firminy church is neither as relaxed nor as sexy as the Seattle library; it is, after all, still a place of worship. But by virtue of the strange relationship it forges with the library, the ". . . Interruptus" of Firminy joins its tale to a favorite theme of imaginative literature, the one that finds a parent reincarnated younger than an offspring by time travel or the numinous exchange of bodies. A variant of "sleeper awake" tales like Rip Van Winkle, the child-becomes-parent story appeared in the nineteenth century but proliferated in the twentieth, once it found its native medium: movies. Tracking modernism's increasing discomfort with received wisdom, these stories confound the orderly succession of authority dictated by a linear conception of history, and so dramatize our desire for deliverance from what literary critic Harold Bloom terms the anxiety of influence, whether Freudian or Darwinian. Our desire, that is, for more freedom.

9 NOLO CONTENDERE

I. Plea
On all charges, I, deconstruction, plead:
Nolo contendere.
Jeffrey Kipnis paid *Assemblage* $150.00 to publish this piece.

II. Abstract
1. The meaning of any work is undecidable.
2. Inasmuch as a work aspires to meaning, it represses undecidability.
3. It is both possible and desirable to work in such a way as to respect undecidability.

III. Brief
1. The meaning of any work is undecidable.
Perhaps the most difficult and virulent aspect of deconstruction is to be found in its many demonstrations of this principle. Every work—written, spoken, performed, drawn, or built—is considered to be decidable in principle, that is, to have an ultimate reason, explanation, meaning, or finite set of meanings (hereafter referred to collectively as "meaning") that could be fully exposed and comprehended. The Western critical and philosophical tradition has been conditioned by this assumption of teleological decidability, conditioned, that is, to a pursuit of the meaning of the underlying work in question, whether a dialog by Plato, an

experiment by Galileo, a play by Shakespeare, or a building by Mies van der Rohe. In this tradition, difficulties encountered in the pursuit of the meaning of any particular work are attributed to exigencies of circumstance. Insufficient or incorrect information, bias, prejudice, and so forth distort the ultimate meaning of the work in question, delaying its achievement.

Deconstruction, on the other hand, contends that the very condition that enables a work to produce any meaning at all guarantees that it must produce many meanings simultaneously, including those that are contradictory, unintended, and undesirable. Thus, a work is in its essence *undecidable*; the difficulties in determining the meaning of a work do not obtain merely from the circumstance of its analysis but are an intrinsic property of the work itself.

To demonstrate undecidability in its most insistent forms, deconstruction has articulated a catalog of notions such as *difference*, *trace*, and *supplement*, a detailed treatment of which is beyond the scope of this brief. Some sense of the argument can be gathered, however, from the following simplification. In order for there to be meaning at all, one entity must refer to another, a signifier must refer to a signified. For this to be possible, two conditions are implied: the signifier must be able to refer and the signified must be able to be referred to. Yet every entity— a word, an object, a building, and so on—can both refer to other entities and be referred to by other entities. For example, a black cat can be referred to by the phrase "that is a black cat" and, as well, can refer to something else, as when it is taken to be an omen of bad luck.

Every "thing," therefore, is constructed as a "thing" in a field of reference. Before there can be meaning as proper reference, there must be reference in general. The conditions of reference in general are primordial and essential, anterior to any thing, origin, or ground. Thus the very conditions that make meaning possible also guarantee its subversion. Inasmuch as the articulation of existence ("that is a black cat") is the fundament of proper referral, it must be concluded that, though the conditions of reference are real, they do not exist. They are the very possibilities of existence, of "things," "presence," "origins," and "grounds," each of which is an aspect of proper reference.

As a consequence, there can be no pure signifier nor any final signified. All "things" are constructed by and construct an interminable web, a textile of referral in which no proper beginning nor authentic end can be located, no privileged path of reference identified. Though the necessary conditions for decidable meaning (origin, linearity, and termination of reference) exist, they are not real. The term *text*, with its constellation of words such as *texture*, *textile*, and *context*, has come to be used in deconstruction to invoke the undecidable matrix of referral.

2. Inasmuch as a work aspires to meaning, it represses undecidability. Meaning is wrought from the undecidable text only when a portion of the field of reference has been provisionally and contingently isolated or "framed," that is, when most of the interminable directions of reference are repressed so that one privileged direction of referral emerges, as if from a signifier to a signified. Yet the other threads of reference cannot simply be erased to yield the desired meaning. Framing produces meaning only in and as the violent repression of other strands of meaning, which nevertheless continue to occupy the text, a condition that deconstruction, borrowing from Sigmund Freud, refers to as *the return of the repressed*.

Recognizing not only the inevitability but the necessity of meaning, deconstruction does not call for an overthrow of all work aspiring to meaning. Rather, deconstruction operates to keep in motion the contingent and provisional status of meaning, thereby preventing any position, radical or conservative, from gaining absolute privilege. Beyond this, deconstruction has no position.

3. It is both possible and desirable to work in such a way as to respect undecidability.

While all frames are provisional and contingent, always changing and context-dependent, frames as such are not optional; there is no such condition as pure, unframed text, present in its naked undecidability. Everything is always already framed text. Thus, the concern of deconstruction is not and cannot be to overthrow meaning per se.

Deconstruction does not render works—artistic, political, social, philosophical, etc.—meaningless, despite the relentless efforts to characterize it as doing so. Nor does it dissolve the object. Though it does indeed subvert every analysis, theory, philosophy, or phenomenology of the object, and thus may be said to dissolve the "classical object," insofar as it articulates the inevitability and irrepressibility of framing, it also maintains the object as such.

The concerns of deconstruction are twofold: first, to destabilize the meaning of apparently stable works and, second, to produce self-destabilizing works. In the first of its concerns, deconstruction displays the contingency of the framing under which any work is held to have canonic meaning by "reframing" that work, that is, by revisiting and respecting it in such a way as to mobilize the many repressed threads of meaning within the work while strictly adhering to the work itself. In so doing, deconstruction not only reads some of the possible but repressed other meanings, but also exposes mechanisms of repression and the agendas that those repressive mechanisms serve.

In the second of its concerns, deconstruction seeks to produce work in respect of undecidability, that is, work that, though not meaningless, does not simply give itself over to meaning. Such works resist, defer, and destabilize meaning by lending themselves to many frames while not allowing any particular frame to gain a foothold from which to narrow and confine the work to one particular meaning.

This aspect of deconstruction aspires to produce a work that is neither meaningful nor meaningless. Hence, strictly speaking, these endeavors cannot be considered as directed toward the development of a new "type" of work inasmuch as "type" is a concept intimately connected to decidability and therefore to a particular frame. Rather, these works seek to destabilize the order, anteriority, and decidability of type as such.

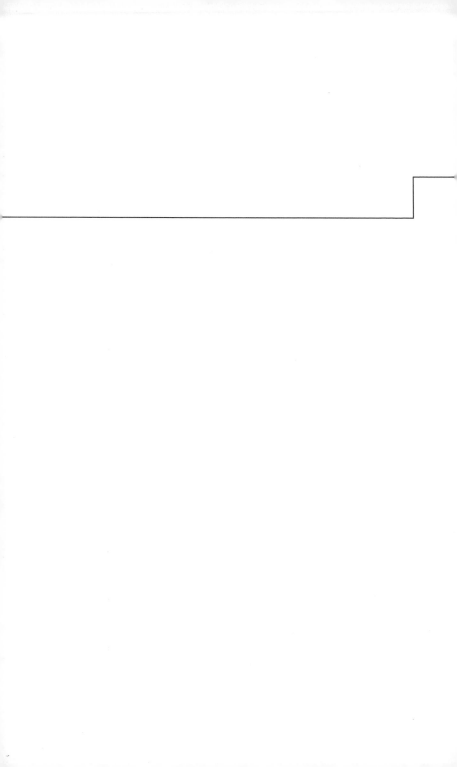

10 /TWISTING THE SEPARATRIX/

From the moment Bernard Tschumi invited Peter Eisenman and Jacques Derrida to collaborate on a design for one of the gardens along the *promenade cinématique* of the Parc de la Villette in Paris, all were agreed. In fact, their collaboration was so obvious that its latecoming felt oddly conspicuous, like an augury that though prepared at a beginning could only mean its meanings at an end. A collaboration between Eisenman and Derrida would be a golden opportunity if the chemistry proved right. Allow me to add immediately that the chemistry between the two was exactly right, better than one could have imagined. It was the right chemistry for the opportunity—the chemistry of gold.

Derrida, of course, is the architect of deconstruction, that contemplation of writing and reading which has shaken and forever destabilized the "solid foundations" of all the humanities, particularly the "serious" disciplines such as philosophy, law, psychoanalysis, literary criticism, and now, at last, architecture. At the risk of repeating a no longer necessary summary of deconstruction, let us accent certain of its themes to better situate the discussion to follow. First, despite the invectives of nihilism hurled at it from the right and the more recent charges of a complicity with conservatism emerging from the traditional left, deconstruction is neither radical nor conservative, at least in the familiar sense of a radical/conservative opposition. A general positioning of its motifs for architectural design: Do not destroy; maintain, renew, and reinscribe. Do battle with the very meaning of architectural meaning without proposing a new order. Avoid a reversal of values aimed at an unaesthetic, uninhabitable, unusable, asymbolic, and meaningless architecture. Instead, destabilize meaning. To destabilize meaning does not imply progression toward any new and stable end, and thus can neither mean to end meaning nor to change meaning. Nor, obviously, does it mean to conserve a "true" meaning. To destabilize meaning is to maintain (a respect for) all of the meanings possible, as a consequence of the congenital instability of writing.[1] "One does not declare war: another strategy weaves itself between hostilities and negotiation."[2]

One of the most powerful techniques of deconstruction is to search out and destabilize the *separatrix*, that divider whose ability to separate the inside from the outside establishes the solid ground upon which all of the foundations of discourse rest. The separatrix is the /, aka *solidus*, *virgule*, *slash*, *slant*, *diagonal*, and, in French, *ligne*, *barre*, *oblique*, *trait*. It marks among its many punctuations: ratios and fractions (2/3), simultaneity (president/commander-in-chief), choice (and/or), opposition (nonserious/serious, inside/outside), and all other manner of structured relationships (signifier/signified, ornament/structure). The separatrix is the incision of decision, the cut that is the possibility of management, of rendering complexity manageable (from the French, *traitable*), of keeping things in line, keeping things straight. Throughout his work, Derrida relentlessly tracks the separatrix in all its operations, overt or covert, so as to twist it, turn it back on itself, and poke holes in it in order to expose the inseparability of those terms that it separates.

Like Holmes on the trail of Moriarty, Derrida pursues his quarry, *le trait*, with a compulsive, icy calculation that often causes his readers to shiver—with excitement of course, but always also with dread and revulsion. Lest we think his chase a matter of mere academic exercise, let us eavesdrop on one of the author's private postcards, sent to a lover but destined for Eisenman: "The *trait* in itself is indiscreet; whatever it traces or represents, it is indecent (my love, free me from the *trait*). And to these obscene *traits* I immediately want to erect a monument or a *house of cards*" (emphasis added).[3] What drives Derrida against the separatrix, against *le trait*, is a violent, puritanical passion. And can it fail to interest us that in this private, expressive moment, Derrida's abhorrence of the separatrix moves him to contemplate committing architecture, Eisenman's architecture?[4] Thanatos and architecture are familiar bedfellows, of course, and, as voyeurs of this postcard well know, eros is always close behind.

Having dogged and disrupted the separatrix, deconstruction can then inquire into the hidden agendas that underlie its efficacy of simple difference. It thereby recovers, and gains respect for, the undecidability that this mark represses so as to make decision possible.[5] Thus, for example, deconstruction deconstructs the project of radicality as well as that of conservatism by destabilizing the network of separatrices that construct the simple directionalities, inclusions, and exclusions of either project, of any project as such. Other than in this sense, deconstruction has no project.

Above all, deconstruction is nothing new. According to its principles, deconstruction is possible only because it is always already occurring. What is new about it, what gets named with the new name "deconstruction," is a new respect for the instability that is always already at work, that is irrepressible and yet that every totality, radical or conservative, and every scene of stability must attempt to repress, to disrespect. Architecture is a major test for deconstruction precisely because it is a scene of the proper, a scene of stability unlike any other—physical, aesthetic, historic, economic, social, and political.

If it is unnecessary to introduce Derrida and deconstruction, then in this context it is even less necessary to identify

Eisenman, who throughout his career has been the foremost advocate of a "depth" architecture. In recent years, largely through the stimulus of Derrida's work, this has come to mean, for Eisenman, an architecture that admits of the clay feet of its own "stable" (historical) foundations of familiarity, orderliness, beauty—all of which he assembles under the term "anthropocentric." What he desires is an architecture that no longer writes the one anthropocentric text that sponsors all traditional theories and processes of architectural design. In Eisenman's view, the architect does not write differently who writes by mere contradiction or idiosyncrasy. Instead, the architect must find methods that at once embody complex organizations of multiple and contradictory meanings and meet the responsibility to shelter, function, and stand. Thus, rather than merely symbolizing a lack of confidence in the traditional terms of architectural stability with a traditional design process given to a contradictory aesthetic (fragments, nonorthogonal angles, sculptural collage, etc.), Eisenman seeks nontraditional design processes that might yield another architecture.

While there are clear allegiances between Eisenman's and Derrida's work, there are also conspicuous tensions and disagreements.[6] The field of these differences may be circumscribed by noting that Derrida has tenaciously worked to render fathomless the "depth," which always means the deeper truths, sought by depth practices. Thus, that deconstruction should become the intellectual stimulus of a depth practice—Eisenman's is always that, above all else—is one of the many contradictions that we will leave to others to ravel. Of course, to stimulate is not the same as to instruct.

Let us pause for a moment, then, to consider the promise of this collaboration before we take up the question of its results. For though the relationship produced exactly what it was prepared for, it is not clear that it produced what was anticipated. In this sense, we might say that the event was fecund but infertile; from it came offspring, but not progeny. Thus, if we hoped for a clear and definitive discourse in both text and design on the relationship between architecture and deconstruction, one that would end the anxious ambiguity and difficulty of this issue, then we would be disappointed. If we desired some demonstration of how simply rigid disciplinary boundaries could be dissolved, as if such boundaries were arbitrary conventions and carried no stakes, then we would be thwarted. If we dreamed of two authorities cutting through all resistances, habits, and vested interests to focus on a common task, then we would be rudely awakened by the defensiveness, duplicity, and conflict in this relationship—most of which has operated through the conduit of an intimate friendship. These were the loftier aspirations for the collaboration, but there were other stakes, more vulgar perhaps, yet stakes nonetheless. So the litany continues: if we hoped that Derrida could be convinced, coerced, tricked, or seduced into anointing one architectural effort from those put forward under his name—and in 1985 that meant Tschumi or Eisenman—then we would be deflected. And if some anticipated that Derrida would, if not vindicate, then at least grant dispensation to Eisenman's misreading of deconstruction and his argument by casual analogy and non sequitur, while others looked forward to this forbidding intellect excommunicating Eisenman and his theories, then both parties would receive their just deserts.

Aside from its naïveté, an irony resides in asking, from whatever position, what the presence "in person" of Derrida "himself" in collaboration would do to, or for, Eisenman. One of the concerns of Derrida's work is to disrupt from within what he terms the "metaphysics of presence," the insatiable desire for an unambiguous standard for truth that shapes the conceptual structure of all that stands and has the status of serious discourse. Derrida argues that such a standard, a "transcendental signified," does not exist. The principal vector for this desire, belief in the possibility of the unambiguous truth of the word, he names "logocentrism," and within logocentrism the particularly important status of the authority of the spoken word he names "phonocentrism."[7] The most disturbing aspects of Derrida's work evolve from these ideas, including the deconstruction of the separatrix that produces the ordered relationships that constitute all discourse as discourse, the analytic of the undecidables such as *différence* and trace,[8] and, ultimately, his call to "write in another way."

Can we, then, avoid a certain discomfort with the very premise of an event whose main attraction is the copresence of these two figures in particular? Moreover, if we overcome this discomfort, we immediately face another. Since Derrida ostensibly operates as the authority on discourse in this joint effort, should we not, according to him, have the deepest suspicion of that which is taken for granted in this event as a unity—that is, "Derrida himself"—but which, in fact, is one of those insidious systems most vulnerable to deconstruction: (Derrida's) writing / (Derrida's) speech. In this event, it seems that logocentrism, phonocentrism, and the metaphysics of presence could not be more dominant—unless we somehow find a way to refuse them. At the very least, let us bear this issue in mind as we ask the question: what are these things (themselves) called Eisenman and Derrida?

To be sure, however, the issues are by no means confined to what Derrida would do to, or for, Eisenman; for some, the reverse is perhaps more interesting. Could Eisenman dislodge what seemed to be an absent-minded architectural conservatism expressed by Derrida? This conservatism, were it that, took several forms, the most conspicuous being a certain suspect voice he gave to public responsibility and the inviolability of domesticity. Consider Eisenman's remarks, made at a conference on deconstruction and architecture in Chicago in 1987:

He wants architecture to stand still and be what he assumes it appropriately should be in order that philosophy can be free to move and speculate. In other words, he wants architecture to be real, to be grounded, to be solid, not to move around—that is what Jacques wants. And so when I made the first crack at the project we were doing together—a public garden in Paris—he said things to me that filled me with horror: "How can it be a garden without plants?" "Where are the trees?" "Where are the benches for people to sit on?" This is what philosophers want, they want to know where the benches are.

The minute architecture begins to move away from its traditional role as the symbolization of customary use, that is when philosophy starts to shake. [Such movement] starts to question its philosophical underpinnings and starts to move it around and suggests that what is under philosophy may be architecture and something that isn't so nice. In other words, perhaps it's not so solid, not so firm, no so well constructed.[9]

To give a deserved benefit of doubt, perhaps all that is evident in this more pedestrian conservativeness that Derrida displays is a struggle between this thinker's intellectual commitment to the consequences of his work and an initial reluctance to face these consequences in architecture, where, as he now often repeats, the stakes are among the highest. In this case, Derrida's conflict would merely be representative of the vested interest in architectural inertia that confirms these stakes as highest, even for those most committed to overcoming this inertia. Let us recall how often Eisenman has asserted his own lack of interest in living in residences designed in the spirit of his work. Is this, too, "wanting architecture to stand still and be what he assumes it appropriately should be in order that he can be free to move and speculate"? If the stakes are truly so high, then no one, including Derrida and Eisenman, is immune.

Hence Eisenman's claim to the contrary; any conservatism of particular interest on Derrida's part will not be found at the level of the humane concerns he expresses during the project. Nor can much be made of the mild xenophobia the philosopher demonstrates when he first encounters Eisenman's efforts to work at the limits of architecture. He was, after all, not at home in architecture, though a certain irony or two sounds here, considering how much abuse his "too foreign" writings have received. To his credit, in fact, Derrida quickly set aside these early resistances—perhaps even too quickly.[10]

But Derrida exhibits another form of conservativeness that is worth closer attention. In the beginning, he assumes as self-evident that architecture, in its essence, is limited to very narrow modes of meaning, namely, depiction or symbolization. Thus, for example, when the discussion turns to the representation of *chora* by the design, Derrida's suggestions always stay close to sculptural depiction.[11] Because *chora* is something of a radical void (though not a void), he recommends that the project be simple, even empty. The role of the four elements—earth, air, fire, water—in Plato's *Timaeus* leads him to propose that they be symbolized in the project (sand for earth, light for fire, and so on). When called upon to contribute form to the design, he draws a picture derived from one of the descriptions of *chora* in Plato's text. Likewise, as the collaboration proceeds, Derrida becomes distressed by the complex, narrative-loaded, and labyrinthine architecture that Eisenman pursues in the name of *chora*. This is all the more curious when we consider what he has to say about the history of the interpretations of *chora* in his own essay on the subject: "Everything happens as if the yet-to-come history of the interpretations of *chora* were written or even prescribed in advance, in advance reproduced and reflected in a few pages of the *Timaeus* 'on the subject' of *chora* 'herself' ('itself'). *With its ceaseless relaunchings . . . this history wipes itself out in advance since it programs itself, reproduces itself, and reflects itself by anticipation. Is a prescribed, programmed, reproductive, reflexive history still a history?"* (emphasis added).[12] Here it is almost as though he were trying to describe Eisenman's design process. While we must point out that at this moment in the essay Derrida is raising questions about the efficacy and agenda of this history, he by no means intends to call for an interpretation that would be somehow more representational.

In putting forward this axiomatic of architecture's limited talents, Derrida repeats a familiar theme found in philosophy's contemplation of the nonlinguistic fine arts. Let us remember that Hegel uses precisely the "self-evidence" of architecture's limited and insufficient possibilities of meaning to relegate it forevermore to the irrelevant. It is particularly conspicuous that Derrida should casually repeat Hegel, since, as the most powerful philosopher of totalization, Derrida endlessly grapples with his thought. Beyond this contradiction, two others are worth attending. First, Derrida knows that such representational strategies are wrong for *chora*. *Chora* is that which cannot be shown, described, or positively represented. He not only says as much in his meetings with Eisenman, but in his essay "Chora" brilliantly conveys both the error of trying to represent *chora* "properly" and the underlying agenda in a history of those efforts in philosophy to do so. Moreover, his essay paradoxically seems to get closer to *chora* by moving away from it in a complex, labyrinthine writing that, like all of his work, is neither philosophy nor literature but something else again. A third kind of writing, a bastard writing, we might say, as long as we avoid meaning a new kind of writing, a bad seed come to flower in the letters. To the issues of this essay we will return. But here we must point out that it is exactly his writing technique wherein lies the last contradiction.

Derrida feels no conflict in the labyrinthine complexity of his writing on *chora*, no need to present blank pages or to use simple representational descriptions, in other words, to depict *chora* in his essay. Quite to the contrary.

Consider these three contradictions: first, the comfortable repetition of themes from a philosophical tradition that he, above all, discomforts; second, the proposition of ideas that he knows are wrong but other than which he cannot conceive; and third, the employment of techniques in his own medium, writing, that he resists in the medium of architecture. If a more complex writing can say something about *chora* that could not otherwise be said, why not a more complex architecture? Certainly it seems in the end that Derrida agrees or at least stipulates the possibility. At least he says in retrospect that he is comfortable with cosigning the work. We will check to make sure.

Before we do so, though, let us note that to challenge the self-evidence of the limitations of architectural meaning to the "aesthetic" and the "representational" is the most persistent theme in Eisenman's work. In his view, these limitations are not due to any essential aspect of architecture; rather, they constitute a resistance, a received value structure by which architecture is repressed. His concepts of "presence of absence" and "absence of presence," his development of "scaling" processes, and so forth, evidence his effort to articulate the terms of and produce another mode of meaning in architecture. Eisenman was attracted to deconstruction, correctly or not, for this reason. Most alluring to him have been its theme of the return of the repressed and such Derridean notions as "arché-writing" and "text," which, in Eisenman's eyes, confirmed that architecture was a writing in its own right, not merely and inferiorly a "writing" by analogy to linguistic models. Deconstruction said to Eisenman that architecture could do something more, something of what writing does, even if that is not what deconstruction says. It promised him the possibility of another architectural meaning and—it must always be repeated—a new relevance for architecture. Thus we might say that the scene of Derrida's resistance coincided with that of Eisenman's greatest interest.

We should return, then, to examine Derrida's signature. But again not yet. Let us look first at Eisenman's resistance. Without doubt, the design process and final project of this collaboration are, in every way, situated firmly within Eisenman's work of the period: the La Villette project belongs among his so-called scaling projects. From this angle, the design process and the "choral work" scheme are interesting enough. The multiple relationships among Tschumi's La Villette scheme, Eisenman's Cannaregio scheme, Paris, and Venice within which the design process operates are rich, highly charged, and provide a fascinating scenario for an architectural text. As a polemic design process, however, the work here is not particularly distinguishable from the others in its species, such as Romeo and Juliet or the Long Beach Museum. Hence, it cannot be said that the garden evidences any significant directional change for Eisenman that can be expressly attributed to Derrida's participation. Eisenman prevented that from happening, as we shall see, though he and Derrida agreed that it must happen.

Throughout their meetings, Derrida reluctantly deferred to Eisenman on each step of the design process ("OK, so we have to do so"). From the transcript of their conversations, we can follow as Eisenman ignores his collaborator, usually by seeming to go along with him ("I hear you"), while Derrida abandons every one of the specific ideas and desires for the design that he had proffered: that it be a place where "something should be printed by reflection and erased as soon as it is printed"; that it be simple ("it will be a simple scheme," "the operation must be simple"); that it be naked—not too labyrinthine, too emotional, or too historical; that it not be a masterwork, an ultimate place, but a place among others; that it provide some mechanism for the user to "affect the forms without leaving a stable trace"; that it make use of material analogies for earth, air, fire, and water, particularly water; that it employ light and sound through photographic and phonographic devices; that, above all, it not be circular, self-contained, totalizing ("now it is my wish to avoid any kind of totalization, and the metonymic structure of which you are speaking approaches such a totalization"). Though scaling is circular, is self-contained, we will leave open for a moment the question of its totalization. Regardless, all of these suggestions, whatever their merits in retrospect, are absent from the garden.

Most conspicuously, Eisenman kept Derrida from affecting the work even when, near the end of their collaboration, Derrida seemed finally to insist on somehow disrupting the circular closure of the process ("what is needed here is some heterogeneity, something impossible to integrate into the scheme"). They arrived at a tactic. Some will say it was too little/too late; it hardly matters, for it, too, was deflected. Derrida was to send a drawing for a contribution that would have nothing to do with Eisenman's design process, making all decisions as to materiality, scale, shape, and location in the scheme, thereby breaching the project's circularity. As agreed, he sent by letter a contribution that was quite specific, if somewhat short of the requested specificity of scale, location, and so on. Upon receiving it, Eisenman and Thomas Leeser, principal design associate on the project, quickly found a way to ignore the contract, to violate both the spirit and the form of the contribution. In brief, they rationalized a loose analogy between Derrida's drawing and the shape of the site, and integrated the site, not the drawing, into the circularity of the scaling scheme, reiterating the closure Derrida desired to break.

It almost seems as if an obsessed Eisenman wanted nothing from Derrida but an endorsement of scaling—that is, Derrida's signature. In turn, it almost seems as if Derrida would sign any-thing in this project but scaling. A closer look at the movements of this signature is thus called for. Derrida, after he and Eisen-man concur on the tactic of his contribution, says of it: "And this will be the place of the real signature. Some little something, I don't mean names, but some signature would be there. So *your work* would be, *on the one hand*, read as a combination of those three elements continually expanding, as an exercise in recon-structing in a sophisticated way, and then, *in the margin, some-thing totally alien* from which and toward which everything had been or would be written" (emphasis added).

"On the one hand," "your work." On the other hand, his signa-ture as "something totally alien," "in the margin." At this point, at least, Derrida is less than willing to sign the design. Can we imagine where Derrida wants to be, where the margin of this project is? Perhaps it is the grid become gridiron, the no-man's-land between Tschumi proper(ty) and Eisenman proper(ty). Indeed, that would be a fascinating place for a separatrix, an Eisenman/Tschumi come to be written:

Eisenman *Derrida* Tschumi

One way or the other, the reader will discover the skirmishes over this border to be well rehearsed.

Derrida has elsewhere placed his signature on this project, most conspicuously in his essay "Why Peter Eisenman Writes Such Good Books." Once we delve into this text and others as-sociated with it, however, any aspiration of finding a simple so-lution to the problem of the role and place of Derrida's signature in this collaboration quickly evaporates. Instead, we confront a complex, dizzying structure—a double labyrinth at least—of sig-natures and autographs, inclusions and omissions, insides and outsides. Keeping in mind all that Derrida has written on the operations of quotation marks, signatures, autographs, and letters, we might have expected as much.

If, to clarify his position, we attempt to compare the idea that Derrida's contribution hosts the signatures as that idea occurs in the meetings with its appearance in "Why Eisenman . . . ," we immediately discover the difficulty at hand. "I believe that nothing else should be inscribed on this sculpture (for this is a sculpture) save perhaps the title, and a signature might figure somewhere (*Chora L Works*, by . . . 1986), as well as one or two Greek words (*plokanon, seiomena*, etc.). To be discussed, among other things."[13]

The cited passage appears within the essay as the end of an extended extract from the letter Derrida sent to Eisenman discussing his contribution. To be precise, however, what Derrida sent to Eisenman was two versions of the same letter differing slightly in the pertinent passage: one, handwritten and unsigned (no doubt a draft, though it, too, was dispatched); another, the one "quoted" in the essay, typed and signed. So, at the very least, a thorough reading must trace the ins and outs of the question of Derrida's signature as it circulates through four variously signed representations of this question: one "in his own words" (the conversation transcript), one unsigned but in his autograph (the draft of the letter), one typed but autographed with his personal signature (the letter), and one retyped with autograph eliminated and placed within an essay that bears his name as author. We begin to wonder whether or not there is any meaning to the questions: what, and where, is Derrida's signature?

Let us outline a portion of one of the several labyrinthine structures at work here. Among the three letters, the typed version is ostensibly the "original." It is the one authorized to appear in the essay; as well, though actually a copy of the original draft, it bears the author's handwritten signature. On the other hand, the handwritten draft sans signature is in the author's autograph;

though merely a draft, it is a letter in autograph. And, after all, both were dispatched to Eisenman at the same time. Furthermore, Derrida introduces the letter within the essay thus: "I write therefore to Eisenman, in the airplane, this letter from which one will permit me to cite a fragment."[14] What is the antecedent of "this"? The fragment "quoted" is not from the draft written on the airplane, but from the version typed later—almost. Additional material (in both autograph and type!) appears in the margins of the typed rewrite, that is, as marginal to the body of the letter. In the letter as it appears in the essay, this material has been brought into the body of the letter as parenthetical; thus, strictly speaking, the essay letter is "original." This original letter is inside the essay, but is inside as outside, as a quotation. It is an inside-outside as outside-inside, since it appears as the representation of Derrida's private communication to Eisenman. Clearly, this trail winds a vertiginous, indissoluble labyrinth that no Ariadne's thread can lead out of. Each line that appears as such a thread is but the lure of Arachne's web. Were we to consider all of the translations, changes, omissions, strikeovers, and other inside-outside mechanisms at work here, which become even more augmented in their complexity as they bear upon to whom these various letters were dispatched (the draft to himself, the draft plus typed letter to Eisenman, the quoted letter to an audience), we could fill a large volume.

Yet for our purpose, let us attend to a few details alone. First, under one of Derrida's signatures, that of the letter, one event is represented as having occurred inside a conversation between Eisenman and Derrida, while another, also part of this conversation, has been removed from this event to appear in the letter as if for the first time. We refer, of course, to the question of Derrida's contribution as the site of the signature. In all versions of the letter, what is to be remembered from the meeting that generated the letter is the agreement for a contribution. "You will recall what we

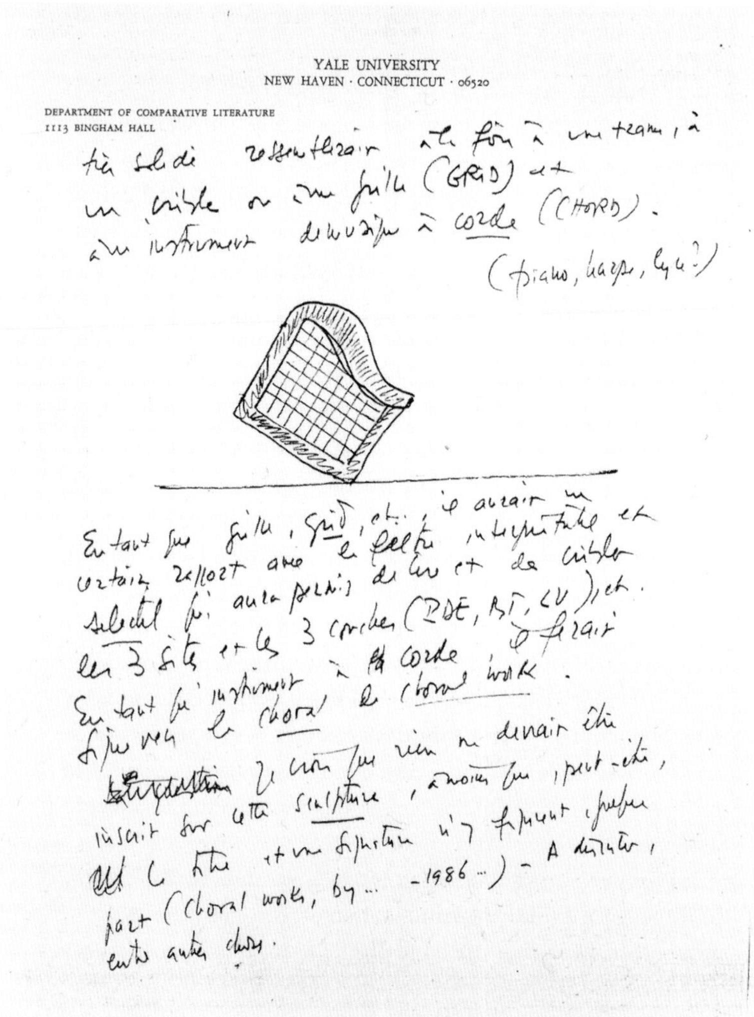

YALE UNIVERSITY
NEW HAVEN · CONNECTICUT · 06520

DEPARTMENT OF COMPARATIVE LITERATURE
1113 BINGHAM HALL

10.1

Jacques Derrida, letter to Peter Eisenman. With drawing for the *chora*, May 30, 1986. Collection Centre Canadien d'Architecture / Canadian Centre for Architecture, Montreal.

envisaged together at Yale: that in order to finish, I 'write,' if one can say, without a word, a heterogeneous piece."[15] What is forgotten, or to be forgotten, is that the question of this piece as the site for a signature was also an issue within the meeting. The issue resides in the tense of the letter: "I believe that nothing else should be inscribed on this sculpture." The signature is never a topic for collaboration; it is always in Derrida's hands.

Compare now the two versions of Derrida's contribution as a site for the signature and other things. In the meeting: the real signature, though perhaps not names. In the letter: the title (*Chora L Works*), names ("by . . . "), and some Greek words. But perhaps not names. Derrida skirts the issue yet again; though his parenthetical inscription suggests names, he refers to "une signature," seemingly leaving room for it with three dots. Or is he suggesting three dots as the signature? So far, neither his signature nor his thoughts on this signature will be pinned down. At the very least, however, he seems willing to have the title, *Chora L Works*, signed.

Before engaging this willingness, let us raise another point or two. Turning back to Derrida's introduction of the letter in the essay, we read: "I write therefore to Eisenman, in the airplane, this letter." Now consider the first sentence of the letter which immediately follows: "You will recall what we envisaged together at Yale: that in order to finish, I 'write,' if one can say, without a word, a heterogeneous piece." Note the quotation marks that distinguish the *I write* of the essay from the *I "write"* of the letter. For Derrida, to write a contribution to architecture requires a not quite writing, an outside of writing proper, a "writing." Not so for letters.

Derrida is comfortable with "real" writing, having rehabilitated writing from its exclusion, its metaphysical exteriorization, and repression vis-à-vis speech. This he was able to do by putting forward a concept of arché-writing—that is, a generalized writing anterior to speech—in large part based on such notions as trace and *différence*. Trace is a material-less, indeed, strictly speaking, nonexistent condition that, as Derrida has demonstrated, is nevertheless necessary for and always anterior to any production of meanings—including architectural meanings.[16] The originary trace frustrates the desire for a transcendental origin, a first and final "actual meaning," and thus guarantees the infinite openness of writing and reading. Yet, though architecture is a zone of the trace and thus within arché-writing, it seems nonetheless to require a hierarchical mark, a trace of its difference (in value) from "real" writing, hence the quotation marks.

In fact, as he himself emphasizes, Derrida never makes an architectural contribution. In the handwritten draft of his letter, he writes of his contribution, "I believe that nothing should be inscribed on this *sculpture*." In the typed version, the emphatic underline is insufficient and is replaced by a parenthetical mark: "nothing should be inscribed on this sculpture (for this is a sculpture)." What is Derrida trying to write so emphatically? Permit another digression to situate this question.

Among other places, Derrida confronts and undoes the metaphysical distinction between speech and writing as it is made in the works of Hegel.[17] Operating in and between Hegel's *Encyclopedia of the Philosophical Sciences* and his *Aesthetics*, Derrida focuses on two issues—the difference between sign and symbol, and the differing materiality of speech and writing—both of which are central to Hegel's privileging of speech. Hegel privileges hearing and speech over sight and writing because the materiality of the former—the breath—internalizes the temporality of the concept, something that the latter cannot do. Hence, like the plastic arts, writing holds back the progress of the spirit. Derrida is able to disrupt this argument by rendering the question of materiality immaterial, that is, by finding again the immaterial originary trace, the spacing that makes possible both writing and speech, as a necessary but repressed aspect of Hegel's argument. Of greater interest here, however, is Derrida's identification of the agenda behind this repression: "This *relevant*, spiritual, and ideal excellence of the phonic makes every spatial language—and in general all spacing—remain *inferior* and *exterior*."[18] Including architecture.

We have already touched on this issue. As an aspect of the question of materiality, Hegel, in his *Aesthetics*, invokes as an essential limitation of the plastic arts a production of meaning restricted to the aesthetic and the representational. From this, he can argue their inferiority and irrelevance within the arts as compared to poetry. Architecture, for example, confined to the massive and immobile material of stone and wood, is thus confined to the symbol. Poetry, to the contrary, living in the mobile and fluid materiality of language, of writing and, even better, of speech, operates with the *sign*. According to Hegel (and many others), the distinction between sign and symbol is that, unlike the symbol, which is motivated and thus limited by its referent, the sign is an unmotivated vector of meaning, arbitrarily related to its referent. Therefore, the sign alone can express the infinite elaboration that is the spirit. Along the way of this linear Hegelian path from the irrelevant to the relevant, from architecture to poetry, and eventually out of the arts to philosophy, architecture—not quite the first art but, in any case, the first expression of the spirit to itself—is superseded by sculpture. Sculpture, the *Aufhebung* of architecture, kills architecture as a relevant activity.[19]

Is Derrida's contribution a monument to the death of architecture, one upon which he would be willing to write, as one does upon a headstone, here lies "*Chora L Works*, by . . . 1986," after which he would say "a few Greek words"? If so, he would have created a marvelous symbol, ironically representing not only the death of architecture and its supersession by sculpture, but the death of sculpture and its supersession by music—for what is more musical than a choral work?—the death of music and its supersession by poetry—the play on words—and, finally, the death of the arts in general and their supersession by philosophy: for the "few Greek words," drawn from the *chora* passage in Plato's *Timaeus*, are to be inscribed, are they not, to symbolize Plato's texts, where poetry and myth move toward philosophy. In other words, he would have created a monument to Hegel's *Aesthetics*.

Let us be neither so hasty nor so harsh. Derrida subverts Hegel's simple sign/symbol distinction precisely by tracking the operations in his writing of the *pyramid*—for Hegel, the quintessence of architecture, proof of both its power and its limitation. Though the particulars of the argument are beyond the scope of this essay, suffice it to say that Derrida follows the pyramid as both concept and object in Hegel's work to show that Hegel himself cannot sustain the simple difference of sign/symbol. Yet another separatrix crumbles.

As we have said, Hegel's philosophy is totalization itself and therefore the constant target of Derrida and deconstruction in every one if its arguments and manifestations. Yet in this collaboration, again and again, we run across a latent Hegelian tendency in Derrida that surfaces in his confrontation with architecture. Whether in stipulating architecture's restriction to the symbolic or in preferring to situate his signature closer to writing than to design, he casts a Hegelian shadow.

Derrida's critique of Eisenman's scaling process as totalizing is, on its surface, accurate and consistent with his attack on totalization in any form. A glance at the scaling diagram for the project reveals that the circular relationships it proposes among Tschumi's design scheme for La Villette and Eisenman's for Cannaregio are not only closed, but determined by fact and presence: a fourth permutation of the cycle returns the system to its origin, a statement of the current condition of the presence of Tschumi's scheme and the absence of Eisenman's.

Eisenman counterargues that the scaling scheme proposes a design process motivated by other criteria than those that have dominated architecture throughout its history, or, more accurately, as its history. From Eisenman's point of view, the history of architecture's limitation to the aesthetic and the representational is the history of architecture as totalization. In this view, the history of architecture is a univocal text of *uomo universale*, the universal man, man as the measure of all things. While the metric of measurement changes and produces what we call architectural history, the origin of that metric—"man"—remains the same. Thus, all of the considerations that dominate traditional design processes—attention to the whole, symmetry, order, ornamentation (whether prescribed or proscribed), function, and so on—are always grounded in the self-evidency that the purpose and meaning of architecture is to express (what is considered to be) the timeless and universal condition of man (at any time). To be sure, throughout Eisenman's writings, particularly those on scaling, we encounter an inconsistent and self-contradictory strain of argument. Eisenman typically grounds his call for a "textual architecture," one that writes of other than the universal man, on the post-Freudian condition. In other words, he argues that, since Sigmund Freud, man has discovered himself to be more complex and multivalent than he is represented to be in traditional architecture. Therefore, architecture should do something new and different—represent this complexity and multivalency. Hence, at the very moment Eisenman demands an end to the domination of the *uomo universale*, he reinvokes it.[20]

The "should do something new and different" tone of Eisenman's writings is antithetical to the position of deconstruction and supports Derrida's criticism, directed not only at the closure of scaling but at scaling as the flagship of this revolutionary aspect of the entire Eisenman enterprise. To summarize, scaling is totalizing, first because it is structured as a closed narrative entirely determined by origin and end; thus, though it can be made to read differently—a central dogma of deconstruction being that every text is essentially undecidable and so open to different readings—it does not respect textual openness. Second, scaling is the vehicle by which Eisenman seeks to replace one totality—traditional design—with a new and different totality. If we grant this last point, and we must, we have nevertheless said nothing of scaling as a design process, merely commented on Eisenman's pronouncements about it. The key question is whether or not Derrida's first criticism is valid.

Certainly, were Eisenman to write the fictional story contained in the recursive diagram of this project in literary language, it would be suspect as totalizing in all of the terms discussed. Yet, Eisenman argues, this is not true of the design process, nor necessarily of its final result. Scaling is not the discussion of scaling or the literary motif within the scaling diagram, but rather these taken together with the manipulation of drawings and forms as one text. The process uses the linear fictional scheme to direct a play with the materials of architecture. In using a linear motive to direct design, scaling is akin to traditional design methods; however, it seeks to avoid the trap of architectural (not literary) totalization by replacing the universalizing discourse that drives traditional design with a local fiction. Scaling also engages aesthetics and representation, scale, solid and void, simultaneity and materiality, in such a way as to stay within the tradition of architectural design while displacing the underlying "anthropocentrism" of this tradition. It searches architecture for something that remains architecture yet is other than a discreet, unified, and universalizing whole. In this regard, Eisenman argues, scaling meets the criteria for design as writing in deconstruction's sense of the term.

Derrida's uneasiness with the linearity and closure of scaling is only legitimate if architectural design results in nothing more, and nothing other, than an exemplification of the ideas that motivate it—a signifier/signified thesis strongly at odds with the themes of deconstruction. Derrida aims his criticism at neither the process nor the final design, but at what is said of them: "Now, it is my wish to avoid any kind of totalization, and the *metonymic structure* of which you are *speaking* approaches such a totalization" (emphasis added). In these terms, his criticism is completely accurate; however, in targeting the word rather than the entire text, is it off target?

Discourse, literary writing, and architectural design are different; they each do things the others cannot. If, before, we took Derrida to task for distinguishing between literary writing and architectural writing (writing vs. "writing"), it was not to suggest that they are identical. Rather, it was to ask why their difference required the hierarchy of quotation marks, which suggest the Hegelian theme of literary writing, "real" writing, as more important and more able than architectural design. Scaling is not a hierarchical chain, a discourse that produces a narrative that then produces drawings and models. It is a text in which discourse, narrative, and design all operate simultaneously to motivate and disrupt each other in their separate realms.

As we indicated, one of the traditions of hierarchical difference between architectural design and writing turns on the question of sign versus symbol. This is not to say that the structure sign/symbol correctly articulates the difference between language and architecture, but that the differences between the two have been incorrectly and hierarchically subsumed under that distinction. Derrida has disturbed the sign/symbol distinction by demonstrating that the unmotivated trace, the required condition for the arbitrariness of the sign, does not exist: "In fact, there is no unmotivated trace: the trace is indefinitely its own becoming-unmotivated. . . . There is neither symbol nor sign, but a becoming-sign of the symbol."[21] Thus, deconstruction respects, and depends on, the irreducible nonarbitrariness—the formality and materiality—of language. It makes its necessary and serious point by playing with spelling, anagrams, puns, homophones, homonyms, formal analogies; in other words, by emphasizing the residual symbolic always within the signification of language.

Architecture poses, in a sense, the opposite problem. If, in language, the "arbitrary signifier" would like to disappear completely into its signified but cannot quite do so, always leaving open the door for deconstruction, then, in architecture, the symbol would like to appear exactly as its referent, be its (own) referent, though neither can it quite do so. Hence, though architecture is another field of the becoming-unmotivated trace, unlike writing it is the one that has been constituted historically as entirely motivated, that is, symbolic. Architecture is the scene in which, so to speak, the always-becoming-symbolic of the ("arbitrary") sign is repressed. Scaling attempts to respect and play with the becoming-symbolic of the arbitrary. Not, of course, the truly arbitrary, which does not exist: scaling does not aspire to invent new forms out of nowhere. Rather, it produces a more playful disposition of the sources of the symbolic (reference, scale, and so forth). Hence, it results in neither an entirely arbitrary sign nor an architectural symbol. It seeks to subvert: the autocratic and authoritative relationship of the word over the object, figure/ground relations, the hierarchy of scale, the hierarchy of solid versus void, the privilege of the "now" of perception, and the traditional presence of the architectural whole. In short, it seeks to subvert all of the bastions of architectural totalization without simply negating these issues.

It must be admitted that, by the end of the collaboration, Derrida, if still somewhat wary, addresses these issues as they apply to scaling. In "Why Eisenman . . . ," he says of the final design, "In this *abyssal* palimpsest, no truth can establish itself on any primitive or final presence of meaning," and later notes "the discontinuous structure of scaling."[22] However, even as he takes up the question of whether or not to sign scaling, he always leans toward, if not on, the word. On the way to a final look at Derrida's contribution in these terms, at his reading of the ongoing text implied by the emphatic sculpturality of this contribution, we should pass by another excerpt from his writings: "One must then, in a single gesture, but doubled, read and write. And that person would have understood nothing of the game who, at this, would feel himself authorized merely to add on; that is, to add any old thing. He would add nothing: the seam would not hold. Reciprocally, he who through 'methodological prudence,' 'norms of objectivity,' or 'safeguards of knowledge' would refrain from committing anything of himself, would not read at all. The same foolishness, the same sterility, obtains in the 'not serious' as in the 'serious.' The reading or writing supplement must be rigorously prescribed, but by the necessities of a *game*, by the logic of *play*, signs to which the system of all textual powers must be accorded and attuned."[23] If all that we have written is wrong, if, contrary to these arguments, the scaling process failed to meet the criteria of rigorously prescribed play and, indeed, was too closed, too circular, too totalizing, was it correct to add "something totally alien," a "sculpture" to introduce "some heterogeneity"? Was not this proposition an example of any old thing merely added on? In restoring the figure/ground relationship by reducing the scaling field to a pedestal for a "totally alien" "sculpture," Derrida's contribution would have homogenized more than heterogenized— just as the Choragic Monument of Lysicrates in Athens does to its famous pedestal. At the very least, the absence of any mention of the Derridean treatment of "supplement" during the discussion of Derrida's contribution is a conspicuous silence.[24]

In a certain sense, Derrida's tactic was, as always, precise and to the point. The idea of contributing an image extracted from the *chora* passage of Plato's *Timaeus* would have introduced, through rigorous play, a heterogeneity into the discussion of a process designed around *chora* that at the same time had nothing of *chora* in it. It would not, in fact, have been adding any old thing. But the drawings and models were of the text, not exemplifications of it. To avoid adding any old thing, to put aside his anaclitic relationship to the word, would it not have been necessary to read in such a way as to respect the drawings and models as text rather than as examples? Then the contribution could have played its game with the entire text, formally, materially, discursively, and so on.

Without having decided anything, then, let us return to the scene that we were reading, return, that is, to the question of Derrida's signature. In his essay "Why Eisenman . . . ," though he praises much of Eisenman's work, again particularly as it concerns writing, Derrida extends his criticism of the architect's totalizing tendencies with stinging irony, thus distinguishing his work from deconstruction proper. The very title of the essay indicates what is to come. Consider what Derrida writes in a chapter, entitled "The End of the Book and the Beginning of Writing," from *Of Grammatology*, held by many to be the premier textbook of deconstruction: "*The idea of the book is the idea of a totality*, finite or infinite, of the signifier: this totality of the signifier cannot be a totality, unless a totality constituted by the signified preexists it, supervises its inscriptions and its signs, and is independent of it in its ideality. *The idea of the book, which always refers to a natural totality, is profoundly alien to the sense of writing*. It is the encyclopedic protection of theology and logocentrism against the disruption of writing, against its aphoristic energy . . . and against difference in general (emphases added)."[25] Does such a writer entitle an essay "Why Peter Eisenman Writes Such Good Books" without irony? Lest we think that, in the Case of Eisenman, Derrida could be referring to "books," not books, and thus perhaps that the text/book distinction does not play here, consider how quickly it arises in the essay. In the second paragraph, the distinction is revived in terms that suggest a choice be made between Derrida and Eisenman. Referring to his own writing strategy, Derrida remarks, "Is this not the best condition for writing good *texts*?" (emphasis added).[26]

The title also opens the door to several other participants in the discussion; some enter forthrightly, some obliquely. Derrida reveals some and conceals others: as he says, this is the best condition for writing good texts; certainly, it is the best condition for writing ironic texts. Besides Derrida and Eisenman, who for a time we require in name only, we will want some of these participants on hand in this reading. Let us call them by name. The most obvious is Friedrich Nietzsche, for the title to this essay is a play on a chapter title, "Why I Write Such Good Books," from Nietzsche's *Ecce Homo*.[27] Then there is, of course, Richard Wagner, for, beyond *The Case of Wagner*, what and who is Nietzsche, in any case, without Wagner? Almost as obvious is John, the gospel according to St. John; after all, Pontius Pilate in John 19:5 delivers Jesus to his accusers and to his eventual crucifixion with the ironic words "Ecce Homo." In that text and this one we also find, among other things, the denial of Peter. Jesus himself has a small role, at least insofar as he knew how to stop a spear, if not an arrow. We need a cameo from Plato, a safecracker, a wrinkle or two to be ironed out, some ice, some diamonds, and, above all, laughter for this irony of ironies.

In "Why Eisenman . . . ," Derrida employs a technique found in much of his writing, though with a twist. Many of the writer's essays play on the name of their underlying subject: *Signéponge* on the poet Francis Ponge and "Parergon" on Immanuel Kant (*Kante* in German means "border" or "edge") come to mind as obvious examples. Such is the case for this essay as well, with the twist that the play extends into the work's very tone. It is an ironic essay first because of what it has to say, but it is also an iron-y essay about Eisenman (*Eisen* is German for "iron").[28] The irony to be worked out, perhaps even heard as a plaint within the title

("Why Eisenman?"), is at once how very similar and how very different the two are to and from each other, and not only in their work. The lever of intervention, the pivot between the two that is also a gap, is ostensibly Nietzsche. The Eisenman/Nietzsche is the old Nietzsche, the simple, radical Nietzsche, the one traditionally read as critic of the human-all-too-human, as nihilist, as revaluer of all values, as the philosopher of the end of the "truth" of everything, which is to say, the end of everything. *La fin de tout*, particularly the end of God, *la fin de Dieu*. Versus the Derrida/Nietzsche, the Nietzsche who would read a text as a *text*, the complex Nietzsche who not only abolishes the "true" world but also in the same gesture abolishes the apparent world, the "apparency" of the apparent world.

But I ask, do we not hear a hint of another voice in the opening strains of the essay, when, as Derrida summons Nietzsche's *Ecce Homo* to bear witness, he takes it upon himself to clear Eisenman of all suspicion? Suspicion of what? At the very least, do we not hear a whisper of Pontius Pilate, who did everything he could to evade the entanglement in which he found himself, who tried to put his responsibility on someone else, who summoned a bearing-witness with the ironic words "Ecce Homo," who took it upon himself to clear someone of all suspicion, but, above all, himself? And Pilate who removed his signature from the act, washed his hands of it, so to speak? Do we not hear him? No? Perhaps not.

Derrida draws the lines among Eisenman, Nietzsche, and himself quickly, and equally quickly seems to take sides. Though Eisenman's antianthropocentric words sound like Nietzsche's, "we should not, however, simply conclude that such an architecture will be Nietzschean." Rather, Derrida suggests that Eisenman is "the most anti-Wagnerian creator of our time."[29] He, Derrida, is more like the real Nietzsche; he writes on a computer as Nietzsche wrote on his typewriter. With Nietzsche, Wagner and I-rony are never far away. It is in the chapter of *Ecce Homo* concerning his *The Case of Wagner* that Nietzsche writes of his "love of irony, particularly world-historical irony." What is it to be the most anti-Wagnerian creator of our time? Wagner was the foremost creator of artistic totalities, the composer par excellence of whole worlds. To be the most anti-Wagnerian creator of the time: is this to be, like Derrida, an arch-deconstructionist totally against all totalization, or is it to be the foremost creator of new totalities, the creator of whole antiworlds? In the end, we must consider the possibility that these are the same.

Great care is called for here, for we are sending letters to "the wrong address" if we think we have a simple twosome in this essay, a Derrida versus an Eisenman. When Derrida writes that "it is not he who speaks, it is I. I who write; I who, using displacements, borrowings, fragmentations, play with identities, with persons and their titles, with the integrity of their proper names," be warned.[30] The initial play from first person to third person, from "I" to "Eisenman," is played back and forth again and again, intentionally and/or not. Throughout, wherever Derrida says "I" listen for "Eisenman." Whenever he writes "Eisenman" listen for "I," as in "I's a man" or "I's de man."

Beyond the tone of the work, the play on the proper name becomes a specifically ironic theme in the essay. Derrida writes, "Peter Eisenman, whose own name embodies both stone and metal," and, a moment later, "it is the truth that this man of iron, determined to break with the anthropocentric scale, with its 'man the measure of all things,' writes such good books! I swear it to you!"[31] As might be expected both in principle and in these particular circumstances, nothing in this essay permits of a conclusion that Derrida is simply opposed to Eisenman's work; to the contrary, much in it explores Eisenman's machinations with both respect and admiration. Yet the reader will be hard pressed to find such ironic heat elsewhere in Derrida's writing, which is usually as cool as ice. As a writer, Derrida is an iceman. If we look deeply enough at the play of proper names, beyond those that Derrida engages, we can discover within them barely imaginable ironies that confirm and overdetermine many themes in this collaboration, including the fluidity of identities. If, for example, Peter comes from the Greek word meaning "stone" and Eisenman means "iron-man," what does Jacques Derrida mean?

Consider the French verb *dérider*; is it close enough to Derrida? An English-speaking reader might guess from the looks of it that *dérider* means "to deride," perhaps ironically. Happily, it does not; it means "to brighten up," "to make less serious." Certainly, in French, Derrida *déride*. Further, since *rider* is the French verb meaning "to wrinkle," *dérider (de-rider)* can also mean "to remove wrinkles," "to unfurrow the brow." To remove wrinkles: could that be "to iron"? And Jacques? Like the English Jack, nickname of John. Does John 19:5 anticipate Derrida's signature, especially since the collaboration began in 1985? No doubt that is too farfetched.[32] Let us treat Jacques a bit more properly. Jacques, French equivalent to Jacob, comes from the Hebrew word meaning "supplanter," one who takes the place of through force or scheming. Jacques Derrida: one who schemes to supplant iron, "I" take the place of "Eisenman"!? One wonders whether "supplant" is ever used to translate Hegel's *Aufhebung*.

Almost at the very beginning of this paper, we introduced the theme of gold, which we will mine further, in particular as we engage the question of *chora*. In anticipation, however, let us read a passage about gold from the *Timaeus* in order to extend our thought on the proper names of this event: "Of all these fusible varieties of water, as we have called them, one that is very dense, being formed of very fine and uniform particles, unique in its kind, tinged with shining and yellow hue is gold, the treasure most highly prized, which has been filtered through rock and compacted. The 'scion of gold,' which is very hard because of its density and is darkly coloured, is called adamant."[33]

In his commentary on the *Timaeus*, Francis Cornford outlines a debate on the meaning here of "adamant": some say iron, some say diamond. In the end, what difference does it make? In German, *Eis* means "ice," American criminal slang for diamonds. At least, as we have seen, Eisenman is adamant about the scaling process, to Derrida's chagrin. And if ice is criminal slang for diamond, a Peterman is criminal slang for a safecracker. Is not Peter (Eisen)man one who seeks to crack the illusion of safety in anthropocentrism, to crack the safe of architecture, break into its pyramid, so to speak? None of this improper play, which nevertheless confirms and elaborates themes within the text proper, would be possible without the originary trace, that is, without writing. Moreover, we are guaranteed by the trace that the proliferation of meaning cannot peter out.[34]

This is why in his essay Derrida stays close to writing and close to Eisenman's play with writing. In the very last sentence of the essay, the climax of his ironic criticism of Eisenman as architectural totalist, as the anti-Wagner—"Ecce homo: end, the end of all, *la fin de tout*"—Derrida is at play. He not only plays with the termination of his essay, but as well extends the many plays on another of Eisenman's wordplay titles, *Fin d'Ou T Hou S*. Therein also are the conflated identities. Derrida: the end of all (I have to write). Eisenman: the end of everything (the anti-Wagner). And Nietzsche: *la fin de Dieu*.

While we play, however, we should not lose sight of our elusive quarry, Derrida's signature. Very early in the essay, Derrida introduces the collaboration as "one of Eisenman's works in progress." Not until after he elaborates Eisenman's skill with titles and wordplay and turns his attention to the title *Chora L Works* does the collaboration become a joint effort, "our common work." And the title alone is entitled to the honor of being of a joint effort: "This title is more than a title. It also designates a signature, a plural signature, written by both of us in concert."

The ever-present qualifier is there, however. In a parenthetical, in the essay as not in the essay, we find that this "(. . . was also a way not to sign while signing)."[35] Until this moment, there was no collaboration. Even though Derrida made an earlier contribution—a fragment of his *chora* text—no duet existed until the title emerged. Eisenman "appropriated by himself and for himself" from this fragment. In fact, after this point, after "our" title, Derrida is reluctant to refer again to the collaboration as a joint effort. Without doubt correctly, despite his efforts; we already know what happened to his final contribution. Moreover, Derrida's analysis of the title *Chora L Works* is very much to the point of the collaboration at the level of discourse, as his unfolding of it more than amply demonstrates. The title did open the work to readings and extensions that were resisted by the discourse of the collaboration before its inception. And it is truly a collaborative moment: though it is spoken by Eisenman, its possibility and desirability come from Derrida.

Throughout "Why Eisenman . . . ," Derrida lends his signature to Eisenman's *play with words* while furrowing his brow at the architect's inclinations toward a totalizing architecture, at his *work with words*. He is virtually silent on the drawings and models; if he describes them or uses them as examples of discourse, he never reads them as text. What interests Derrida most is how Eisenman's wordplay "participates with full legitimacy in the invention of architecture without being submitted to the order of discourse."[36] What interests him least, besides the themes of totalization already discussed, is Eisenman's reliance on traditional rhetorical modes. He stops short of crucifying the architect on this issue, though he comes very close: "And we could say something *analogous* on the subject of this active/passive opposition in the texts of Eisenman, something analogous as well on what he says about analogies. But one must also know how to stop an arrow. He, too, knows how to do that."[37]

If our conjecture on the interplay of "I's" is to the point, Derrida also stops short of allowing his arrow to strike home because he must stop short of suicide. This is not a Freudian question of unconscious projection or identification; that moment was reserved for Eisenman. During the first meeting, following upon a period spent apologizing for their respective lack of expertise in each other's discipline, was this exchange:

> **Derrida:** *I will stop apologizing for not being an architect.*

> **Eisenman:** *And I will stop apologizing for not being an architect.*

It is telling that no one in the meeting heard the slip. Derrida stopped short rather because, as he well knows and despite his effort to the contrary, *he writes such good books*.

So what are our conclusions? Where is Derrida's signature, and does he sign the project?

In this collaboration, Derrida, master of the word as an open door, is somewhat of a victim of words, Eisenman's words. He believes them and is upset by them. He hears closure, dialectic, circularity, allegory, etc., and closes his eyes.[38] He signs most easily some of Eisenman's words, but others stop him short of simply signing the project. He chooses his words carefully, so carefully, in fact, that he comes close to choosing nothing but words. Thus, despite what he has done for writing, Derrida never moves very far either from his name or from the book of John. Though he has done much to unfetter writing from its false bondage to a desire for the truth of the word, Derrida remains devoted to the power and priority of the word. "In the beginning was the word" is the haunting opening of John, as we all know. It is also worth recalling that the gospel according to St. John is a text concerned with logocentrism versus anthropocentrism.[39]

Let us also remember that in the Old Testament, at least, logo-centrism as phonocentrism in mortal man was first a question of power, not truth. In Genesis 27, the metaphysical power of the word extends from God's breath to man's, even though what is spoken is false. Though he was tricked into giving his blessing to the wrong son, Isaac could do nothing to take back his word. It was through the power of the word, not the truth, that *Jacob* supplanted Esau.

Clearly, to the question, "Where is Derrida's signature?" the answer must be that it is always with the word. Equally clearly, that this is the case does not indicate merely some trivial failing on Derrida's part. Rather, it speaks to the stakes of a deeply problematic issue in architecture: the role and privilege of the word with/in design. Does he sign the project? The answer to that must be both yes and no, neither yes nor no. That is the final irony, for this familiar double bind is his most genuine, most authentic signature. It is the one signature of Derrida that is absolutely resistant to deconstruction. Irreducible in every reduction, it is Derrida's transcendental signature itself.

Thus far we have outlined the expectations for this collaboration and pointed out the deflections and deferrals that they inevitably encountered. Are we gaining much? Or have we taken the path of least resistance by following the paths of most resistance through this event? Everyone that studies the transcripts of their meetings and the designs will no doubt quickly and correctly identify many more fascinating defenses and resistances than we have discussed. And it must be said, in this regard, that Eisenman and Derrida each exceed the typical in their capability of and givenness to the inert, above and beyond the machinations of this joint effort. If elsewhere Derrida has proclaimed this potential inertness of his work, has written that he risks not meaning anything, not a few in architecture would say that Eisenman has for some time now repeatedly accomplished the fact.

Though we recognize now a collaboration on the word, however convoluted, do we claim that there was never an effort at collaboration on design? No. Let us run a risk and try to identify one point in this event when a mutual commitment to work together, to become a duet, came briefly to fruition only to dissolve again into an "aggregate of solos." For such a moment, certain preliminary criteria would have to be met out of respect for the players. It could not be a singular origin, the singularity of a beginning, the point of the big bang; rather, it would have to be a moment of originary coincidence. A coincidence, a co-incident, the doubling of a co-inside, of an originary two, the condition made possible by the originary trace, which is to say, all conditions. It would thus leave traces, footprints that rippled both ways in the event, forward and backward.

Our nomination for such a moment would be the conversation between Eisenman and Derrida that took place in Trento, Italy, on December 16, 1985, during the third of their six meetings. As in the early stages of all such opera, in the first two meetings the universe had begun to take shape, which Eisenman and Derrida would perform. The program, Plato's *chora* in a new scoring by Derrida; the choreography, Eisenman's scaling; the cast; the scenery—all these had undergone a first negotiation and had been preliminarily endorsed. The first act, then, of this opera occurs in scene three. Staged as a pas de deux with chorus, it is the sparest scene in the entire opera, the one and only time the two are alone together and at one together, almost. If it is correct that this is the scene of two become one become two again, it could not have been better staged in any other form, keeping in mind that in French, *pas de deux*, a ballet duet—literally, a "step of two"—means, at the same time, coincidentally, "not of two" or "no two." Here we find the classical form of the pas de deux, consisting of an entrée, an adagio, a set of variations for each of the two, and a coda. For the question at hand, we turn our attention to the variations that begin with Derrida, "Repeat it once more, I'm not sure I got it," to which Eisenman responds, "Look, you are pushing me to invent this as I go along." Thus, the curtain rises on a set of variations on metaphorical and literal language played out through misunderstandings of the meaning of words. It is a scene with both the hilarity of Abbott and Costello's "Who's on First" and the sadness engendered by all of the hitches, contretemps, and misunderstandings of *Romeo and Juliet*.

Eisenman is attempting to convey metaphorically how the scaling he has in mind might be related to *chora*, in particular to the theme of imprinting: "our writing leaves a trace on a palimpsest, *whatever the material*, and we freeze that. Now, the imprint could be the plan of La Villette" (emphasis added). Derrida, perhaps confused by the mention of a specific, is no longer sure whether Eisenman speaks metaphorically or literally. To confirm his thought that the conversation may have moved to specifics, he interjects: "In concrete." To a French-speaking philosopher, his remark is unambiguous; it means "I take it we are speaking literally now, no longer figuratively." To an English-speaking architect, it is equally unambiguous and means "in the material concrete." Thus, Eisenman answers, "Let's say concrete," confirming to Derrida that they are now speaking of reality while confirming to himself that they continue to speak metaphorically. Though Derrida hears the variation on concrete, he now talks of reality: "The problem is, what substance will you use for this? If the floor layer is concrete, then you need something which is not hard." Eisenman, still completely within metaphor, says, "That is correct. . . . Let's say paste," elaborating the false confirmations and the slippages among materiality, the real, and the metaphorical. And so ensues an extraordinary conversation that climaxes in the moment of unstable unity in which Derrida makes an effort at concrete design, or should we say paste design? As funny and sad as this exchange may be, what is important is that, however short-lived, in this attempt Derrida abandons the traditional design assumptions he came with and tries to design in Eisenman's terms.

The variations are brief, and the pas de deux soon moves to the beginning of the end, the coda, the tail that tells the tale of the rest of the opera. Derrida: "It is as if you were the dreamer and I were the architect, the technician. So, you are the theoretician and I am thinking all the time of the practical consequences of everything in the place," and indeed will be for the rest of the story. There will be fluidities of identity, as we have seen, but never again an effort at unity. Later in the same scene, Eisenman will strongly protest when Derrida asserts that the work has moved from a duet to an "aggregate of solos."

> **Derrida:** *I am less sure that the rest of our, your . . .*
>
> **Eisenman:** *No! No! Of* OUR.
>
> **Derrida:** *. . . is physically possible for the moment.*

Derrida never recants his "your." *La fin de deux.*

So, now that we have acquitted our responsibility to take the presence of these two figures seriously, to consider their personalities, inclinations, and disinclinations, let us simply grant the obvious. Defenses and resistances abound: above all, the mark of an implied contract of noninteraction is inscribed in this event. In fact, come to think of it, how could this have been otherwise, considering the chemistry of gold? Therefore, can we be satisfied merely to continue this litigation? To do so would be to stipulate the question of presence: psychological presence, artistic and intellectual presence, and, especially, the "metaphysics of presence" that, as we noted early on, could render this potent event mundane, if not mute, unless we find a way to refuse it. We need a place of refusal, a way to sift through this collaboration and shake more out of it. Shake out of it what it was prepared for rather than what we anticipated for it. Shake out of it something for architecture.

Chora

is a common word in ancient Greek for place. It differs, though, from *topos*, "the place where something is located." Neither does it mean "finite void," *kenon*, or "infinite space," *apeiron*. *Chora* designates the container of something and has associations with words that convey "to hold" or "to have room for." It is used for the post, station, office, the place that a person holds, or a room that is filled. For Derrida and this event, however, the word takes on special significance for the unthinkable place it holds in the *Timaeus*, Plato's account of the cosmogony, the making of the known universe. According to Plato, the universe that we know was born as the Demiurge, architect of the cosmos, forged the sensible, material universe while contemplating the Forms (the Ideas, the *eidos*, the members of the true, perfect, immutable, and intelligible realm of being) as models (*paradigmata*) for the creation.[40] Though the Demiurge did the best possible job in making the universe, the necessities of his work—that is, materiality—insured that the sensible universe would be inferior to, and other than, the realm of true and ideal being; the sensible universe, then, is the realm of becoming. During the course of this discussion, a problematic question arises: into what place does the Demiurge inscribe the copies?[41] As Plato takes up this question, a wonderfully obscure and conflicted discourse emerges, unlike any other in the philosopher's writings. Generations of philosophers have struggled to make more precise Plato's problematic treatment of this dizzying question.

Before we examine Derrida's meditation on *chora* and take a second look at the collaboration through this lens, let us review some of the characteristics of this place unlike any other. When Plato turns his attention to *chora*, he does so as a retelling of the cosmogony, having discussed it once already in terms of the paradigms and the copies, being and becoming. As a prelude to this first telling, Plato says that any account of the physical world is, at best, a "likely story" because the world itself is a likeness; he reiterates this contingency before turning to this second "strange and unfamiliar exposition." In his first account, Plato distinguishes only two types, the intelligible and the sensible, the paradigm and the copy. In his second, his thought of *chora* requires that it be a "third kind," neither sensible nor intelligible, a form "difficult and obscure." What is its nature? "This more than anything else: that it is the Receptacle—as it were, the nurse—of all Becoming." After arguing that a figure molded in gold should always be referred to as "gold," for gold remains the same though the figure may be remolded, Plato notes that the same principle applies to that which receives all: "It must be called always the same; for it never departs at all from its own character; since it is always receiving all things, and never in any way whatsoever takes on any character that is like any of the things that enter it. By nature it is there as a matrix for everything, changed and diversified by the things that enter it, and on their account it *appears* to have different qualities at different times; it takes impressions from [the copies] in a strange manner that is hard to express." Plato goes on to compare the receptacle to a mother, the paradigm to a father, and the copy to a child. Yet the receptacle/mother/nurse is neuter; it has no qualities of its own. It is "free from all those characters which it is to receive from elsewhere"; "that which is to receive in itself all kinds must be free from all characters." Thus, it is not earth, air, fire, or water; rather, "it is invisible and characterless, all-receiving, partaking in some very puzzling way of the intelligible and very hard to apprehend."

This third genus, *chora*, is everlasting, indestructible. "It provides a situation for all things that come into being, but [is] hardly an object of belief"; *chora* can only be thought "as in a dream." Not (exactly) one of the Forms yet nevertheless everlasting, *chora* was of the chaos before the Demiurge brought forth the ordered universe. Before the ordering by the Demiurge, *chora*, receptacle of the chaos, "had every sort of diverse appearance to the sight" and "was everywhere swayed and unevenly shaken by these things and by its motion shook them in turn." "And they, being thus moved, were perpetually being separated and carried in different directions, just as things are shaken and winnowed by means of winnowing-baskets. . . . The dense and heavy go one way, while the rare and light are carried to another place and settle there." Thus, *chora* moved and ordered the chaos before the origin of true motion and ordering, "whereby the different kinds came to have different regions, even before the ordered whole consisting of them came to be."

The problem of *chora* is an anomaly in Plato's oeuvre; *chora* is therefore an outside that is inside—an irresistible temptation for Derrida. Let us skim quickly his reading of this enigma to situate some of the issues that arise in the discussions and to extract some guidelines for another look at the Eisenman/Derrida event. Derrida first attends to the history of the interpretations of *chora*, all of which aspire to speak the terms of *chora*'s existence, or at least its condition, better than Plato—that is, more seriously, more philosophically. "Rich, numerous, inexhaustible, the interpretations come, in short, to give form to the meaning of *chora*. They always consist in giving it form by determining it, it which however can offer itself only by removing itself from any determination, from all the marks or impressions to which we said it was exposed."[42]

All "serious" interpretations, then, try to recover the philosophic essence of *chora* from the apparent metaphoricity of Plato's descriptions and the mythological form of his argument, assuming, first, that the structures metaphor/referent and mythos/logos exist, second, that from these structures metaphor and myth can be identified as such and isolated, and (therefore), third, that the logos and referent as such can be recovered, disencumbered from myth or metaphor. Thus, and we might finally begin to say as always, this history, the history of the interpretations of *chora*, is a metonymy for history as the production of logocentrism.

Operating strictly with and within Plato's text, Derrida determines that the difficulty is not a failure of interpretation that might someday be overcome with more powerful exegetical or hermeneutic technique, but that the assumptions underlying what is called serious philosophic interpretation are precisely those resisted essentially by *chora*. *Chora*, as what, above all, is not, but what also is not nothing, emerges as that which cannot not be thought, but cannot be thought as such. To think toward a recovery of *chora-itself* is to re-cover *chora*. Thus, on the one hand, though we can write about *chora*, we cannot get to, achieve, expose, define, determine, or reveal *chora*, we cannot "give form to the meaning of *chora*." Beyond the negative rule, however, Derrida writes to us that, on the other hand, we cannot but write *chora*, something that all writing as inscription will always do.

The history of interpretations seeking to correct the "problems" of Plato's treatment of *chora* begins by criticizing Plato's reliance on metaphor and myth—philosophically inadequate forms of argument. Derrida demonstrates that the concepts of metaphor and myth, strictly speaking, cannot apply to a meditation on *chora*. There is no metaphor, at least in the structure metaphor/referent, nor is there myth, at least in the structure mythos/logos, if there is no referent, no logos. *Chora* is always anterior to inscription, though only after the fact; it is after the fact as before the fact, after the fact as such. *Chora* has no existence, no pure being anterior to and free from inscription, outside of rhetoric and trope: it *is*, though it *is* only and always in the text as before it.

In a lengthy digression to and against Hegel, Derrida reminds us that the mythos/logos structure embodies one of the underlying oppositions within Western philosophy, nonserious/serious. His reading of *chora* here twists this opposition into a form that can no longer be taken seriously. Moving from and with his thought on *chora* and the problematic of its history of interpretations, Derrida then develops a new strategy for reading (Plato), one that finds the evidence of *chora* already at work in (Plato's) text. In brief, he combs out formal analogies between the textual structures of the *Timaeus* and what is said of *chora* within the text. Thus, for example, he locates compelling analogies to what is said there of *chora* in an extended consideration of the place of Socrates in the early passages of the *Timaeus*. As Derrida writes, "Socrates is not *chora* but he would look a lot like it/her if it/she were someone or something." So, too, of the architecture of the text, which occurs as a "theater of irony where the scenes interlock in a series of receptacles without end and without bottom."[43]

Derrida stops short of it, but his reading seems to insist that *chora* be inscribed into his list of undecidables. We can at least draw the vector of such a conclusion by connecting those points in his essay where *chora* takes on the traits of the other, more familiar undecidables—the contradiction in terms notwithstanding. Like the others, *chora* is neither word nor concept, neither proper noun nor common noun, and it is a condition of absolute anteriority. Moreover, though Derrida treats of it only in passing, *chora* shakes, shakes the whole, separating before the separation; it is a movement before movement begins, since in the *Timaeus* all true movement begins with the world-soul and comes after the Demiurge does his work. Yet *chora* shakes and orders even the chaos. Thus *chora solicits*, in the Derridean sense of the terms.[44]

For the sake of expediency, let us limit ourselves to extracting from Derrida's reading only a few directions. The first comes by way of a caution: "these formal analogies are not considered . . .

as artifices, boldnesses, or secrets of formal composition: the art of Plato the writer!" His reading is not of a Plato who, with totalizing skill, deploys his discourse on *chora* in both the content and the structural form of the *Timaeus*, but of a Plato who, as he engages the question of the space of inscription, is inextricably bound by the very fact of his inscription to repeat by resemblance and before the fact his discourse on *chora*, as do all those who follow him. Including Derrida and Eisenman. *By resemblance and before the fact.* Recalling that his reading depends on formal analogy and authorizes this dependence in the name of *chora*, we find in Derrida's essay that *chora* is also the inevitability, the structural law, of anachronism in all inscriptions, including events. "We would like to show that [*chora*] is the structure that makes them inevitable, makes of them something other than accidents, weaknesses, or provisional moments," Derrida writes. "*Chora* 'is' the anachrony within being, or better, the anachrony of being, it anachronizes being." We might add, it analogizes being.

Our guide, our Greek chorus, then, shall be the law of the *ana-* that *chora* reflects into every inscription. Though we concentrate on but two paragraphs of that law, *analogy* and *anachronism*, we should not lose sight of its dimension, which would embrace the evidence of *chora* in an entire field of *ana-*: anabiosis, anabolism, anaclisis, anagnoresis, anaglyph, anagram, analysis, anamnesis, anastrophe, anastylosis, anatomy, and so forth, even extending by formal analogy to Ananke, Anaximander, and Anaxagoras, each of which operates in this event and could lead to yet another reading. Even more care is necessary here, however. Though not incorrect, it would underestimate the breadth of this law if all we read in it was that *chora* guarantees that no chronology be free of anachrony, that no logic be free of analogy. The law of *ana-* is not merely a law of impropriety; it is not a law of the contamination of the proper (*logos*, *chronos*) by the improper (*ana-logos*, *ana-chronos*), but a law anterior to the separation of the proper from the improper, a law anterior to the possibility of law, a law of laws. The law of *ana-* is the law of originary *ana-*, of originary anachrony, originary analogy.

Today we think of anachronism as error or, at best, as a form of literary play or joke. We treat analogy as an illegitimate, bastard form of reasoning.[45] Similarly, we consider coincidence to be merely a striking analogy arising by accident. Yet, since *chora* is the meeting place in which things that are not together in time or space nevertheless participate in one another in time and space, the place in which others co-inside, it reflects a law of analogy, anachrony, and coincidence that is not only their possibility but their necessity.[46] *Chora* makes inevitability of what we call mere accident and error.

On the way to an end, then, let us test our law with respect to analogies, anachronies, and coincidences in this event, test it with a second look, remembering that *chora* is in evidence only in a second look, a re-spect of the text. To inscribe *chora*, the Demiurge took a second look at the Forms,[47] Plato a second look at the Demiurge, the history of interpretations a second look at Plato, Derrida a second look at the history of interpretations, Tschumi a second look at Derrida,[48] and Eisenman a second look at Tschumi. As Eisenman says, "In retrospect, we were already working toward *chora*" and, later, "I feel I was actually making *chora* before I ever knew about it."

We begin again with the separatrix.

Though cautioned by Derrida not to dare too much with plays on feminine suffices, note that, like *chora*, the separatrix is an it/she.[49] The ending *-trix*, as in *aviatrix*, is the feminine form of the suffix of action, *-or*, as in *aviator*. That is, except in geometry where *-trix* is neutered and used to name various straight lines, not without irony, as in *directrix*. Like Derrida's Socrates, the separatrix is not *chora* but it/she would look a lot like it/her if *chora* were something. The separatrix is the third kind in those tripartite systems called "binary," such as word/meaning, becoming/being, or copy/paradigm. It forms all manner of relationships, yet it is "always called the same" and "never departs from its own character"; it "never in any way whatsoever takes on any character that is like any of the things that enter it." The separatrix is there as "a matrix for everything," though in its ability to forge different relationships it "appears to have different qualities at different times." Moreover, though it never belongs to one side or the other—for example, it is neither signifier nor signified—nevertheless the separatrix "partakes in some very puzzling and hard to apprehend way of the intelligible: though it does not mean anything, it is the place and possibility of meaning, of something meaning something else." As Derrida says of *chora*, so may we say of the separatrix: "Giving place to oppositions, it would itself not submit to any reversal. And this, another consequence, would not be because it would inalterably be *itself* but because in carrying beyond the polarity of sense (metaphorical or proper), it would no longer belong to the horizon of sense, nor to that of meaning as the meaning of being." No logic can put the separatrix into opposition, although without it there is no meaning; no meaningful / / / is possible.

If earlier we characterized deconstruction as preying upon the separatrix to destabilize it—and here we draw an analogy between the separatrix and *chora* that seems to valorize the former—there is, nonetheless, no contradiction or paradox. Deconstruction is not destruction, it does not pursue the separatrix to destroy it and the laws it enables; it does not seek the chaos that would result from destruction of either the separatrix or *chora*. It seeks, instead, to expose the hidden agenda behind an untenable reification of the order that the separatrix imposes. Deconstruction questions the repressions of the instability that the separatrix, like *chora*, reflects into order, making order possible. Deconstruction, returning to Nietzsche's question,

"What if truth were a woman?," respects the mark for what it/she is.

And so it seems, in a bit of bastard reasoning, does Eisenman. Is it not the separatrix as *chora* that Eisenman struggles to articulate during the fourth meeting, right in the middle of the dialogs, in his strange and unfamiliar exposition of the "wedge," the cut between metonymy and metaphor? We may be uncomfortable when he uses "allegory" as a metaphor for this between, this wedge, but have we not read a similar exposition on such a "between" already, one also strange, also in the middle of a dialog, also confined to, yet discomfited by, inadequate metaphor? To be sure, the proliferating analogies among the themes and structures of the dialog of the *Timaeus* and those that occurred during this event are uncanny. The curtain rising, the introductory conversations among Socrates, Timaeus, Critias, and Hermocrates, and those among Eisenman, Derrida, Renato Rizzi, and myself, each shaped around the identification of expertise and incompetence, render these dialogs as virtual mirror images.

As mirrors reverse left and right, so does the analogic/anachronistic mirror between these dialogs, *chora*, reverse before and after. Just *after* Socrates discusses what Derrida demonstrates to be a key structural analogy for *chora* in the early part of the *Timaeus,* he states his own incompetence to conduct this dialog: "My judgment upon myself is that to celebrate our city and its citizens as they deserve would be beyond my powers. My incapacity is not surprising." Socrates goes on to relate his unsurprising incompetence to his resemblance to the poets, the artists, the imitators. Though he is not an imitator, he is incompetent because he feels like one; thus Socrates silences himself, preparing to receive all. Derrida uses this very moment in the dialog to begin constructing his analogy between Socrates and *chora*. Now, in his first meeting with Eisenman, just *before* he introduces *chora*, Derrida mirrors Socrates with startling precision. First he states his incompetence for the dialog: "I have no competence in architecture at all." Then he adds that he is like an imitator, an architect: "Yet I have always had the feeling of being an architect." Finally, as in the case of Socrates, Derrida constructs himself in terms belonging to *chora*. He says, "When Tschumi first asked me to participate in this project, I was excited, but, at the same time, I was totally, totally empty. I mean, I had no ideas at all."

Let us simply list a few more of these analogies.

Early in the *Timaeus*, Socrates states the desirability of contriving so that no parent "should recognize his own offspring." This theme recurs in the first meeting: it is noted that one of the most interesting and important features of the scaling process is that, when finished, no one knows the results, no one person understands all of the features in the final design, not even Eisenman.

The question in the *Timaeus* that lead to the discussion of *chora* concerns the relationship between idea and necessity—the very issue that governs the collaboration. Countless times during the event, necessity encroaches upon the idea: "in the end, it must be sensible, it must have physicality."

The *Timaeus* itself was to be the first of a trilogy; it stands now with the partially finished *Critias* and the never-begun *Hermocrates*. The final design was also to be the first of a trilogy, a three-site scheme; need we point out that the second site was started but left unfinished and the third site never begun?

Consider Eisenman's initial speech on the anthropocentrism of architecture. He takes as his principal motif that function, considered by many to be the primary cause of architecture, is only accessory to its deeper cause, the manifestation of meaning, of the idea. Compare this to the discussion of accessory cause in the *Timaeus*: "Now all these things are among the accessory causes which the god uses as subservient in achieving the best result that is possible. But the great mass of mankind regards them, not as accessories, but as the sole cause of things." Plato, too, goes on to privilege the idea as first cause.

And just as the Demiurge, after beginning the process of making the sensible universe, delegates it to those lesser gods he has created, so Eisenman turns the design process over to his protégés, Thomas Leeser and Renato Rizzi: "These people work full-time on it, I have only been overseeing."

Where analogy reigns, anachronism cannot be far behind. One of the most striking anachronistic analogies concerns the much-discussed title of this collaboration, *Chora L Works*. The law of *ana-* should guarantee that this title was already at work as architecture in the *Timaeus*. In fact, is not the name of the architect in the *Timaeus* already like *Chora L Works*, a likeness that emerges after the fact as before the fact? Demiurge (*demi-urgos*) is a word constructed from the Greek roots *demos* meaning "a group of people," such as a chorus, and *ergon* meaning "work."

If we made much of Derrida adding a sculpture to the scheme to introduce some heterogeneity, we cannot now be surprised that before this issue arose in the meetings, Renato Rizzi simply added a diagonal ground line to the scaling diagram for the very same reason, to add some heterogeneity. This is the source of the skew to the ground in the scheme. Like Derrida, he derived this addition by rereading a source text, Eisenman's Cannaregio project.

Also worth attending is the anachronism of authorship in the dialog of the final meeting. When he first sees the second model, Derrida remarks, "It's really a creative space; so many things about it call for going in and under." Afterward, a discussion ensues concerning whether or not people will be allowed onto the scheme. Derrida wants access so that the design will not become a precious object. Several suggestions are made and rejected, when Rizzi finally says, "Or we could create an access level beneath." Derrida: "I do not understand. Under?" Eisenman: "Like

10.2
Eisenman Architects, La Villette, Paris, 1987.
Presentation model. Courtesy Eisenman Architects.

a tunnel." Derrida: "Yes, it's a wonderful idea." On this occasion, it is Derrida who has Rizzi's "original" idea first.

There can be little doubt, then, that in reflecting the wonders of the law of *ana-* the event of the collaboration is inscribed in *chora*. Yet does the law operate within the design produced by this event? Scaling, of course, is a design process entirely constructed around anachronism, analogy, and coincidence. In this case, a fictional narrative anachronizes the relationship between Eisenman's housing project for Cannaregio and Tschumi's design for the Parc de la Villette. This narrative gains its foothold by taking opportunistic advantage of the formal analogy that exists between the point grids in these two designs. Elements from (the history of) Venice and Paris and Eisenman's and Tschumi' s projects coincide at three different scales and in various notations for presence, absence, and "time." For instance, the Paris of Louis-Philippe is represented in a fragment of the last Parisian wall raised by Adolphe Thiers, while a subsequent Paris is represented by the forms of the abattoirs that took the place of the wall on this site after it was razed by Georges-Eugène Haussmann.

As well, we see at differing scales a positive representation of the Cannaregio Canal, positive and negative representations of Eisenman's housing blocks, imprints of Tschumi's plan, the analogous point grids characteristic of these two schemes, and the lyre/site form that displaced Derrida's contribution. These are made to participate in one another by registering one ensemble of forms to another along the seam of an analogic feature. Thus, for example, the dominant axes of the two point grids serve to register Tschumi's scheme to Eisenman's. Decisions as to scale, solid (positive) or void (negative), and so forth derive from the scaling diagram as modified by Rizzi's rotation of the ground datum.

These aspects of the scaling process are straightforward, and with a little study the reader could easily understand the process and confirm its results in the second model. Yet merely to affirm that anachronism and analogy have been built into the design process is not to test the process in terms of the law of *ana-*. Indeed, if the final design closes off an extended field of reading, if it interrupts the proliferation of analogy, anachronism, and coincidence as it seeks to take control of them, then we must acknowledge that, though scaling as a process symbolizes *chora*, it does not respect it/her. As we now know, symbolization is particularly antithetical to the undecidability of the place that this event seeks.

So, for our purposes, a test of the final design cannot stand either on its beauty or on the legibility of the fictional history that was its nominal genealogy.[50] These are insufficient to determine whether or not this work finds its place. For this measurement, we must turn our attention to a feature within the design that nevertheless eludes the clarifying grasp of the design's history and logic, an inside that is outside. We can then track this feature to read what, if any, internal analogies, anachronies, and coincidences unfold from it.

In examining the second model, we soon notice the color, which participates as a design notation. Most of the elements remain the natural color of basswood. The reds of the Eisenman housing forms, the silver of the lyre/site forms, and the gold of the Paris wall and abattoirs are the exceptions. The reds recall the original color of the housing for Cannaregio; the silver indicates aspects of the discussion of the lyre form in the meetings and in Derrida's letter. In all these discussions, it was thought that Derrida's sculpture should be in metal. In fact, in his letter, the philosopher specifically suggests it be gold, noting that gold appears both in relevant passages of the *Timaeus* and in one of the models of the Cannaregio project. Instead, the golden sections of the second *Chora L Works* model belong to the Paris forms. Nothing in the discussions or the scaling logic accounts for this notation, yet it is one of the most prominent features of the model. Let us choose this feature, then, for our test.

As we have said, gold is not arbitrary, not simply outside of the motifs of this event. Beyond the several appearances of gold in the *Timaeus* already noted, in certain ways, in fact in its very heart, *chora* already heralds gold. Gold opens a place for a key analogy in Derrida's essays "Chora" and "Why Eisenman . . . ". Derrida also attends gold in other of his writings on Plato, most notably in his pair of essays "Plato's Pharmacy." And if we trust our ear, surely we can hear that what we began by calling gold opportunity became exactly that, an aural opportunity, an oral exchange become choral. Yet, in the model, gold fails to mold any of these possible figures; considering this, it seems rather oddly unmotivated.

In Eisenman's Cannaregio project, gold and Venetian red appear for symbolic reasons, gold symbolizing the alchemical pursuits of Giordano Bruno and red the blood of his execution. After Cannaregio, however, something else takes place in Eisenman's designs. Some projects, such as the Wexner Center for the Visual Arts and the Berlin housing, are dominated by multiple grids. In the rest, including Romeo and Juliet, the Long Beach museum, and the Progressive Corporation project, an anomalous golden area appears in one or more of their representations. If the grid is Eisenman's most famous signature, we must begin to wonder whether gold is becoming another, alternative, signature. Remembering that Hebrew law forbids the name of God to be spoken or written, a prohibition that requires English-speaking Jews to write "G-d" in the word's place, then perhaps the g-d structure that persists as Eisenman's signature moves from grid to gold suggests that the "arbitrary" gold in this project is Eisenman's signature as Architect/Demiurge.[51]

Yet this reading of the golden section of the model as Eisenman's signature is, at first glance, somewhat disappointing in that, unlike *chora* and its law of *ana-*, it seems to have a precise beginning at the Cannaregio project. It thus lacks the anachrony that should be inscribed in the movement of the signature. An endpoint enters the reading, blocking off the proliferation of analogies and coincidences that we seek. Or does it? Are there golden sections at work in this model and in Eisenman's signature before the fact? A paradoxical lapse in Eisenman's early houses might help us to break through this block.

From his earliest endeavor, Eisenman was interested in using intellectualized processes to move away from the anthropocentrism of architecture. In keeping with this interest, he venerated the rational design process of Le Corbusier while criticizing the unabashed anthropocentrism that motivated the Paris-based Swiss architect. Le Corbusier's "Modulor," avatar of the rationalized anthropocentrism underlying his processes, should therefore have been an anathema to Eisenman, yet his early houses each deployed proportional systems drawn from the Modulor. Of interest to us here, however, is that Corb based his proportional analysis of man on the Fibonacci series, the mathematical extension of the geometric proportion known as the *golden ratio* or *golden section*. A well-known signature device in several of Le Corbusier's drawings is the boldly proclaimed algebraic ratio of the golden section, $A/B = B/(A+B)$. Thus, from the beginning and before he first signs with an anomalous golden section, Eisenman was already signing his works with anomalous golden sections.

The golden section does not occur in the *Timaeus* as such, but Plato opens a place for it in his discussion of the most perfect triangle out of which the Demiurge is to build perfect bodies. Before stating his nominations for the best of the isosceles and scalene triangles, he writes that "if anyone can tell us of a better kind . . . his will be the victory, not of an enemy, but of a friend." Now, the geometry and mathematics of the *Timaeus* are thoroughly Pythagorean. The symbol of the Pythagorean Society, which the Pythagoreans named *health*—they, too, posited the relationships among triangles, ratios, and the perfect body—is today called the *triple triangle*. It consists of three identical one-hundred-eight-degree isosceles triangles superimposed to create a five-point star with a regular pentagram as its center. Other than its cosmological symbolism, the most outstanding feature of this figure, and a source of its mystical power for the Pythagoreans, is the extraordinary number of golden sections that it contains, well over two hundred. At the very least, armed with the golden section, we could ably take up Plato's challenge to name a better triangle.

Through the lens of the golden section, a second look at the project unfolds yet another series of startling anachronisms and coincidences. Eisenman has already spoken of the analogy between Le Corbusier and Tschumi, another Swiss-born architect based in Paris. And it was Corb's unrealized project for a hospital in Cannaregio that provided the source of the point grid in Eisenman's housing design. Recalling Plato's problematic metaphors for *chora*, mother/nurse, can we resist the coincidental presence of absence in this project of the house/hospital, those architectural places par excellence for the mother/nurse that already occupied Eisenman's Cannaregio scheme before being reinscribed and multiplied here, even before Eisenman feels as though he is already "making *chora*"? Lest the reader think this track of the golden section a contrivance imposed upon the event by a mere play on words, note Eisenman's remarks in the second meeting as he describes the details of the scaling he has in mind: "In this case we also have three texts: Bernard Tschumi's, Jacques Derrida's, and Peter Eisenman's, which is not yet given. Interestingly, each of these is a text on a text: Bernard's can be seen as a text on mine for Venice; mine will be a text on Jacques Derrida's; his is a text on Plato's *Timaeus*. We therefore have both a closed and an open circle. Derrida opens the circle, changing it into a spiral. But the process will be as much conditioned by Tschumi's text as by Derrida's. Let's see. Tschumi is to Eisenman as Eisenman is to Tschumi plus Eisenman. Then, Plato is to Derrida as

Derrida is to Plato plus Derrida. Then a third which connects the two. Something like that." "Tschumi is to Eisenman as Eisenman is to Tschumi plus Eisenman. Then, Plato is to Derrida as Derrida is to Plato plus Derrida." This is, of course, $A/B = B/(A+B)$, the classical algebraic statement of the golden section. Eisenman here extends this ratio from its geometric beginnings through its mathematization into the realm of textual analogy.

If the reader remains unconvinced, if he or she still finds this only a coincidence of words, then consider the design process itself. Though the details of scaling as a process varied in each of the projects in which it was employed, nevertheless one characteristic remained constant, the notion of recursivity. In every case, the texts—the ensembles of forms—in question were recapitulated at three spiraling scales to destabilize any dominant, original scale. Yet such spiraling is one of the characteristic features of the golden section as embodied in the golden rectangle. This analogic spiraling can easily be seen in the second model if we follow the lyre/site form at its three scales. Eisenman disrupts the self-same repetition of the golden rectangle diagram by employing, instead, a temporal notion of self-similarity; but does this not actually improve the architectural translation of the regress of the golden section by embodying in it one of the most important factors distinguishing architecture from geometry—time?

If this brief excursion along a golden pathway is to be trusted, then perhaps we have found what we were looking for. Clearly, in the context of the event, the design does operate as a signpost for many readings, does, that is, obey the law of *ana-* with respect to anachronisms, analogies, and coincidences. Considering that no event has a true beginning or a true end, we can expect more readings to unfold, readings unanticipated by the project but for which it will have always been prepared. On the other hand, *chora* and the law of *ana-* guaranteed this result from the beginning, guaranteed it absolutely, not only in this project but in any and all projects, any and all inscriptions. What was at stake in the collaboration was therefore less a work in which undecidability could be found than a work that began to explore, to celebrate, to *respect* undecidability as an essential aspect of architectural design. Did Eisenman's scaling accomplish this respect, or was it yet another, more sophisticated version of architecture's traditional desire to exercise complete control? Let us, for the time being, leave these questions without answers. They must be discussed and elaborated at length, perhaps in terms not yet conceived and not restricted to the circles of Eisenman and Derrida.[52]

As we bring our second telling to a close, then, let us remind ourselves that the motive for our reembarkation was not to determine the success or failure of this collaboration. Rather, we wanted to shake something out of it for architecture. And it does seem that we have winnowed a positive possibility. We have at least begun to articulate the terms, not of a new architecture or anarchi-tecture, new first principles or anarchy, but of a new respect for the imprint that *chora* reflects into all writing, including architecture. The respect is nothing other, but nothing less, than the recognition that what marks and makes possible the opposition arché/anarchy is the entire field of *ana-*, ana-architecture. To close without ending, let us call up one last separatrix for a twist, let us shake a bit the massive structure of lie/truth. Perhaps then, we will understand that this respect is not a new possibility, but only the movement that always already lies within what we call the truth of architecture.

11 TOWARD A NEW ARCHITECTURE

Well, I stand up next to a mountain,
and I chop it down with the edge of my hand.
Well, I pick up all the pieces and make an island,
might even make a little sand.
—Jimi Hendrix, "Voodoo Child"

Over the last few years, a few projects by a handful of architects have broached discussions of a New Architecture. The themes of this discussion are only now coming into sufficient focus to allow for the preliminary efforts to articulate some of them in this volume. Before we turn our attention to that specific task, however, let us consider for a moment what is at stake in the endeavor.

"A New Architecture." Today one whispers this phrase with trepidation and embarrassment, perhaps for good reason. True enough, most New Architectures are so ill-conceived that they are stillborn or die a merciful death early in infancy. But the prognosis is poor even for those with the strength to survive their hatching, for the majority of these are killed by a well-coordinated, two-pronged attack.

There are several variations, but the general schema of this attack is well known: first, critics from the right decry the destabilizing anarchism of New Architecture and the empty egotism of its architects; then, critics from the left rail against the architecture as irresponsible and immoral and the architects as corrupt collaborationists. Sapped by this onslaught, the eviscerated remainders are quickly mopped up by historians, with their uncanny ability to convince us that the supposed New Architecture is actually not new at all, and was in fact explored with greater depth and authenticity in Europe some time ago.[1]

Today, historians and critics alike sermonize upon the creed that there is nothing new worthwhile in architecture, particularly no new form. Their doxology is relentless: "praise the past from which all blessings flow." Thus, we retreat from the new and have become ashamed to look for it. I have colleagues who comb drafts of their work before publication in order to replace the word "new" as often as possible; I have done it myself. As a result, PoMo, whose guiding first principle is its unabashed and accurate claim to offer nothing new, has become the only architecture to mature over the last twenty years.

"Nonsense!" it will be argued; "During the same period a flourishing revival of the avant-garde has developed," and fingers will point to the Museum of Modern Art's "Deconstructivist Architecture" exhibition and to the buildings of Eisenman, Gehry, Libeskind, Tschumi, Koolhaas, Hadid, and others. Yet, upon closer examination, is it not more accurate to say that these works have been executed under the auspices of an implicit contract of disavowal? In other words, is it not the case that these designs are celebrated as auratic, signature buildings of interest only for their irreproducible singularity, rather than as sources of new principles for a general architectural practice? In that sense, the discipline of architecture has recognized them as exotic, precisely so as to suppress their contribution to a New Architecture.

Yet within these disparate works are insights that might well contribute to formulating a framework for a New Architecture: one that promises both formal vitality and political relevance.

Consider the work of Daniel Libeskind, for example. From *Chamber Works* to his recent projects in Germany and elsewhere, one finds a sustained, penetrating critique of the axis and its constellation of linear organizations. Considering the political, social, and spatial history of the axis in architecture and urbanism, this is no minor issue. Yet very little on this subject can be found in the critical literature treating these projects. Instead, Libeskind is configured as an avatar of the esoteric, and the status and power of the axis in quotidian architectural practice, so thoroughly rethought in his projects, are left unquestioned.

On the surface, our retreat from the new seems both historically and theoretically well informed. With its utopian aspirations, architectural modernism sought to overthrow obsolete spatial hierarchies and establish a new and more democratic, homogeneous space. However well-meaning this goal, insofar as its search for the new was implicated in an Enlightenment-derived, progressivist project, it was also implicated in the tragedies that resulted. The instrumental logic of architectural modernism's project of the new necessarily calls for erasure and replacement; for example, Le Corbusier's proposal for old Paris.

In the name of heterogeneity, postmodern discourse has mounted a critique of the project of the new along several fronts. It has demonstrated both the impossibility of inventing a tabula rasa and the necessity to celebrate the very differences modernism sought to erase. Its own version of the search for the new, a giddy logic of play, of reiteration and recombination, of collage and montage, supplants modernism's sober, self-serious search for the Brave New. In postmodernism's play, history regains renewed respect, though on different terms. Rejected as a linear, teleological process that underwrites its own erasure and replacement, history is now understood as a shapeless well of recombinatorial material: always deep, always full, always open to the public.

In postmodernism's most virulent practices—those that use reiteration and recombination to insinuate themselves into and undermine received systems of power—a relationship to the new is maintained that is optimistic and even progressive, albeit not teleologically directed. In such postmodern practices as deconstruction, the project of the new is rejected. New intellectual, aesthetic, and institutional forms, as well as forms of social arrangements, are generated not by proposition but by constantly destabilizing existing forms. New forms result as temporary restabilizations, which are then destabilized. Accelerated evolution replaces revolution, the mechanisms of empowerment are disseminated, heterogeneous spaces that reject established categorical hierarchies are sought, and a respect for diversity and difference is encouraged. Far from being nihilistic, postmodernism in this conception is broadly affirmative.

Unfortunately, however, postmodernism's critique of the politics of erasure/replacement and emphasis on recombination have also led to its greatest abuse, for it has enabled a reactionary discourse that reestablishes traditional hierarchies and supports received systems of power, such as the discourse of the nothing new employed by Ronald Reagan and Margaret Thatcher for their political ends, and by Prince Charles, Roger Scruton, and even Charles Jencks to prop up PoMo.

I believe, therefore, that it is not postmodernism itself but another, more insidious pathology, a kind of cultural progeria, that underlies our current withdrawal from the new. The symptoms of this disorder were first diagnosed by Friedrich Nietzsche and more recently have been thoroughly analyzed by neomodern social theorist Roberto Mangabeira Unger.[2] Manifested as a rationale, it holds that the catalog of possible forms—institutional, social, political, and aesthetic—is virtually complete and well known. We may debate the relative merits of this form or that, but we will no longer discover nor invent any new forms. This position is far from the suppositions of post-modern combinatorics.

Is it possible that "Westernity" as a cultural experiment is finished and, put simply, that we are old? Only in that context could our current, excessive veneration for the received catalog of forms be valid. Frankly, I cannot believe that in the short span of our history we have experimented with and exhausted the possibilities of form. It seems to me that every indication today is to the contrary, whether one considers the political transformation in Eastern Europe or the technological transformations that characterize today's society. The building of the catalog of available aesthetic, institutional, and social forms has only just begun.

If this New Architecture is not to repeat the mistakes of modernism, it must continue to avoid the logic of erasure and replacement by participating in recombinations. As far as possible, it must seek to engender a heterogeneity that resists settling into fixed hierarchies. Furthermore, it must be an architecture—that is, a proposal of principles (though not prescriptions) for design. Finally, it must experiment with and project new forms.

The first two of these criteria already belong to architectural postmodernism. However, the last two criteria—the call for principles and the projection of new forms—fundamentally detach the theorization of a New Architecture from postmodernism proper, however much it draws upon the resources of the latter.

Indicative of that detachment is the degree to which some New Architecture theorists, notably Sanford Kwinter and Greg Lynn, have shifted their attention from poststructural semiotics to a consideration of recent developments in geometry, science, and the transformations of political space, a shift that is often marked as a move from a Derridean toward a Deleuzian discourse.[3]

In these writings, the Deleuzian cast is reinforced with references to catastrophe theory—the geometry of event space transformations—and to the new biology. Geometry and science are traditional sources par excellence of principles and form for architecture, but within each of these areas of study the paramount concern is morphogenesis, the generation of new form. However provocative and invaluable these studies in philosophy or science are as resources, neither provides the impetus for a New Architecture nor the particulars of its terms and conditions. Rather, these have grown entirely out of architectural projects and developments within the discipline itself.

One contributing factor to the search for a New Architecture is the exhaustion of collage as the prevailing paradigm of architectural heterogeneity. In order to oppose modernism's destituting proclivity for erasure and replacement, postmodernism emphasized grafting as the recombinatorial instrument of choice. The constellation of collage, in all its variations,[4] offered the most effective model of grafting strategies. From Colin Rowe to Robert Venturi to Peter Eisenman,[5] from PoMo to the deconstructivists, collage has served as the dominant mode of the architectural graft. There are indications, however, to suggest that collage is unable to sustain the heterogeneity architecture aspires to achieve. In lieu of the meticulous study necessary to support this claim, allow the suggestion of two of its themes, the first historical and the second theoretical. First, postmodern collage is an extensive practice wholly dependent on effecting incoherent contradictions within and against a dominant frame. As it becomes the prevailing institutional practice, it loses both its contradictory force and its affirmative incoherence. Rather than destabilizing an existing context, it operates more and more to inscribe its own institutional space. The only form collage produces, therefore, is the form of collage.

Secondly, and perhaps more importantly, collage is limited to a particular order of semiotic recombinations. Each element in a collage, even in the aleatoric process-collages of Dada, must be known and rosterable in its own right. Thus, although collage may engender new compositions as well as shifts, slips, accidents, and other chimerical effects, the long-term effect of collage is to valorize a finite catalog of elements and/or processes.

Collage is only able to renew itself by constantly identifying and tapping into previously unrostered material. Thus, collage can never be projective. The exhaustion of collage derives from the conclusion that the desire to engender a broadly empowering political space with respect to diversity and difference cannot be accomplished by a detailed cataloguing and specific enfranchisement of each of the species of differentiation that operate within a space. Such a process is not only economically and politically implausible but theoretically impossible.[6] If collage is exhausted as a recombinatorial strategy—a matter still debated[7]—then the problem becomes one of identifying grafts other than collages. The key distinction from collage would be that such grafts would seek to produce heterogeneity within an intensive cohesion rather than out of extensive incoherence and contradiction.[8]

In a lecture delivered in 1990 to the Anyone conference in Los Angeles, Unger took issue with current postmodern practices in architecture, primarily in terms of what he saw as the "ironic distancing" effected by both PoMo and deconstructivist architecture. At the conclusion of his lecture, he outlined five criteria for any New Architecture seeking to contribute to a nonhierarchical, heterogeneous political space.

According to Unger, such architecture must be *vast* and *blank*; it must *point* and be *incongruous* and *incoherent*.[9] It is not clear from the lecture how Unger intended his criteria to be interpreted, but I was struck by the degree to which, with one exception, they lent themselves to a discourse on grafting alternatives to collage. Particularly interesting to me was how well these criteria read as generalizations of the spatial/formal project of modernism outlined in Le Corbusier's five points. While Le Corbusier's points are directed toward producing a broadly democratic space through homogeneity, Unger's are directed toward a similar political goal through a spatial heterogeneity that does not settle into stable alignments or hierarchies. I interpret and modify Unger's criteria as follows: (i) Vastness—negotiates a middle ground between the homogeneity of infinite or universal space and the fixed hierarchies of closely articulated space. Recognizing the necessity of finitude for heterogeneity, vastness seeks sufficient spatial extension to preclude the inscription of traditional, hierarchical, and spatial patterns. Design implications: generalization of free plan to include disjunction and discontinuity; extension of free plan to "free section"; emphasis on residual and interstitial spaces. (ii) Blankness—extrapolates the modernist project of formal abstraction, understood as the suppression of quotation or reference through the erasure of decoration and ornament, to include canonic form and type. By avoiding formal or figural reference, architecture can engage in unexpected formal and semiotic affiliations without entering into fixed alignments. Design implications: generalization of free facade to free massing. (iii) Pointing—architecture must be projective, that is, it must point to the emergence of new social arrangements and the construction of new institutional forms. In order to accomplish this, the building must have a point, that is, project a transformation of a prevailing political context. The notion of pointing should not be confused with signifying; it is in fact a challenge to the determined structure of the signifier/signified, whether monosemic or polysemic. The indeterminacy of pointing shifts the emphasis from the formation of stable alignments and/or allegiances to the formation of provisional affiliations. (iv) Incongruity—a requirement to maintain yet subvert received data, including, for example, the existing site as a given condition and/or program brief. Maintenance and subversion are equally important; neither alone leads inexorably to spatial hypostatization. Design implications: a repeat of the architectural postulates of harmony and proportion, structural perspicuity, and system coordination, for example among plan, section, and facade, or between detail and formal organization. (v) Intensive coherence—Unger stresses the necessity for incoherence, understood as a repeat of the architectural postulate of unity or wholeness. However, because incoherence is the hallmark of postmodern collage, I suggest, as an alternative, a coherence forged out of incongruity. Intensive coherence implies that the properties of certain monolithic arrangements enable the architecture to enter into multiple, even contradictory relationships. This should not be confused with Venturi's notion of the "difficult whole," in which a collage of multiplicity is then unified compositionally.

At the beginning of this essay, I noted that a few recent projects offer specific terms and conditions for a New Architecture. While in general these projects show a shift away from a concern for semiotics toward a concern for geometry, topology, space, and events, in my view they subdivide broadly into two camps, which I term DeFormation and InFormation. DeFormation seeks to engender shifting affiliations that nevertheless resist entering into stable alignments. It does so by grafting abstract topologies that can neither be decomposed into simple, planar components nor analyzed by the received language of architectural formalism. On the other hand, the strategy of InFormation, of which Rem Koolhaas's Karlsruhe and Bernard Tschumi's Le Fresnoy are exemplary cases, is to form a collecting graft, usually by encasing disparate formal and programmatic elements within a neutral, modernist monolith. The resultant incongruous, residual spaces are then activated with visual layering, programmatic innovation, technological effects, and events.

Although both evolve from the same problem, the architectures of DeFormation and InFormation are by no means simply

11.1
Bernard Tschumi Architects, Le Fresnoy Art Center,
Tourcoing, France, 1991–1997. Peter Mauss © Esto.

collaborative. In general, both agree on certain architectural tactics that can be understood in terms of Unger's criteria (as modified). Both, for example, rely on such devices as box-within-box sections with an emphasis on interstitial and residual spaces (vast, incongruous). They also deploy monolithic forms and avoid any obvious applied ornament or figurative reference (blank, intensive cohesion).

Yet the tensions between them are pronounced. While De-Formation emphasizes the role of new aesthetic form and therefore the visual in the engenderment of new spaces, InFormation deemphasizes the role of aesthetic form in favor of new institutional form, and therefore of program and events. The event spaces of new geometries tend to drive the former, while the event spaces of new technologies occupy the latter.

One of the pervasive characteristics of InFormation is its unapologetic use of the orthogonal language of modernism. When postmodernist architecture first emerged, the formal language of modernism was simply condemned as oppressive and monotonous—recall Venturi's "Less is a bore." Subsequently, that critique was deepened as architects and theorists demonstrated that, far from being essentialist, the language of modernism constituted a sign system. Once the demonstration that architecture was irreducibly semiotic was complete, the essentialist justification for the austere language of modernism dissolved and the door opened to the use of any and all architectural signs in any and every arrangement.

InFormation posits that the exhaustion of collage is tantamount to rendering irrelevant all aesthetic gestures.[10] The architectural contribution to the production of new forms and the inflection of political space therefore can no longer be accomplished by transformations of style. Furthermore, InFormation argues that the collective architectural effect of modernism's orthogonal forms is such that it persists in being blank, often stressing that blankness by using the forms as screens for projected images. Pointing is accomplished by transformations of institutional programs and events. For DeFormation, on the other hand, architecture's most important contribution to the production of new forms and the inflection of political space continues to be aesthetic. Far from being blank, DeFormation perceives the modernist language of InFormation as nothing less than historical reference and the use of projected images as no more than applied ornament. Instead, DeFormation searches for blankness by extending modernism's exploration of monolithic form, while rejecting essentialist appeals to Platonic/Euclidean/Cartesian geometries. Pointing is accomplished in the aesthetics; the forms transform their context by entering into undisciplined and incongruous formal relationships. InFormation sees the gestured geometries of DeFormation as predominantly a matter of ornament.

To examine the design consequences of these issues, let us briefly compare Tschumi's InFormation at the National Center of Contemporary Arts at Le Fresnoy with Bahram Shirdel's DeFormation at the Nara Convention Hall. Le Fresnoy offered a perfect circumstance in which to reconsider the graft. In his description of the problem, Tschumi was specific in outlining the various possibilities. Since many of the existing structures were in disrepair, a return to an erase-and-replace approach was perfectly plausible. On the other hand, the quality of the historical forms and spaces at Le Fresnoy also suggested a renovation/restoration approach à la collage. Tschumi eschewed both, however, and enveloped the entire complex within a partially enclosed modernist roof to create a cohesive graft. The graft does not produce a collage; rather than creating a compositionally resolved collection of fragments, the roof reorganizes and redefines each of the elements into a blank, monolithic unity whose incongruity is internalized. Tschumi sutures together the broad array of resulting

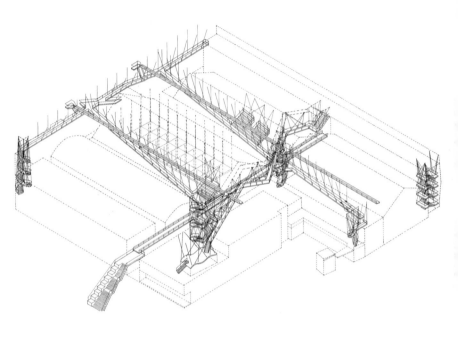

11.2
Bernard Tschumi Architects, Le Fresnoy Art Center,
Tourcoing, France, 1991–1997. Courtesy Bernard
Tschumi Architects.

spaces with a system of catwalks and stairs, visually interlacing them with cuts, partial enclosures, ribbon windows, and broad transparencies. Wherever one is in the complex, one sees partial, disjointed views of several zones from inside to outside at the same time.

Like the visual effects, the role of programming in this project concerns the production of space as much as, if not more than, the accommodation of function. Tschumi programs all the resultant spaces, even treating the tiled roofs of the old building as a mezzanine. Where direct programming is not possible, he elaborates the differential activation in material/events. In the structural trusses of the new roof, he projects videos as an architectural material in order to activate those residual spaces with events.

The resultant project promises a spatial heterogeneity that defies any simple hierarchy: a collection of differentiated spaces capable of supporting a wide variety of social encounters without privileging or subordinating any. Le Fresnoy undermines the classical architectural/political dialectic between hierarchical heterogeneity and homogeneity and points to a potentially new institutional/architectural form.

Like Tschumi at Le Fresnoy, Shirdel also uses a collecting graft to unify an incongruous, box-in-box section at Nara. Unlike Tschumi, however, he shapes the form and internal structure of the graft by folding a three-bar parti with two complex, regulating line geometries. The first geometry involutes the exterior of the building into an abstract, nonreferential monolith whose form flows into the landscaping of the site. The second geometry has a similar effect on the major structural piers that hold the three theaters suspended in action, each one a box whose form is determined simply by exigent functional requirements.

The internal and external geometries connect in such a way that the "major" spaces of the complex are entirely residual—alleys, so to speak, rived in the provisional links between two invaginated geometries. The residual-space effect is reinforced by the fact that all of the explicit program of the building is concentrated in the theaters and lobbies that float as objects above and away from the main space. In a sense, Shirdel's attitude toward program is the opposite of Tschumi's. Although the building functions according to its brief, there is no architectural program other than the given function, neither informing choreography nor any use of technology to activate spaces. Shirdel's computer renderings of Japanese dancers performing in eerie isolation in the emptied, residual space underline that point. Spatial heterogeneity rests in the aesthetics of the form and in the opposition between unprogrammed event and function. In passing, it is worth noting that the risk of proposing that the dominant (and most expensive) space of a building be nothing other than residual space should not be underestimated.

I pursue the development of DeFormation in greater detail below and will return to Shirdel's Nara project. However, I believe that the brief comparison above is sufficient to indicate both the similarities and divergences in the routes being mapped by In-Formation and DeFormation toward a New Architecture.

DeFormation[11]

As is always the case in architectural design theory, DeFormation is an artifact, a construction of principles that have emerged after the fact from projects by diverse architects that were originally forged with different intentions and under different terms and conditions. Thus, strictly speaking, there are no DeFormation-ist architects (yet), just as there were no mannerist or baroque architects. It is a minor point, perhaps too obvious to belabor; yet as we move toward a development of principles and a technical language with which to articulate them, we must be cautious not to allow these to prematurely circumscribe and regulate a motion in design whose fertility derives as much from its lack of discipline as from its obedience to policy. If there is a DeFormation, it has only just begun.

Much has been written and no doubt more will be written that consigns the work of DeFormation (and InFormation) to this or that contemporary philosopher, particularly Gilles Deleuze. It cannot be denied that a powerful consonance exists between the field of effects sought by these architectures and various formulations of Deleuze and Guattari in *A Thousand Plateaus* or by Deleuze in *The Fold*. The sheer number of terms that the architectural literature has borrowed from the Deleuzian discourse (affiliation, pliancy, smooth and striated space, etc.), not to mention such fortuities as the shared thematization of folding, testify to the value of this correspondence. However, for all of the profitability of this dialog, there are costs to which we should be attentive. Obligating any architecture to a philosophy or theory maintains a powerful but suspect tradition in which architecture is understood as an applied practice. In that tradition, the measure of architectural design is the degree to which it exemplifies a theory or philosophy, rather than the degree to which it continuously produces new architectural effects; as a consequence, the generative force of design effects in their own right is subordinated to the limited capacity of architecture to produce philosophical (or theoretical) effects.

In his reading of Gottfried Wilhelm Leibniz in *The Fold*, Deleuze stages his meditation on the fold as part of an interpretation of the space of baroque architecture; thus, it might be assumed that baroque architecture stands as a paradigm for the architectural effects of the fold. Such an assumption, however careless, would underwrite the configuration of DeFormation as nothing more than a neo-baroque.

Now, though Deleuze's reading of baroque architecture is adequate to exemplify his thought on the fold, it is by no means an adequate reading of the architectural effects of the baroque.

Baroque architecture is no more able to realize the contemporary architectural effects of the fold than Leibniz's philosophy is able to realize the contemporary philosophical effects of Deleuze's thought. In other words, Deleuze's philosophy is no more (merely) neo-Leibnizian than DeFormation is (merely) neo-baroque.

However much Deleuze's philosophy profits from the generative effects of Leibniz's texts, its payoff, what it has new to say, does not rest on the accuracy of its scholarly recapitulation of Leibniz's philosophy, but rather on the differences between what Deleuze writes and what Leibniz writes. Similarly, the interest of DeFormation does not rest on its recapitulation of baroque themes, but primarily on the difference it effects with the baroque and its other predecessors.

But perhaps the dearest cost to which we must be attentive is the degree to which formulating DeFormation in terms of a Deleuzian language belies the independent development of the consonant ideas within architecture. No doubt this development, more a genealogy than a history, lacks the grace and pedigree that it would obtain from architecture conceived as applied philosophy. Yet the halting, circuitous pathways of DeFormation's evolution—here lighting on cloth folds depicted in a painting by Michelangelo, there on train tracks, here a desperate attempt to win a competition, there a last-minute effort to satisfy a nervous client, and always drawing upon the previous work of others— not only bears a dignity all its own, but also materially augments the substance of the philosophy.

Allow me, then, to retrace some of these paths, collecting my effects along the way. Neither arbitrarily nor decisively, I begin with three contemporaneous projects: Bahram Shirdel and Andrew Zago's Alexandria Library competition entry, Peter Eisenman's Columbus Convention Center, and Frank Gehry's Vitra Design Museum.[12]

For a number of years beginning in the early 1980s, Shirdel, in association with Zago, pursued an architecture that he termed black-stuff. Ironic as the term may first appear, black-stuff is quite an accurate name for the effects Shirdel sought to achieve. Rejecting the deconstructivist themes of fragments, signs, assemblages, and accreted space, he pursued a new, abstract monolithicity that broached neither reference nor resemblance. Shirdel was interested in generating disciplined architectural forms that were not easily decomposable into the dynamics of point, line, plane, and volume of modern formalism. We will come to refer to these forms in terms of anexact geometries and nondevelopable surfaces, but Shirdel's black-stuff set the stage for the DeFormationist principle of nonreferential, monolithic abstraction we have already discussed.

To generate these forms, Shirdel developed a technique in which he would begin with one or more recognizable figures whose underlying organization possessed the desired internal complexity. Then, in a series of steps, he would map the architectural geometry of these figures in meticulous detail, carefully abstracting or erasing in each progressive step aspects of the original figure that were referential or recognizable—a process I termed disciplined relaxation at the time.

The culmination of the black-stuff investigations was the Shirdel/Zago entry premiated in the Alexandria Library competition, a design that evolved from a disciplined relaxation of a painting of folded cloth by Michelangelo. In that figure of the fold, Shirdel found precisely the formal qualities he sought. Although the final form shows no obvious traces of the original painting, relationships among surface, form, and space are captured in the architecture.

Similar processes appeared in the work of Eisenman and Gehry. Shortly after the Alexandria competition, Eisenman entered a limited competition against Holt Hinshaw Pfau Jones

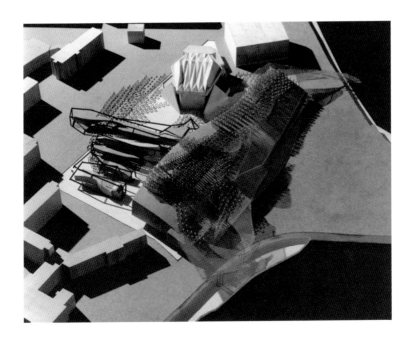

11.3
AKS RUNO, The Library of Alexandria, 1989.
Photo: Tom Bonner.

11.4
Eisenman Architects, Greater Columbus Convention
Center, Columbus, Ohio, 1990–1993. Photo Courtesy
Eisenman Architects.

and Michael Graves[13] to design a convention center for Columbus, Ohio. Because the City of Columbus framed the opening of the center in terms of its quincentennial celebration of Christopher Columbus's first voyage, Eisenman's initial strategy was to design a collage project based on the nautical architecture of the *Santa Maria*. With only three weeks remaining in the twelve-week competition period, Eisenman learned that Graves, too, was basing his design on a nautical theme. Anxious to win the competition (he had only just opened his own office), Eisenman took the extreme risk of abandoning nine weeks of work and shifting to an entirely different scheme, taking a moment to send Graves a postcard of a sinking ship en passant.

The new scheme was based on the notion of "weak form" Eisenman had only just begun to formulate.[14] Working from two oddly similar diagrams, one of a fiber optics cable cross-section and the other of the train track switching system that once occupied the site in Columbus, Eisenman produced the winning design: a monolithic box knitted out of vermiform tendrils. The likeness shared by the two diagrams is important to note, for in that weak resemblance Eisenman first saw the potential of weak form.[15]

Although similar in many respects, Eisenman's weak-form projects are different from Shirdel's black-stuff in one aspect that is of fundamental significance to the principles of DeFormation. Eisenman also attempts to achieve an abstract monolith free of explicit reference. But while the black-stuff projects were intended to be radically other, Eisenman's notion of weakness requires the form to retain a hint of resemblance so that it might enter into unexpected relationships, like the one that connects the two diagrams.

True enough, once alerted, one is quite able to read both the train track and fiber optic diagrams in the convention center's form. However, the most surprising weak link occurs when the scheme is placed on the site. As is to be expected, the design addressed many traditional architectural relationships to the site, such as reinforcing the street edge and negotiating a severe scale transition. On the other hand, almost as if it had been planned from the beginning, the braided forms of Eisenman's project connected the mundane three-story commercial buildings across the street from the center to the complex highway system interchange behind it. Though entirely unplanned, this connection had the effect of transforming the prevailing architectural logic of the site.

Borrowing from Deleuze, DeFormation refers to these tentative formal links with contingent influences as affiliations, and engendering affiliations is the foremost mechanism by which DeFormation attempts to point. Affiliations are distinct from traditional site relations in that they are not predetermined relationships built into the design, but effects that flow from the intrinsic formal, topological, or spatial character of the design.

Typically, one identifies important site influences such as manifest or latent typological/morphological diagrams, prevailing architectural language, material, detailing, and the like, and incorporates some or all of these influences into a design, often by collage. Such relationships are not affiliations but alignments, and serve to reinforce the dominant architectural modes governing a context.

Affiliations, on the other hand, are provisional, ad hoc links that are made with secondary contingencies that exist within the site or extended context. Rather than reinforcing the dominant modes of the site, affiliations amplify suppressed or minor organizations that also operate within the site, thereby reconfiguring the context into a new coherence.[16] Because they link disjoint, stratified organizations into a coherent heterogeneity, the effect of such affiliations is termed "smoothing."[17]

In order to complete our initial survey of affiliative effects, we must pick up a few threads from Gehry's Vitra Design Museum.

Gehry's design process, not unrelated to Shirdel's disciplined relaxation and Eisenman's weakening, involves the incessant modeling and remodeling of an initial figure or set of figures. Though he distorts and deforms these figures toward architectural abstraction, Gehry is even more concerned than Eisenman to preserve a representational heritage in the design.

Gehry's Vitra commission called for a site master plan, a chair assembly factory, and a museum for the furniture collection. In the preliminary design, he simply aligned the new factory with the factory buildings previously on the site, while his museum, a geometer's Medusa, stood in stark contrast. Though Gehry reduced the difference to some extent by surfacing the museum in white plaster so as to relate to the factory buildings, nevertheless, as a graft on the site, the form of the museum installed the familiar disjunctive incoherence I have associated with collage. The client, fearful of employees' complaints that all of the design attention was being invested in the museum and none in the workplace, asked Gehry as an afterthought to enliven the new factory building. In response, he appended some circulation elements that reiterated the stretched and twisted tentacles of the museum to the two corners of the new factory nearest the museum.

The architectural effect was dramatic; like Eisenman's convention center, the additions knit affiliative links between the factory buildings and the museum, smoothing the site into a heterogeneous but cohesive whole. However, unlike in the convention center, the staircases entered the site as a field rather than as an object, pointing to the possibility of intensive coherence generating a smoothing effect at an urban scale. From this perspective, the circulation additions contribute as much to the architecture of DeFormation as the museum itself.

Because other genealogies tracing through other projects can also be drawn, it cannot be said that DeFormation is born from these three projects, though they exemplify two of its key

11.5
Frank O. Gehry, Vitra Design Museum, Weil am Rhein,
Germany, 1989. © Vitra.

principles. In summary, these are: (i) an emphasis on abstract, monolithic architectural form that offers minimal direct references or resemblance and is alien to the dominant architectural modes of a given site; (ii) the development of smoothing affiliations with minor organizations operating within a context, engendered by the intrinsic geometric, topological, and/or spatial qualities of the form. However, before we examine the discussions that have developed around these issues, the evolution of one last principle must be traced.

In analyzing these and related projects, Bahram Shirdel and I noticed that, for all of their other movements, they tend to leave the classical congruity between massing and section largely intact. As a result, the skin of the building continues to be partitioned into the familiar program-driven hierarchies of major, minor, and service spaces implied by the massing. The most important issue, as we saw it, was to avoid both the continuous, homogeneous space of the free plan and the finite, hierarchical space of more traditional sectional strategies.

Several projects suggested different ways to approach the problem of section. Among the more influential of these were Eisenman's Carnegie Mellon research institute, the Jean Nouvel/Philippe Starck entry for the Tokyo Opera House competition, and Koolhaas's Bibliothèque de France. In the Eisenman scheme, essentially a chain of Boolean pods, a large sculptural object whose form was congruent with the pod floated concentrically within each unit, in effect rendering the primary space of the building interstitial. The striking Nouvel/Starck opera house was noteworthy for the way its theater was embedded as an incongruent object into the urban object massing. In the Bibliothèque de France, a seminal example of InFormation, Koolhaas achieved an extreme detachment of sectional space from the massing. Shirdel, Zago, and I formed a partnership in order to continue to develop methods for generating affiliative, monolithic forms, as well as to develop these sectional ideas. Our event structure entry for the Place Jacques-Cartier competition in Montreal, for example, called for a large deformed envelope within which three independently deformed theaters floated as sectional objects. As in InFormation, every surface, including the outside and inside of both the exterior envelope and the floating theaters, was programmed. Our goal was to render all of the spaces in the building interstitial and/or residual and to activate them as a nonhierarchical, differential structure. However, the formal similarity between the two systems, the envelope and the sectional object-theaters, resulted in spaces that were less interstitial than homogeneous.[18]

Our subsequent design for the Scottish National Museum competition produced somewhat more interesting results. The typical section of such museums partitions the space into well-defined compartments determined by the categories of the different collections. In order to counter this alignment between form and program, we devised a section and circulation system in which elements of differing collections would enter into various and shifting associations as one moved through the museum. The effect of encouraging provisional, weak links among the items in the collection was further augmented with a series of windows calculated to frame objects in the urban setting as if they were objects within the collection. Finally, two of the major lobes of the building itself stood as objects within the basement galleries.

This section/circulation system was embedded within a three-lobed, articulated monolith. Though conspicuously alien to the classical language and other dominant architectural influences of the site, the geometry of the massing took good advantage of several subordinate organizations within both Edinburgh and the larger context of Scotland to extend the production of affiliative effects. A catalog of over two dozen of these relationships generated by Douglas Graf, an architectural theorist specializing

11.6
Jeffrey Kipnis, Bahram Shirdel, Andrew Zago
(with Allan Murray), National Museum of Scotland,
Edinburgh, 1991.

in formal relations, was included with the competition submission. As we, and others, worked on similar problems, the two major sectional themes of DeFormation began to emerge. First, the section space of the building should not be congruent with the internal space implied by the monolith. Second, residual, interstitial, and other artifactual spaces should be emphasized over primary spaces wherever possible. Because the box-within-box section is effective at producing both of these effects, it is often the tactic of choice, though by no means the only one possible. The impetus to programmatic saturation so central to InFormation plays a much less significant role in DeFormation.[19]

With these sectional themes, the last of the preliminary principles of DeFormation is in place. Yet we should not prematurely draw the conclusion that DeFormation is complete and a prescription for its architecture written. Indeed, though paradigmatic building projects such as Eisenman's Max Reinhardt Haus[20] or Shirdel's Nara Convention Hall can be identified, the internal debates among these and other related projects assure us that there are principles and projects to follow. The most interesting of these debates revolve around design techniques for producing smoothing affiliations.[21] Because such affiliations require that loose links be made among dominant and contingent organizations operating within a context, some architects work by identifying examples of both types of organization and then driving the design toward their connection, while others rely entirely on the intrinsic contextual affiliations, as engendered by Eisenman's convention center or the Shirdel, Zago, Kipnis Scottish National Museum; in each case, most of the links were unplanned and occurred only after grafting the project to the site.

Shoei Yoh's Odawara Sports Complex, on the other hand, is a conspicuous case of the former. Yoh designed the complex's roof by mapping a detailed study of a variety of contingent forces confronting the roof, such as snow loads, into a structural diagram.

He fine-tuned the mapping by abandoning the coarse, triangulated structural geometries that generalize force diagrams, using instead computer-generated structural analysis to resolve force differentials at an ultrasensitive scale and produce the unusual undulating form of the roof. This process enabled Yoh to avoid the pitfalls of stylistic necessities of the project. As computer-aided manufacturing techniques proliferate, such approaches that maximize efficient use of material will no doubt gain popularity.

Undoubtedly, such an approach to contingency is attractive, yet questions arise. At the very least, these processes threaten to turn DeFormation into a single-theme architecture based on a search for contingent influences, much as Arnold Schoenberg's dodecaphonic theories of atonal music composition resulted in a decade during which serious composers devoted all of their attention to finding new tone rows. As Lynn has quipped, "Soon we'll be designing form based on the air turbulence generated by pedestrians walking near the building." More significant, however, is the degree to which such processes are actually aligning rather than affiliative. It seems to me that by predetermining the contingent influences to be addressed, the process simply redefines the dominant architectural influences on the site. The test of whether or not the results are DeFormative, therefore, will depend not on the success of the project in embodying responses to those influences, but on the other contingent effects it continuously generates.

If embodying effects into the design a priori is problematic, then the central issue for DeFormation becomes the elucidation of methods that generate monolithic, nonrepresentational forms that lend themselves well to affiliative relationships a posteriori. If all that were required were gesture and articulation, then the problem would pose no particular difficulty and could be solved by employing familiar expressionist techniques.

Yet the DeFormationist principle of minimal representation also prohibits explicit reference to expressionist architecture, much as it criticizes InFormation for its explicit reference to formalist modernism. I have already mentioned a group of related techniques that start with a complex figure or set of figures and then move these toward nonrepresentational abstraction while preserving intrinsic complexity. These techniques have stimulated investigations into a variety of methods for accomplishing that movement toward nonrepresentation; for example, the study of camouflage methods, experimenting with computer "morphing" programs that smoothly transform one figure into another, or employing topological meshing techniques such as splines, NURBS (nonuniform rational B-splines), etc., that join surfaces delimited by the perimeters of disjoint two-dimensional figures into a smoothed solid. Because these methods often yield anexact geometries—forms not describable by an algebraic expression yet which show a high degree of internal self-consistency—and nondevelopable surfaces—surfaces that cannot be flattened into a plane—other architects have turned their attention to these areas of study.

As far as I am concerned, it is in the context of the development of architectural technique rather than as applied philosophy that the issue of the fold in DeFormation is best understood. Clearly, the initial figure and transforming process in any DeForming technique does not in itself guarantee the results. Nevertheless, both of these mainly contribute to the effective properties of the results. Long before any of them even heard of *The Fold* or paid any attention to the diagrammatic folds found in Jacques Lacan or René Thom's catastrophe theory, it occurred to many architects that the fold as a figure and folding as a transformative process offer many advantages.

Neither pure figure nor pure organization, folds link the two; they are monolithic and often nonrepresentational, replete with interstitial and residual spaces, and intrinsic to nondevelopable surfaces. As a process exercised in a matrix such as the urban site, folding holds out the possibility of generating field organizations that negotiate between the infinite homogeneity of the grid and the hierarchical heterogeneity of finite geometric patterns, an effect which Eisenman employs in the Rebstock Park housing and office project in Germany.[22] Finally, when exercised as a process on two or more organizations simultaneously, folding is a potential smoothing strategy.

All of these aspects of the fold are related to architectural effects. Although they may be attracted to the underlying work, none of the architects who make use of Thom's fold diagrams, for example, make any claim, as far as I know, to inscribing the four-dimensional event space that the diagrams depict for mathematicians in the resultant architecture, any more than any architect claims to be inscribing the effects of René Descartes's philosophy when employing a Cartesian grid. Fortunately, there do not seem to be too many people suffering from a radical mind/body split walking around midtown Manhattan. In both cases, architects employ these diagrams for the architectural effects they engender.

As is typical of Eisenman, both Rebstock Park and the Alteka Tower are driven more by folding as a process than by any particular fold as a diagram or spatial organization. In the former, Eisenman inscribes an initial parti derived from the modern housing scheme by Ernst May on the site. Then, operating strictly in the representational field of drawing, he projects both extended site and parti into the respective figures formed by the boundaries of these two sites. The resulting drawings create the representational illusion that these two organizations have been folded. This drawing, neither axonometric nor perspective or fold, is then massed as the project. Through this process, he attempts to transform the modern, axonometric space characteristic of the original scheme into a visual space that hovers between an axonometric and a perspectival space with multiple vanishing points. The figure of the fold, a quotation of sections cut through a Thomian diagram, appears on the tops of the building to effect the weak, cross-disciplinary links of which Eisenman is so fond.[23] Similarly, the Alteka Tower begins with the high-rise type and folds it in a process reminiscent of origami in order to deform the type and to produce multiple residual spaces.

Many diagrams, such as those depicting Lacan's "mirror stage" or the parabolic and hyperbolic umbilic folds associated with Thom's catastrophe theory, have attracted architectural interest for several reasons. They offer a level of discipline to the work and avoid the pitfalls of expressionist processes. Using these diagrams as a source of regulating lines, so to speak, allows the architect to design with greater rigor. As Le Corbusier writes, "The regulating line is a guarantee against willfulness." Moreover, such diagrams are neither purely figural nor purely abstract, and therefore hold the potential to generate weak, resemblance effects. Finally, the multiple and disjoint formal organizations that compose these compound diagrams themselves have many of the desired spatial characteristics in section described previously.

A more sophisticated use of these diagrams as regulating lines can be found, again, in Shirdel's Nara Convention Hall. Rather than beginning with a typological or formal parti, Shirdel initiated the design for the hall by grafting a carefully excerpted portion of the Scottish National Museum project to the site. He chose a portion of the museum where two independent lobes of the museum joined obliquely and subtended a constricted, interstitial space. Transferred to Nara, this graft had the advantage of already being incongruent but coherent, an aftereffect of excerpting the connection between the two disjointed lobes.

Shirdel reinforced this effect by using the resultant interstitial space as the main entryway into the new building.

Studying the famous Todaiji temple in Nara, Shirdel found the temple space dominated by three figures: a giant central Buddha and two smaller flanking attendant figures. Stimulated by this analysis, he decided to encase each of the hall's three theaters in objects that would float in section. The forms of these theater-objects were determined simply by functional exigencies. Other than their patinated copper cladding, chosen to link the sectional objects to the figures in the temple, the theaters were entirely undesigned.

Visitors to the Todaiji temple encounter the Buddha figures frontally, a classical arrangement that emphasizes the subject/object relationship between the two. Shirdel, on the other hand, arranged his three sectional objects axially. Visitors entering the convention hall confront nothing but empty space—the enormous mass of the three theaters hovering off to the side. In order to design the envelope of the hall and to configure the main entry as residual space, Shirdel used two folds. First, he reconfigured the massing of the original graft with a Thomian diagram of a hyperbolic umbilic fold, extending this fold into the surrounding landscape so as to smooth the connection of the building with its immediate site. Then he shaped the concrete piers holding up the three theaters and the lobby of the small music theater according to the parabolic umbilic fold. As a result, the main space of the hall is the residual space between the topology of these two folds, an effect that the constricted entryway again reinforces. Shirdel's scheme introduces into Nara an entirely new form in both the architectural and institutional sense. More interestingly, it effects its affiliations spatially as well as formally. At the level of the building, it accomplishes the effects that the preliminary principles of DeFormation seek to engender. I also believe that it meets the five criteria for a New

Architecture: it points, and is blank, vast, incongruent, and intensively coherent.

Whether or not DeFormation and/or InFormation mature into a New Architecture remains to be seen. Certainly, the rate of realization for DeFormation is not yet as promising as it is for InFormation. Yet I believe it can be said with some confidence that these architectures have at least broached the problem of the New and thus offer a measure of optimism, while the critics and historians have not begun to circle them in earnest. Yet.

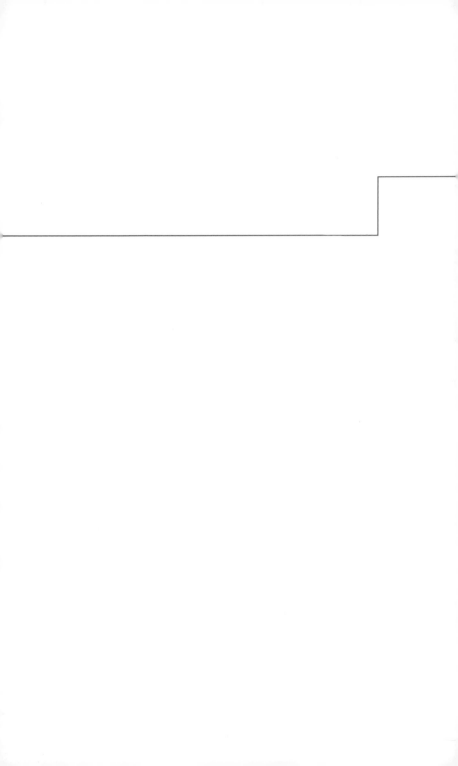

NOTES

1 A QUESTION OF QUALITIES

1. *Morphosis: Buildings and Projects 1999–2008* (New York: Rizzoli, 2009).

2. See Peter Eisenman, "Presentness and the Being-Only-Once of Architecture," in *Written into the Void* (New Haven: Yale University Press, 2007).

3. For this reason, conceptual discourse is intrinsically historical—its fundamental difference with phenomenology. An interesting tendency today is the effort to transform the notion of history into the larger construct of an ecology, since ecologies grasp the temporalities and the intricate subtleties of multivariate processes as well as or better than historical thought, without the heritage of teleology that continues to plague historical thought.

4. Listen, for example, to Charles Ives, *The Unanswered Question*. The full title Ives originally gave the piece was *A Contemplation of a Serious Matter or The Unanswered Perennial Question*. His biographer Jan Swafford called it "a kind of collage in three distinct layers, roughly coordinated." The three layers involve the scoring for a string quartet, woodwind quartet, and solo trumpet. Each layer has its own tempo and key. Ives himself described the work as a "cosmic landscape" in which the strings represent "the Silences of the Druids—who Know, See and Hear Nothing." The trumpet then asks "The Perennial Question of Existence" and the woodwinds seek "The Invisible Answer" but abandon it in frustration, so that ultimately the question is answered only by the "Silences." See "The Unanswered Question," *Wikipedia, The Free Encyclopedia*, http://en.wikipedia.org/wiki/The_Unanswered_Question (accessed July 31, 2012).

5. See Paul Mies, *Beethoven's Sketches: An Analysis of His Style Based on a Study of His Sketchbooks* (New York: Dover, 1974), 5–16.

6. Thom Mayne, "Some Scattered Thoughts Instead of a Foreword," in *Morphosis: Buildings and Projects 1999–2008*.

7. Heinrich Wölfflin, *Renaissance and Baroque*, trans. Kathrin Simon (Ithaca: Cornell University Press, 1966), 80–81.

8. Josie Glausiusz, "Your Body Is a Planet: 90% of the Cells within Us Are Not Ours but Microbes," *Discover Magazine*, June 19, 2007, http://discovermagazine.com/2007/jun/ your-body-is-a-planet (accessed August 1, 2012). "At least 500 species of bacteria, weighing about 3.3 pounds, live inside the human gut. . . . They break down carbohydrates and make essential nutrients like vitamins K and B12."

9. Gilles Deleuze, *Francis Bacon: The Logic of Sensation*, trans. Daniel W. Smith (London: Continuum, 2003), 56.

10. Ibid., 44–54.

2 EXILE ON RINGSTRASSE; EXCITATIONS ON MAIN STREET

This essay first appeared in the book *Coop Himmelb(l)au: Beyond the Blue*, ed. Peter Noever (Munich: Prestel, 2007).

1. Arbeitsgruppe 4: an Austrian group of architects formed in 1952 by Wilhelm Holzbauer, Friedrich Kurrent, and Johannes Spalt at the Akademie der bildenden Künste (Academy of Fine Arts), Vienna, then under Clemens Holzmeister.

    Der Bau: official magazine of the Central Association of Austrian Architects, 1965, radicalized by Hans Hollein and his colleagues as *Bau* with the takeover.

    Sergeant Pepper's Lonely Hearts Club Band: the eighth album by The Beatles, 1967.

    Bonnie and Clyde: a 1967 film about two bank robbers who roamed the U.S. during the Great Depression, directed by Arthur Penn and starring Warren Beatty as Clyde Barrow and Faye Dunaway as Bonnie Parker. It was considered a landmark film in cinema history for breaking taboos about the portrayal in film of sex, crime, and antiestablishment behavior.

2. Hans Hollein, "Alles ist Architektur," *Bau* 23, no. 1/2 (1968). A thousand-word rant against the traditional view of architecture that captured the imagination of the radical architectural movement worldwide.

    "Structures Gonflables": an exhibition and catalog by the group Utopie, presented at the ARC/Musée d'Art Moderne de la Ville de Paris in Paris, March 1968.

3. *Electric Ladyland*, *Beggars Banquet*, *Cheap Thrills*: influential rock concept albums by Jimi Hendrix, The Rolling Stones, and Janis Joplin, respectively.

    2001: A Space Odyssey, *Barbarella*: sci-fi films by Stanley Kubrick and Roger Vadim, respectively.

    Schamlos (Shameless): an exceptional Austrian movie by Eddy Saller. While Austrian movies in the '60s were mainly *Heimatfilme*, that is, colorful pictures about the better days during the monarchy, Saller produced a black-and-white crime exploitation film exploring the gritty truth of postwar Austria that shocked Austrians.

    Moos auf den Steinen (Moss on the Stones): the most remarkable and memorable Austrian film of the decade, directed by Georg Lhotsky. Based on the 1956 novel by Austrian author Gerhard Fritsch, who cowrote the script, the film successfully adapted French New Wave ideas, while providing a brilliant allegory for Austria's identity crisis and the sociocultural problems emerging in a postwar republic haunted by memories of its once powerful empire.

4. Kunst und Revolution: an event organized by the Vienna actionists Otto Muehl, Günter Brus, and Oswald Wiener at the University of Vienna. The event caused a scandal in the press, and Muehl and Brus were arrested.

5. Herbert Muschamp, "Critic's Notebook: When Design Huffed and Puffed, Then Went Pop," *New York Times*, June 18, 1998, http://www.nytimes.com/1998/06/18/garden/critic-s-notebook-when-design-huffed-and-puffed-then-went-pop.html.

6. "Coop Himme(l)blau: Beyond the Blue," an exhibition at the Österreichisches Museum für Angewandte Kunst, Vienna, 2007–2008, for the catalog of which this essay was originally written.

7. Wolf D. Prix, Helmut Swiczinsky, and Michael Holzer founded Coop Himmelb(l)au in 1968. Holzer left in 1971. Even before Coop Himmelb(l)au began, from their time together as students Swiczinsky and Prix were utterly inseparable, collaborating in mind and method on every project until Swiczinsky's retirement in 2006.

   "Gimme Shelter": song by The Rolling Stones that first appeared in 1969 on the *Let It Bleed* album.

8. Endless House: unbuilt project by Frederick Kiesler, exhibited in model form in 1959–1960 at the Museum of Modern Art in New York. In it, the architect sought to dissolve the visual, real, image, and environment into a freely flowing space.

9. "I Heard It through the Grapevine": R&B song written by Motown songwriters Norman Whitfield and Barrett Strong. Whitfield recorded several different versions of the song with several different Motown acts, two of which became hits: the version by Gladys Knight & the Pips became the no. 2 hit in the U.S. in 1967, while the version by Marvin Gaye became the no. 1 hit in the U.K. and the U.S. in 1968.

   The Rite of Spring: a ballet with music by the Russian composer Igor Stravinsky, with the first performance in Paris, 1913.

3 . . . AND THEN, SOMETHING MAGICAL

This essay first appeared in the book *Stone & Feather: Steven Holl Architects/The Nelson-Atkins Museum Expansion* (Munich: Prestel, 2007).

1. Throughout this essay, the theme of inclusiveness will recur, and in that spirit let us be reminded that the name "Steven Holl" herein refers not just to an architect but to a collaboration between a firm and a team assembled to complete the building that includes engineers, consultants, associate architects, landscape architects, and construction personnel—all indispensable to the work. In terms of the design, the fundamental contribution of project architect and partner-in-charge Chris McVoy, the project's co-principal architect, must be singled out.

2. Kristie C. Wolferman, *The Nelson-Atkins Museum of Art: Culture Comes to Kansas City* (Columbia: University of Missouri Press, 1993), 122.

   This essay is deeply indebted to Chief Curator Deborah Emont Scott for her guidance on the collection and the museum's history. Among her many acts of generosity was to provide this delightful book, from which most of the stories and facts regarding the architecture of the original building have been taken.

Some of the tales that Wolferman narrates of the early beginnings of the museum border on the miraculous, such as the fact that the prestigious permanent collection covering Oriental, European, and American fine and decorative arts with which the museum opened in 1933 was acquired entirely from scratch in just three scant years. It is hard to imagine the combination of will, audacity, scholarship, management, logistics, energy, and wealth it took to accomplish such a feat, not to mention sheer luck: the curators were spending their generous budget just at the moment the world was suffering one of its worst depressions. Wolferman's account of this amazing episode is made all the more delicious by the tidbits of controversy and intrigue she adds: "Meanwhile, the [Kansas City] Post continued to raise doubts about both the quality and authenticity of various new purchases. At one point, the Post tried to convince its readers that the trustees had paid a ring of crooks more than $1 million for fake art" (97).

3. The dramatic staging of the sculpture—also known as the *Winged Victory*—by the architecture produces the inescapable effect of convincing everyone that it is the most important of masterpieces. The placement of the sculpture is notorious because it enables the work to look down on an approaching viewer, in keeping with the tradition of Roman sculpture. However, the optimum view of the *Nike*, a Greek sculpture, is on the same level as the visitor, at a 45-degree angle. The work depicts a goddess on a ship's prow, a scene a viewer would expect to see from the side; if you really want to see the miracle of the sculpture, when her stone fabric becomes weightless and ripples in the wind, in its placement in the Louvre you must press your back as far into the corner of the staircase platform wall as you can. In other words, to achieve the spectacular hyperbole in its presentation of the work, the architecture violently subverts the artwork itself.

4. The indeterminacy of Venus's stare in *Tracer* as compared to the activity in the painting's four corners calls attention to the genius, ineptitude, psychology, and dumb luck found in any good work of art, including the Bloch. The pictorial calculations behind Rauschenberg's dissection of the Rubens are truly remarkable. In the original, Cupid holds up a hand mirror mounted in a heavy wood frame, as an African handmaiden stands to Venus's right combing her hair. Formally, the goddess's view terminates at Cupid's left hand, a vertex of a triangle that confines the zone of attention (the other vertices are her eye and his right shoulder). Rauschenberg cuts out Cupid, the wood frame of the mirror, and everything else to the left and above the bevel of mirror glass to allow Venus's gaze to reach out toward the helicopters, the mirror to float, and the white cloud of paint to wash into blue ether.

His handling of the corners is something else. He leaves intact the figure of the African handmaiden on the right, barely visible in the transfer (look for the white dots of her bead necklace just above the bottom line of the floating box). Formally, the handmaiden held the upper right corner of the Rubens, and probably was intended to do the same for *Tracer*, but the transfers of it and the helicopter negative in the lower right corner misalign, warping into the field to leave raw canvas in both corners.

At the top, the artist has painted a geometric half-box, recapturing the head of the handmaiden to resolve the corner brilliantly. At the bottom, he tries to fix the corner by extending the diagonal of the black floor with an afterthought daub of black overpainting, but does not quite get it to line up with the diagonal exactly. Still, his clumsiness yields a satisfying irresolution to the corner that makes the relationship between the pictorial field, the perspectival space, and the canvas itself all the more complex.

Now, one might attribute these corner effects to the artist's plans, but given the resolve of the other two corners, it seems more likely that both were lucky recoveries from accidents, his stock-in-trade. Yet many of Rauschenberg's transfer paintings of 1963–1964 show a struggle at the corners whose character—more fidgety and insecure—is markedly different from the swaggering spontaneity with which he approaches the main canvas.

Perhaps the corner dramas are not so surprising. After leaving the Kansas City Art Institute (across the street from the Nelson-Atkins), the artist landed at Black Mountain College to study painting with the disciplined and methodical Bauhaus formalist Josef Albers. To say the least, the two got on each other's nerves; while crediting Albers as his most influential teacher, Rauschenberg also describes his lifelong compulsion to do exactly the reverse of everything his teacher stood for. The corner is a classical problem in painting, and perhaps no other painter in history has given as much consideration to it as Albers, whose magnum opus, *Homage to the Square*, included over 1,000 works and spanned twenty-five years.

5. See, for example, Rosalind Krauss's seminal essay "Sculpture in the Expanded Field," *October* 8 (Spring 1979), 30–44.

6. Although the steeple of light was part of Wright's 1940 proposal, it was not realized until 1994.

4 THE CUNNING OF COSMETICS (A PERSONAL REFLECTION ON THE ARCHITECTURE OF HERZOG & DE MEURON)

This essay first appeared in *El Croquis* 84 (1997).

1. *Arch+* 129/130 (December 1995). Included in this volume is a reprint of Alejandro Zaera-Polo's excellent "Between the Face and the Landscape," from *El Croquis* 60 (1993) on HdM, and Rem Koolhaas's "Architectures of Herzog and de Meuron," republished under the title "New Discipline," as well as insightful comments by Mark C. Taylor, Terence Riley, and Hans Frei.

2. The electronic equipment in all facilities such as switching stations is already adequately shielded from interference. Thus, though the copper banding system does indeed technically produce a Faraday cage, it is far from a functional necessity.

3. See Marcel Detienne and Jean-Pierre Vernant, *Les ruses de l'intelligence: la mètis des Grecs* [Cunning Intelligence in Greek Culture and Society] (Paris: Flammarion, 1974).

4. Rem Koolhaas, "New Discipline," *Arch+* 129/130 (December 1995), 123.

5. See my remarks in *El Croquis* 83 (1997) on Peter Eisenman.

5 RECENT KOOLHAAS

This essay first appeared in *El Croquis* 79 (1996).

1. See Jonathan Crary, "Notes on Koolhaas and Modernization," *ANY* 9 (November/December 1994), 14, an excellent collection of Koolhaas's work.

2. The work's ascendancy to this position is confirmed by every standard indicator: the frequent appearance of the architect on short lists for high-profile projects; the popularity of publications by him and about his work; the number and popularity of his personal appearances; the number of student imitations; the number of professional knockoffs, piracies, counterfeits, and forgeries; the virulence of practitioners who explicitly position their own work against his; and the number of practitioners, both renowned and uncelebrated, who have openly declared a debt to him.

3. Jeffrey Kipnis, "Recent Koolhaas," *El Croquis* 79 (1996), 420–431.

4. I cite these architects as Koolhaas's confederates not so much because of any shared manifesto but by virtue of historical institutional affiliations: for example, the Architectural Association, the Institute for Architecture and Urban Studies, their participation in more recent alliances, such as the Museum of Modern Art's "Deconstructivist Architecture" exhibition and the ANY conferences, and a general commitment to pursue contemporary design as a progressive, intellectual enterprise. On the other hand, it has always been an uneasy alliance that recalls Mies van der Rohe's ambivalent fraternization with members of the Berlin avant-garde of the late 1910s and early 1920s.

5. See Denis Hollier, *Against Architecture: The Writings of Georges Bataille*, trans. Betsy Wing (Cambridge, MA: MIT Press, 1989).

6. See Rafael Moneo, Pritzker Prize acceptance speech, Getty Center, Los Angeles, June 12, 1996.

7. Throughout his career, Koolhaas has openly shown affection for the work of Mies van der Rohe and Le Corbusier. References to these architects are often found in Koolhaas's earlier designs: Villa Savoye and Farnsworth House (and Philip Johnson's Glass House) in Villa dall'Ava, Le Corbusier's student housing in Nexus World, Mies van der Rohe's National Gallery in the Kunsthal and Agadir. The Miesian stamp on the entry pavilion to the Cardiff Opera House will be evident to all.

8. The term "event structure" is used to indicate all of the social activities and chance events, desirable or not, that an architectural setting stages and conditions. These include, but are not limited to, the expressed activities of the program. An event structure is congruent with the program when no significant events in a setting are encouraged by the architecture other than those prewritten in the program, though, of course, absolute congruence can never be achieved. An architect may reasonably strive for a congruent event structure in a prison or a hospital, but such extreme congruence would be intolerable in a house. The event structure of a sidewalk on a busy city street far exceeds its program—sometimes dangerously. An unexpectedly high level of event structure incongruity occurred in early shopping malls, particularly in the U.S. and Japan. Though the program of the mall was confined to circulation and shopping, the event structure in these buildings so burgeoned that they became the public spaces of choice, particularly for adolescents and young adults.

9. This list is descriptive of the general effects of the projects, not a list of how Koolhaas and OMA actually work in the design process. By the time a project emerges from OMA, it appears so elementary, so guileless, so obvious that one aches with frustration over the question of its actual design technique. The mathematician Carl Friedrich Gauss, it is said, protected his work by first proving a proposition, then refining the proof until its argument, though incontestable, offered no hint of his original thought patterns to other mathematicians. One always suspects a similar process at OMA.

10. There are no urban-scale, formal devices in the scheme of OMA's invention. That OMA was uncomfortable with the chimney is well indicated by the fact that it is conspicuously absent from most of the drawings and models. When OMA stripped the chimney of its brick, it violated a rule of the competition requiring the chimney to be retained in its original form. As ludicrous as the requirement was, the OMA violation was cited by the jury as adequate cause for disqualification.

6 MONEO'S ANXIETY

This essay first appeared in *Harvard Design Magazine* 23 (Fall 2005).

1. "The success of deconstructionist literary criticism in the United States made him [Eisenman] consider coining a new 'ism' and agglutinating an entire architectural movement around himself. Bear in mind that the term 'deconstructivism' was associated with architecture some time later, when Eisenman became the patron of a new tendency by bringing together architects as disparate as Gehry, Koolhaas, Zaha Hadid, Tschumi, and himself in a 1988 exhibition in New York's Museum of Modern Art." Besides Johnson and Wigley, also effaced are Joseph Giovannini, who actually coined the term *deconstructivism* and first suggested the exhibition, and the other two exhibited practices, Coop Himmelb(l)au

and Studio Daniel Libeskind. Rafael Moneo, *Theoretical Anxiety and Design Strategies in the Work of Eight Contemporary Architects* (Cambridge, MA: MIT Press, 2004), 171.

2. This quarrel with the fountainhead trope as it operates in the book should not be confused with its more familiar role in a welling *ressentiment* in architecture, the petty malice that masquerades as moral repugnance toward fame. *Ressentiment* names the corruption of authentic morality by petty negativity such as anger, rage, rancor, spite, *Schadenfreude*, hatred, malice, jealousy, envy, or the desire for revenge. First analyzed by Friedrich Nietzsche in *On the Genealogy of Morals*, its insidious operation as a social and political affect are elaborated in Max Scheler's 1915 classic *Ressentiment*, trans. Lewis B. Coser and William W. Holdheim (Milwaukee: Marquette University Press, 1994).

    Another and perhaps greater disservice perpetrated by the fountainhead trope is the impression it leaves of creativity as sui generis, at the expense of the discipline as an active discourse. Master practices don't exist in isolation; they draw upon the achievements of colleagues. Moneo narrates the genealogy and patrimony of these architects with pleasure but neglects the key influences of contemporaries. Many examples are possible, but one seems to me all but unforgivable: to broach Koolhaas's attitude toward program without mentioning Cedric Price's work on event structures or Bernard Tschumi's influential writings on program, including his theories of cross-programming. Surely when the author writes a passage that entertains "crossbreeding" as a possible name for Koolhaas's ideas, he must cast at least a thought toward Tschumi, whose only presence in the book is parenthetically as the architect who won the La Villette competition "with a project not unlike Koolhaas's."

3. Moneo, *Theoretical Anxiety*, 366.

4. Ibid., 181.

5. Ibid., 65.

6. Ibid., 160.

7. Ibid., 350–353.

8. Ibid., 63.

9. Ibid., 399.

10. Moneo does offer scattershot comparisons. In one inspired paragraph, he outlines divergent attitudes toward models (in the sense of paradigms) in six of the practices: "Curiously, Siza's work emerges full of references for modern architecture, but without models. Rossi's concepts of type and model pertain to the Platonic ambit of a dream world. Eisenman's models give form to a phantom where the basic syntactic structure prevails. Stirling was more preoccupied with style—ultimately with history—than with models. Gehry tries to do away with them altogether. So surely Koolhaas is the only one of the architects discussed in this book who knows

... his models [modern cities] and, like a realist painter, tries to make his buildings get as close to them as possible" (313). In those ninety-six words lies an outline for rethinking the clichéd concept of precedent, which today serves as little more than an excuse for knee-jerk repetition of program-based building patterns. Here at least, a reader can use the author's sketch as a basis for a more sustained inquiry.

11. Moneo, *Theoretical Anxiety*, 313–314.

12. Ibid., 305.

13. Ibid., 341–342. In addition to its invaluable contribution discussed here, the Bibliothèque proposal developed a major variant of the box-in-box scheme, reanimated research into the then-dormant Vierendeel truss (launching engineer Cecil Balmond to fame), and set the stage for both the blob and surface architectural researches that followed soon after: "May 24. Imagine a room where floor becomes wall becomes ceiling becomes wall and floor again" (OMA, Rem Koolhaas, and Bruce Mau, *S,M,L,XL*, ed. Jennifer Sigler [New York: Monacelli Press, 1998], 634). Few lines of design research active today do not trace to this project. It should be remembered, however, that the OMA proposal was itself clearly a development of the captivating Jean Nouvel/Philippe Starck proposal for the Tokyo Opera House competition of 1986, which introduced, among other things, the free section variant of the box in box. Major international competitions of the period that followed evidenced the extraordinary impact of the Nouvel/Starck project, which in addition to the Bibliothèque can be seen, for example, in Arata Isozaki's winning entry for the Nara Convention Hall.

14. It would not be much of an exaggeration to say that almost every OMA project uses a mechanical device as a critique. Besides the Zeebrugge Sea Terminal, ZKM, and the Bibliothèque de France, the Tate Modern proposal, the Bordeaux House, and the Seattle Public Library immediately come to mind. If we extend the argument from circulation to mechanical devices in general, one would have to add the mechanical wall that made the seminal Cardiff Opera House proposal possible. Even the sliding door of Villa dall'Ava plays an important role in its architectural speculation.

15. *S,M,L,XL*, 642.

16. Rafael Moneo, "Reflecting on Two Concert Halls: Gehry vs. Venturi" (lecture, Harvard University Graduate School of Design, Cambridge, MA, April 25, 1990), quoted in "Rafael Moneo 1996 Laureate Biography," The Pritzker Architecture Prize, http://www. pritzkerprize.com/sites/default/files/file_fields/field_files_inline/1996_bio.pdf.

7 THROWING STONES—THE INCIDENTAL EFFECTS OF A GLASS HOUSE

This essay first appeared in the book *Philip Johnson: The Glass House*, ed. David Whitney and Jeffrey Kipnis (New York: Pantheon, 1993).

1. Following Johnson, I will, on occasion, use the name Glass House to refer both to the house itself and to the complex as a whole.

2. Philip Johnson, "House at New Canaan, Connecticut," *Architectural Review* 108, no. 645 (September 1950), 152–159, reprinted in *Philip Johnson: Writings* (New York: Oxford University Press, 1979), 219.

3. Mabel Haeberly, "This New House in Connecticut Needs No Windows," *New York Times*, December 12, 1948.

4. Arthur Drexler, "Architecture Opaque and Transparent," *Interiors and Industrial Design* 109 (October 1949), 90–101, reprinted in Whitney and Kipnis, *Philip Johnson: The Glass House*, 3–7.

5. See Kenneth Frampton, "The Glass House Revisited," in *Philip Johnson, Processes: The Glass House, 1949, and the AT&T Corporate Headquarters, 1978*, IAUS Catalogue 9 (New York: Institute for Architecture and Urban Studies, 1978), 38–59; reprinted in Whitney and Kipnis, *Philip Johnson*, 91–113.

6. Philip Johnson, "Whence and Whither: The Processional Element in Architecture," *Perspecta* 9/10 (1965), 167–178.

7. Robert Stern, "The Evolution of Philip Johnson's Glass House, 1947–1948," *Oppositions* 10 (Fall 1977), 56–67.

8. Peter Eisenman, "Behind the Mirror: On the Writings of Philip Johnson," *Oppositions* 10 (Fall 1977), 1–13.

9. See Johnson, "House at New Canaan, Connecticut."

10. Robert Dell Vuyosevich, "Semper and Two American Glass Houses," *Reflections* 8 (Spring 1991), 4–11, reprinted in Whitney and Kipnis, *Philip Johnson*, 163–171.

11. Francesco Dal Co, "The House of Dreams and Memories," *Lotus* 35 (1982), 122–128, reprinted in Whitney and Kipnis, *Philip Johnson*, 115–122.

12. I am indebted to Professor Douglas Graf for this observation.

8 A TIME FOR FREEDOM

This essay first appeared in the book *Architecture Interruptus* (Columbus: Wexner Center for the Arts, 2007).

1. Nor does the posthumous completion of unfinished works of art belong to architecture exclusively. After extensive study of Edith Wharton's notes and drafts, Marion Mainwaring completed her unfinished last novel, *The Buccaneers*, a half-century after the author's death. Literary critics consider the finished novel flawed, though whether the fault lies with Wharton or Mainwaring continues to be debated. Mozart's *Requiem Mass in D Minor*, though well outlined, remained barely half-completed. His widow, who desperately needed the balance of the commission fee, begged a series of composers to finish the work. Eventually, a young friend of Mozart, Franz Xaver Süssmayr, did so with contributions from others.

2. Bataille discusses these ideas in his essay "Architecture" that appeared in the May 1929 issue of *Documents*, a French journal he edited. His thoughts are more familiar to most readers in architecture from Denis Hollier's *Against Architecture: The*

Writings of Georges Bataille, trans. Betsy Wing (Cambridge, MA: MIT Press, 1992). The Koolhaas quote is from OMA, Rem Koolhaas, and Bruce Mau, *S,M,L,XL*, ed. Jennifer Sigler (New York: Monacelli Press, 1998), 199.

3. Le Corbusier's famed pronouncement, as well as his five points, can be found in the articles he wrote for the magazine *L'esprit nouveau* and collected in *Vers une architecture* (Paris: G. Crès, 1923). *Pilotis* and free facades complete the five points.

4. On the Miller House, see *American Masterworks: The Twentieth Century House*, ed. Kenneth Frampton and David Larkin (New York: Rizzoli, 1995).

5. *Italica*, s.v. "Three Theaters" (by Alice Jarrard), http://www.italica.rai.it/scheda. php?monografia=rinascimento&scheda=rinascimento_parole_chiave_schede_ teatri&hl=eng (accessed August 3, 2012).

6. Le Corbusier's books *When the Cathedrals Were White* and *Travels in the Orient* express his spiritual beliefs. Anthony Eardley discusses the background of the Firminy church commission and Le Corbusier's initial reluctance and eventual acceptance of it in his essay "Grandeur Is in the Intention," original published in *Le Corbusier's Firminy Church*, ed. Kenneth Frampton and Silvia Kolbowski (New York: Institute for Architecture and Urban Studies and Rizzoli International, 1981). He points out that Le Corbusier's ambivalence might have been exacerbated, given that all of his religious commissions were from the Catholic Church, by the fact that the architect "came from a Cathar family whose Protestant heresies embraced the sun as the provider and regulator of all human life." In the Firminy church, signs of that heresy are insinuated not only in the symbolism of the circular top reigning over the square base, but covertly in the dualist yellow sun and red moon oculi in the ceiling and the pagan constellation that replaced the rose window.

7. Le Corbusier, *Oeuvre complète 1957–65*, ed. Willy Boesiger (Basel: Birkhäuser, 1995), 7: 137.

8. Oubrerie began his career as a painter and maintains an active interest in modern and contemporary painting. Though the door is certainly a device derived from his knowledge of minimalist painting, its uncanny resemblance to Kelly's *Red, Yellow, Blue II* is a coincidence. Still, though there is nothing to it, it is fun for the imagination to mull over some circumstances that surround the coincidence: the painting is one of a number of works by the artist treating the same three colors in similar formal arrangements, horizontal and vertical. Most date from 1961 to 1965, but Kelly has continued to revisit the theme occasionally to the present day. *Red, Yellow, Blue II* itself dates from 1965, the same year as Le Corbusier's death. Finally, Oubrerie began his studies at the École des Beaux-Arts in Paris the year after Kelly completed his at the same school.

9. José Oubrerie, "Architecture before Geometry, or the Primacy of Imagination," *Assemblage* 39 (August 1999), 97.

10. Oubrerie's caution that the computer's seductiveness might lessen the responsiveness of the architect is opposite to that issued by author Joyce Carol Oates. She warns that the computer's power to cut and paste threatens to transform the novelist from a focused storyteller into a compulsive editor who cannot stop adding to and changing the story. "I used a word processor for two years (in the composition of *American Appetites*) and found that I was too obsessively attached to the process, reluctant to move away from the screen and back into the 'real' world. I realized that such an addiction was a very bad idea." What makes this dichotomy interesting is that it is not a result of the ethos of the different disciplines, but is at least in part technical: a matter of a computer's relation to file size and memory. Text files are small and all too easy for a computer to manipulate; three-dimensional digital models of buildings are large, complex files that are very difficult to edit piecemeal. Oates's comments are quoted by Jennifer Greenstein Altmann in "Oates Chooses Fresh Identity but Familiar Setting for Novel," *Princeton Weekly Bulletin*, October 11, 2004, http://www.princeton.edu/pr/pwb/04/1011/2a.shtml.

9 NOLO CONTENDERE

This essay first appeared in *Assemblage* 11 (1990).

10 /TWISTING THE SEPARATRIX/

This essay was first published in *Assemblage* 14 (1991).

1. This congenital instability is the necessary consequence of the "originary trace," the condition that Derrida finds preceding all writing, making it possible. Derrida's meditation on writing, extended to the notion of "arché-writing," includes not only what we call writing, but as well speech, reading, and, in general, all acts and ensembles from which meanings flow. Contrary to the tradition in which thought on architectural meaning derives from thought on linguistic meaning, the notion of arché-writing is, or should be, a thought of architectural design necessarily and from the beginning. Moreover, in that the thought of arché-writing is from its outset a questioning of status and repression vis-à-vis meaning, it interrogates the agendas that underlie the privilege of the linguistic model over other disciplines. See text below.

2. This paragraph has been reconstructed from phrases extracted from Derrida's essay on the work of Bernard Tschumi, "Point de folie: Maintenant l'architecture," in *La Case Vide: La Villette*, trans. Kate Linker (London: Architectural Association, 1985). I have refrained from using quotation marks on these phrases, with the exception of the last sentence, because my extraction and reconstruction has been violent. For example, the context of each phrase has been ignored. In deciding how to notate this reconstruction, I have considered it the lesser of evils to elect not to put these words forward under quotation marks, that is, under Derrida's signature.

3. "Le trait en lui-même est indiscret; quoi qu'il trace ou représente, il est indécent (mon amour, libère-moi du trait). Et à ces traits obscènes j'ai tout de suite envie d'élever un monument, ou un château de cartes." Jacques Derrida, *La carte postale: de Socrate à Freud et au-delà* (Paris: Flammarion, 1980), 22. For the English translation, see *The Post Card: From Socrates to Freud and Beyond*, trans. Alan Bass (Chicago: University of Chicago Press, 1987), 17.

4. Beyond, and because of, its idiomatic use, "house of cards" is strongly associated with Eisenman. The architect first employed it as a sobriquet for his work in the essays on Houses I and II, and it subsequently appeared as the title of his book concerning the early houses: Peter Eisenman, *House of Cards* (New York: Oxford University Press, 1987).

5. Throughout this essay, I always employ *respect* toward two meanings. First, I use it in its most familiar sense as indicating appreciation and consideration. In addition, I intend it to echo its etymology: "to re-spect," "to look again," "to take a second look." In this sense, the term reflects not only an important, particular theme of the essay but the necessary condition for any deconstruction, which always consists in taking a second look at a text to see what other meanings unfold in it. In this combined sense, deconstruction is always a form of respect.

6. For an excellent discussion of these differences, see Geoff Bennington, "Complexity without Contradiction in Architecture," *AA Files* 15 (Summer 1987), 15–18.

7. For example, consider these themes as they unfold in the first two chapters of Derrida's *Of Grammatology*, trans. Gayatri Chakravorty Spivak (Baltimore: Johns Hopkins University Press, 1976):

"That logocentrism which is also a phonocentrism: absolute proximity of voice and being, of voice and the meaning of being, of voice and the ideality of meaning" (11–12).

"We already have a foreboding that phonocentrism merges with the historical determination of the meaning of being in general as *presence*, with all the subdeterminations which depend on this general form and which organize within it their system and their historical sequence (*presence of the thing to the sight as* eidos, *presence as substance/essence/existence, temporal presence as point of the now or of the moment, the self-presence of the cogito, consciousness, subjectivity, the co-presence of the other and of the self, intersubjectivity as the intentional phenomenon of the ego, and so forth*). Logocentrism would thus support the determination of the being of the entity as presence" (12, emphasis added).

"I have identified logocentrism and the metaphysics of presence as the exigent, powerful, systematic, and irrepressible desire for such a [transcendental] signified" (49).

"There is thus no phenomenality reducing the sign or representer so that the thing signified may be allowed to glow finally in the luminosity of its presence. The so-called 'thing itself' is always already a *representamen*" (49).

8. In one sense, an *undecidable* is a thing that appears to be a word and/or a concept but, because within it is its own destabilization, is best thought of as a mark within a text. As a simple example, *ravel* means both to entangle and to disentangle, to confuse and to make clear. Thus when an argument uses the mark *ravel* with the intention of invoking one of these meanings, the other is repressed, though a careful reading can find hints of its continuing to operate within the text, a condition Derrida refers to as the return of the repressed, borrowing from Freud. One tactic of deconstruction is to seek out the multiple and covert operations of such marks within a text, respecting all the meanings of undecidable marks on which every text relies (notice, for example, that *relies* can mean both "depends on" and "tells a lie again"). In doing so, a reading produces irresolvable gaps within a text and exposes its apparent meaning as dependent on the operation of an untenable metaphysics, an assumption that the context reveals the correct or intended meaning. Beyond this, however, the "list of undecidables" refers to some three dozen or so marks, including *différence*, *trace*, *remark*, and *supplement*, that Derrida has produced in his analysis of that which resides between the members of apparently self-evident oppositional pairs. Such pairs—same/other, in/out, etc.—seem to consist of unambiguous poles of a switch, free from the undecidability that plagues (or enriches) marks such as *ravel*. All philosophical argument can be shown to rely on the unambiguous hierarchy and decidability of these pairs. In his analysis of these oppositions, Derrida demonstrates that their seeming clarity depends on the repression of an undeniable condition that must be thought anterior to the opposition, producing it and residing within it. His list of undecidables consists of marks for those conditions that he has shown to be always operating in all apparently decidable texts. He thus extends the tactic of deconstruction discussed above with a more powerful technique able to render undecidable even the most resistant texts. For further discussion, see notes 10, 19, and 38 below.

9. Eisenman's comments are quoted with modification from Ann Bergren's essay "Architecture Gender Philosophy," in *Strategies in Architectural Thinking*, ed. John Whiteman, Jeffrey Kipnis, and Richard Burdett (Cambridge, MA: MIT Press, 1992). This essay, delivered in 1988 at a Chicago Institute for Architecture and Urbanism (CIAU) conference on architectural theory, weaves its three themes through a reading of classical texts that blends philological considerations with contemporary gender-structure analysis. It adds an invaluable dimension to the reading of the meetings of Derrida and Eisenman and thus, though it does not appear in *Chora L Works*, forms part of the work. As the reader will confirm in the transcripts of their discussions published in *Chora L Works*, though Derrida exhibits some of the conservatism indicated by Eisenman's statement, Eisenman takes a good deal of liberty in dramatizing this point. All future citations from the meetings of Derrida and Eisenman refer to these transcripts. See *Chora L Works: Jacques*

Derrida and Peter Eisenman, ed. Jeffrey Kipnis and Thomas Leeser (New York: Monacelli Press, 1997).

10. In light of this discussion, it is interesting to note how easily some of Derrida's writings and comments on architecture lend themselves to arguments for an architectural conservatism. At the CIAU conference on architectural theory, Giovanna Borradori, proponent of Italian "weak thought," delivered a response to an essay by Catherine Ingraham, with a decidedly deconstructive flavor, that concerned the role of the proper in architecture. (See Catherine Ingraham, "The Faults of Architecture: Troping the Proper," *Assemblage* 7 [October 1988], 6–13.) Weak thought is one of the philosophical countermovements to deconstruction; it claims to locate and criticize a modernist residue of global idealism and ideologism in the poststructuralist discourse and to offer alternatives. Weak thought would direct architecture, if Borradori's remarks are representative, toward a somewhat conservative, mildly historical, domesticated design with a dash of the safely liberal. Borradori's propositions were grounded on a nonglobal notion of the "architecturally good" that isolates architectural judgment from the interrogation of the foundations of judgments as such, thereby immunizing the architectural tradition from scrutiny and doubt. Thus it was fascinating to hear Borradori construct her response to Ingraham—a response that was conservative, if not reactionary, in its views on dwelling, domesticity, and history—around an argument authorized entirely by quotations from Derrida's writings and interviews about architecture. Though these quotations suffered all of the abuses one might expect (removal from context, systematic misconstrual, etc.), one could ignore neither the availability of the material for such an argument nor its persuasiveness.

11. A well-known and problematic segment of Plato's *Timaeus* (48e–53a) concerns the place (*chora*) into which the universe was inscribed at the time of its creation. Derrida's treatment of this issue provided the program for the collaboration. See his essay "Chora," published in *Chora L Works* (15–23); *chora* is also discussed extensively throughout the transcripts in *Chora L Works*, as well as in the latter part of this essay.

12. All quotations from Derrida's essay "Chora" are from *Chora L Works*.

13. Jacques Derrida, "Why Peter Eisenman Writes Such Good Books," *Threshold* 4 (Spring 1988), 102–103 (translation modified).

14. Ibid., 102 (translation modified). In French: "J'écris donc à Eisenman, dans l'avion, cette lettre dont on me permettra de citer un fragment."

15. Ibid. (translation modified). In French: "Vous vous rappelez ce que nous avons envisagé ensemble à Yale: que pour finir j'écrive,' si on peut dire, sans un mot, un pièce hétérogène . . ."

16. "*The (pure) trace is difference.* It does not depend on any sensible plenitude, audible or visible, phonic or graphic. It is, on the contrary, the condition of such a

plenitude. Although it *does not exist*, although it is never a *being-present* outside of all plenitude, its possibility is by rights anterior to all that one calls sign (signifier/signified, content/expression, etc.), concept or operation, motor or sensory." Derrida, *Of Grammatology*, 62.

17. Cf. Jacques Derrida, "The Pit and the Pyramid: Introduction to Hegel's Semiology," in *Margins of Philosophy*, trans. Alan Bass (Chicago: University of Chicago Press, 1982).

18. Ibid., 94.

19. *Aufhebung*, a key term in Hegel's work, is the process by which the spirit fulfills its telos, coming to know itself in itself as itself. In *Aufhebung*, an insufficient representation of the spirit for itself to itself is at once suppressed as insufficient but retained in an elevated second term. By virtue of its abstraction, architecture is an insufficient representation of the spirit to itself. Sculpture retains the residue of architecture's limited capacity, but in the *Aufhebung* resolves the insufficiency by raising the representation to a new and higher level. Because of the retention, the verb is often, but not quite adequately, translated into English as *sublimation* or *sublation*.

20. Cf. Eisenman's essay in *Moving Arrows, Eros, and Other Errors: An Architecture of Absence* (London: Architectural Association, 1986).

21. Derrida, *Of Grammatology*, 47.

22. Derrida, "Why Eisenman . . . ," 103, 104 (translation modified).

23. Jacques Derrida, "Plato's Pharmacy," in *Dissemination*, trans. Barbara Johnson (Chicago: University of Chicago Press, 1981), 64.

24. Mark Wigley has observed that the very notion of "to add" presupposes a totality to which the addition is made. For example, it is under the logic of addition that an "ornament" is "added to" an independent, self-contained, and whole receiver, such as "the building itself." The metaphysics of presence operating in the logic of such "additions" is exposed under Derrida's scrutiny of the supplement, one of the aforementioned undecidables. In his analysis, Derrida shows that the classical addition logic of the supplement presupposes the presence of existences that cannot exist. Thus, in the most famous example, "culture" can only supplement "nature" if the latter always already lacks, that is, if nature is always already naturally supplemented. "The supplement comes naturally to put itself in Nature's place." The logic of addition is but a desire for a whole nature, without need of supplementation, to which culture comes as an external exigent, and is thus another manifestation of the dream of a transcendental signified. An entire family of separatrices traceable to the culture/nature structure (disease/health, evil/good, etc.) is shaken by this reading of the supplement.

Wigley has observed as well that the "translation" of Derrida's contribution letter as a writing within which a drawing, nominally "the contribution," stands incorporated as non-writing also evidences familiar mechanisms of the metaphysics of presence. Another translation, perhaps a better deconstructive reading in that it would not violate the letter, but at the same time would not obey its properties, would have been to treat the entire letter as the contribution; "cette sculpture" would then have referred not to a drawing of an object within a letter, but to the letter itself. Ample and well-known precedent for this treatment was available, considering the proliferation of "correspondence art." This tactic, too, would have emphasized that Derrida, ostensible origin and author of the letter, was also always "translating," even at the moment of first writing. The theme of translation can be found throughout Derrida's work, for example in the essays "Des Tours de Babel," in *Difference in Translation*, ed. and trans. Joseph F. Graham (Ithaca: Cornell University Press, 1985), and "*Fors*: The Anglish Words of Nicolas Abraham and Maria Torok," trans. Barbara Johnson, foreword to Abraham and Torok, *The Wolf Man's Magic Word: A Cryptonymy*, trans. Nicholas Rand (Minneapolis: University of Minnesota Press, 1986). The latter essay is especially interesting here for its discussion of "incorporation."

25. Derrida, *Of Grammatology*, 18.

26. Derrida, "Why Eisenman . . . ," 99.

27. The reader will find further elaboration of Nietzsche's *Ecce Homo* in Derrida's "Otobiographies: The Teaching of Nietzsche and the Politics of the Proper Name," trans. Avital Ronell, in *The Ear of the Other: Otobiography, Transference, Translation*, ed. Christie McDonald, trans. Peggy Kamut (New York: Schocken Books, 1985), particularly in the first section "The Logic of the Living Feminine." The signature, *le trait*, even life and death are therein considered.

28. Derrida's interest in the proper name derives, in part, from his discussion of writing as the always-becoming-sign of symbol. The history of writing as the phoneticization of speech is intimately connected to the name, the proper noun. Thus, for example, foreign names in the cartouches of Egypt were "spelled out" by a series of hieroglyphs in which the initial sounds of the nominal symbol combined to produce the name. Recall that a key issue in his meditation on writing is the destabilization of the privilege of speech over writing, a manifestation of the metaphysics of presence. This privilege seems confirmed as long as writing is nothing other than and nothing but the picture of speech. Derrida first demonstrates that, strictly speaking, a purely phonetic writing does not exist and then turns his attention to reading texts by emphasizing the nonphonetic content that always resides within any writing, including speech. His reading and writing of texts in terms of the proper name is therefore a tactic in this strategy and works to destabilize the repression of the symbol within the sign. Cf. Gregory Ulmer, *Applied Grammatology: Post(e)-Pedagogy from Jacques Derrida to Joseph Beuys* (Baltimore: Johns Hopkins University Press, 1985), 3–153.

29. Derrida, "Why Eisenman . . . ," 99.

30. Ibid.

31. Ibid., 104.

32. But why does the play between the colon and the 8 in 19:5 seem too farfetched, seem out of bounds even for textual play? This reading uses the forms within text other than letters, and perhaps the properties of punctuational form, like architecture, must remain inviolate. Clearly, the "ornamental" scale and other aspects of the architectonics of punctuation are necessary for it to be outside of the "text itself" yet irreplaceably within the text, the condition that always calls for a deconstruction.

33. See Francis M. Cornford, *Plato's Cosmology* (New York: Harcourt, Brace, 1937). All excerpts from the *Timaeus* herein are from the Cornford translation.

34. The play of proper names also suggests interventions into the design that might have avoided the problems of "adding a sculpture," discussed above, by unfolding the proper name into the design. Thus, as proposed in the meetings, coral or a corral might have been used. But might not consideration have been given as well to iron, peat, and/or jade?—JA cques DE rrida; the French word *déjà* is already a well-known Derridean signature. For Plato's sake, perhaps something could have been made of the Khorat Plateau in Thailand, and not only in respect of the play on names that it affords, but also because this plateau has an uncanny similarity to the project: its shape is roughly the same and it, too, is skewed with respect to the ground plane. Finally, though it may be inexcusably frivolous, the important dialog of the "homogenous paste," discussed later in the text, almost demands naming a material that not only meets all the characteristics sought in this conversation but moreover inscribes a proper name, namely *Playdough*.

35. Derrida, "Why Eisenman . . . ," 101.

36. Ibid., 100.

37. Ibid., 104 (trans. modified).

38. There should be little doubt that Derrida can not only "see" but read drawings as text brilliantly. For example, consider his extended reading of the engraved frontispiece from Matthew Paris's thirteenth-century fortune-telling book. This image, which Derrida discovered reprinted on a postcard, provides the armature for the "Envois" in his *Carte postale*. To say the least, his translations of this image are astonishing.

39. Cf. William Barclay, *The Gospel of John* (Philadelphia: Westminster Press, 1975), 29–37.

40. In the *Timaeus*, the Demiurge is the creator of the sensible universe. In most English translations, the word is rendered as god or God, but to preserve interesting connections—for example, at certain times and locations in ancient Greece the architect was termed *demiurge*—I have maintained the term in transliterated Greek.

41. We might liken the difficulty of this problem to the question that young students often ponder after learning that the universe is expanding. It is a familiar

conundrum: If the universe is everything—all matter, energy, and space—then *into what* does it expand? Another version of the same problem is: if the all-inclusive universe was infinitesimally small at the time of the Big Bang, in what space was it located? Of course, the problem of the space of inscription that Plato contemplates is not identical to the problem of the bounded universe. Indeed, it is even more difficult and subtle, yet the two problems share conceptual similarities.

42. Derrida, "Chora," in *Chora L Works*, 17.

43. The architecture of the text, particularly its center, seems to intrigue Derrida as he reads Plato. In "Chora," he appeals to the appearance of *chora* in the *Timaeus* as a theme "right in the middle of the book." In "Plato's Pharmacy," written some twelve years earlier, this architectural argument is even more emphatic as Derrida reads Plato's *Phaedrus*: "Let us read this more closely. At the precisely calculated center of the text—the reader can count the lines—the question of logography is raised." Other similar architectures might interest us. Consider, for example, that, though Derridean thought is devoted to destabilizing the metaphysics and status of the Idea, there is, nonetheless, an idea embedded inextricably within Derridean thought.

44. Derrida writes of deconstruction as a *soliciting* of the text, a shaking of the wholeness of the text to see what falls out. This play derives from the Latin etymology of *solicit*, from *sollus*, "the whole," and *citus*, from *ciere*, "to arouse."

45. Yet in the *Timaeus* (31c), *analogia* was calculation par excellence and opposed to bastard reasoning, *logismoi nothoi*, which was calculation leading to impossible results. In reading this passage, an analogy between analogy and *chora* is evident: "But two things alone cannot be satisfactorily united without a third, for there must be some bond between them drawing them together." *Chora*, of course, does not unite the Forms (Ideas, *eidos*) to the copies (*eidolon*); rather, it is the place in which one participates in the other.

46. Derrida alluded to this: "I would rather speak of meetings, and of what takes *place* at the intersection of chance and program, of risk and necessity." Derrida, "Why Eisenman . . . ," 100 (translation modified).

47. In this regard, consider an interesting anachrony implied in the *Timaeus*. As we have said, the Forms constitute the permanent, timeless realm of being. The Demiurge, looking upon them and using them as models (*paradigmata*), forges the material universe, the realm of becoming. Yet, strictly speaking, there must be becoming in the realm of being before the realm of becoming is created in order for the Forms to *become* Paradigms in the eyes of the Demiurge. Clearly, this has profound implications for all of metaphysics: it implies that translation is of the essence and, moreover, that the essence is not fulfilled until translation occurs. The "thing itself" is always already translated.

48. Tschumi's first look at Derrida and deconstruction was in his highly regarded *Manhattan Transcripts* of 1981. His second look was the publication of his La Villette project in the AA Files folio *La Case Vide*, which included the essay by Derrida cited earlier. *Case vide*, French for "empty box," can be taken as an obvious if somewhat coarse metaphor for *chora*. Thus, in a sense, before Eisenman and Derrida became the first architect/philosopher pair to collaborate on *chora*, Tschumi and Derrida had already done so.

49. "In the final *l*, choral, *chora* becomes more liquid, more aerial, I do not dare to say more feminine," playing on the French *elle*. Derrida, "Why Eisenman . . . ," 101 (translation modified).

50. As is well known, beauty is one of the three canonic conjugates of Platonic perfection: the True, the Good, and the Beautiful. For many reasons touched upon herein, not least of which is the collaboration's interest in shaking (soliciting) the Platonic foundation of architecture that continues to operate even today, beauty, though not excluded as such, cannot be a measure of the results. In this regard, it is noteworthy to find Eisenman and Derrida in the sixth meeting beginning their assessment of the final design with a discussion of its beauty. I examine this moment and the question of beauty in further detail in an unpublished essay entitled "The Irrelevance of Beauty."

51. It is interesting to note the relationship between this movement of gold in Eisenman's work from motivated symbol to the (almost) arbitrary sign of a signature, a proper name, and Derrida's interest in this same movement. See note 24.

52. Eisenman and Derrida have continued their discussions on these matters in an open correspondence published in *Assemblage* 12 (August 1990). While taking issue with some of Derrida's inferences about the possible implications of the philosopher's work for architecture, Eisenman tacitly acknowledges Derrida's critique of the architect's scaling work and begins to outline a new design response, a belated "collaboration," which he terms "weak form." For a discussion of weak form, see Jeffrey Kipnis, "A Matter of Respect," *A+U* 232 (January 1990), 134–137.

11 TOWARD A NEW ARCHITECTURE

This essay first appeared in *AD Profile* 102 (1993).

1. Historians may note similarities in the work discussed here to the spatial character of baroque architecture and/or to the formal character of German expressionism. I predict their observations will conclude that none of the architects or theorists working in this area are aware of these similarities. Because the writing and projects are not salted with analyses of Francesco Borromini, Camillo-Guarino Guarini, and Gian Lorenzo Bernini, or references to Hermann Finsterlin, Bruno and Max Taut, Hans Poelzig, Hugo Häring, Erich Mendelsohn, Hans Scharoun, Rudolf Steiner, etc., it will be assumed that the work was conducted in blissful ignorance of these similarities. This first conclusion is necessary to support the second, namely, that the similarities are far more important than the differences. Thus, recalling Marx, they will argue that the second instance is but a parody of the tragic profundity of the first (a tautological argument, since the first instance establishes the terms and conditions of similarity; by coincidence, this argument also happens to support the capitalization of their professional activities). However interesting and worthy of study the similarities are, greater stakes are found in the differences: historians will again miss the point.

2. See Roberto Mangabeira Unger, *Knowledge and Politics* (New York: Free Press, 1975). See also Unger's *Social Theory: Its Situation and Its Tasks* (Cambridge, UK: Cambridge University Press, 1987).

3. Other poststructural architectural theorists, notably Jennifer Bloomer and Robert Somol, have appealed to the writings of Deleuze and Guattari, though to different ends.

4. "Collage" is used here as a convenient, if coarse, umbrella term for an entire constellation of practices, for example bricolage, assemblage, and a history of collage with many important distinctions and developments. This argument is strengthened by a study of the architectural translations of the various models of collage and its associated practices. As we proceed into a discussion of affiliative effects below, one might be inclined to argue that surrealist collage, with its emphasis on smoothing the seams of the graft, might provide an apt model. Though there is merit in this position, it seems to me that the so-called seamlessness of surrealist collage, like all collages, acts to emphasize by irony the distinct nature of the elements of the collage and therefore the incoherent disjunctions at work.

    A better model might be Jasper Johns's crosshatch paintings, prints, and drawings. Though these works certainly employ many techniques associated with collage, their effect is quite different. In them, nonideal, gridlike organizations are materialized by grafting elements whose form is disjoint from the overall organization. Moreover, in some of these works, cloudlike shapes entirely outside of the dominant formal/tonal language are built up from the medium itself and camouflaged within the work. For me, these paintings are good examples of a cohesive heterogeneity engendered out of an intensive coherence in the elements themselves.

5. See Eisenman's Wexner Center for the Visual Arts and his "scaling" projects, for example Romeo and Juliet for the 1986 Venice Biennale.

6. Clearly, the economic and political difficulties that result from a model of heterogeneity based on rostering definable species of difference I have associated with collage have broad implications across many institutional frontiers. In the 1992 U.S. presidential election, for example, a key issue was the widely felt frustration over the number of officially recognized special interest groups (now numbering in the thousands) seeking to influence decisions made by the federal government. However cynical one may be about this situation, it is an inevitable consequence of a social arrangement that attempts to negotiate the classical conflict between individual and community, and to achieve a democracy by offering the right to adequate voice and recognition of

differences, that is, a democracy through extensive incoherence. Models of heterogeneity achieved through intensive coherence would not only need to rethink the individual/community conflict, but the entire notion of a democracy achieved by systems of rights.

7. See Robert Somol, "Speciating Sites," in *Anywhere*, ed. Cynthia Davidson (New York: Rizzoli, 1992), 92–97.

8. To be sure, we have already seen possibilities for such grafts, for example in the work of John Hejduk or Aldo Rossi. It is entirely unpersuasive to account for the effects of Rossi's incongruous grafts of received institutions with his catalog of autonomous architectural forms, or for the effects of Hejduk's mytho-poetic, scenographic urban grafts with the logic of collage.

9. See Roberto Mangabeira Unger, "The Better Futures of Architecture," in *Anyone*, ed. Cynthia Davidson (New York: Rizzoli, 1991), 28–36.

10. Rem Koolhaas stresses this point in his short program for the 1992 Shinkenchiku Housing competition, "House with No Style." See *Japan Architect* 9 (Spring 1993).

11. Many of the ideas introduced in the second part of this text grew out of discussions I have enjoyed with Greg Lynn and Sanford Kwinter as well as from their writing. That I do not cite these writings in particular in this text is merely a testimony to how thoroughly it is suffused with their influence. See Greg Lynn's "Multiplicitous and Inorganic Bodies," *Assemblage* 19 (December 1992), 32–49, or Sanford Kwinter's "'Quelli che partono' as a General Theory of Models," in *Architecture, Space, Painting: Journal of Philosophy and the Visual Arts*, ed. Andrew Benjamin (London: Academy Editions, 1992), 36–44. For related issues, see *Incorporations*, ed. Jonathan Crary and Sanford Kwinter (New York: Zone Books, 1992).

12. In this account, I stress DeFormation primarily as a matter of building design and touch on urban issues only as they arise in that context. Several projects have attempted to extend the themes I here identify with DeFormation to urban design, such as Eisenman's Rebstock Park and the Shirdel, Zago, Kipnis competition entry for the Place Jacques-Cartier in Montreal. There are also projects incorporating the themes of InFormation, such as Koolhaas's Lille and La Défense or Tschumi's Chartres.

13. For a discussion of these three projects, see Jeffrey Kipnis, "Freudian Slippers, or What Were We to Make of the Fetish," in *Fetish, Princeton Papers on Architecture*, ed. Sarah Whiting, Edward Mitchell, and Greg Lynn (Princeton: Princeton Architectural Press, 1992).

14. For a discussion of Eisenman's weak-form projects, see Jeffrey Kipnis, "A Matter of Respect," *A+U* 232 (January 1990), 134–137.

15. One of the most fascinating aspects of Eisenman's design career is his uncanny ability to derive an entire architectural design thesis from a key word or phrase happened upon in his reading of criticism or philosophy. While not underestimating the significance of his eventual arrival at some understanding of the source of

the term in question, the fact of the matter is that Eisenman's design inventions virtually always evolve from his initial reaction to what he sees as the architectural implication of the term or phrase, loosened from its original discursive context. Whether Noam Chomsky's "deep structure," Jacques Derrida's "trace," Benoît Mandelbrot's "fractal scaling," or Gianni Vattimo's "weak thought," Eisenman's architectural derivations have much more to do with his stimulated intuition of potential architectural effects than with an attempt to embody the original philosophical effect in question. Eisenman's "deep structure," "trace," "scaling," and "weak form" therefore have little to do with philosophy, but much to do with architecture. This comment is by no means meant to disparage. Indeed, to the contrary—the way in which Eisenman's work has at one and the same time maintained a dialog with philosophical discourse while loosening the domain of architectural effects from and exemplifying/embodying obligation to philosophical effects may be its most important contribution. The conspicuous absence of this issue from the critical literature on Eisenman's work—including my own—testifies to an institutional need for critical literature to maintain a metaphysic of embodiment at any cost, even at the cost of paying attention to the architecture.

16. Though the discussion of affiliation to this point emphasizes form-to-form effects, a meditation on the weak links of affiliative effects also undermines the most preeminent of strongly aligned relations in architecture: the correlation between form and program. "Form follows function" is, of course, the declaration par excellence of an alignment between architectural design and program. Yet does a close attention to the history of architecture actually sustain that position? I believe a careful reading of that history would require a negative answer to this question.

Throughout its history, the relationship between form and program has been far more affiliative than aligned, a fact to which the endless numbers of reprogrammings more than testify (houses to museums, fascist headquarters to state treasury facilities, fire stations to Ghostbusters' offices, etc.). This is not to say that there is no relationship between form and function, but that the relationship is in its essence weak. It is the affiliative character of the form/program relationship that allows Rossi to produce his typological grafts and Tschumi to theorize about dis-cross and trans-programming. After all, has the design of any building significant to architectural history ever achieved its status due to how well it functioned? But the most glaring case of form/program affiliation is to be found in the house, for no one ever lives in a house according to its architectural program. Can a theory of strong alignment between form and program account for reading in the bathroom or eating in the living room, or for the particular pleasures of having sex anywhere but the bedroom? No doubt it was out of a frustration over the failure of affiliations to congeal into alignments that drove Mies van der Rohe to nail down the furniture. The affiliative nature of the relationship between form and program largely accounts for DeFormation's relative complacency vis-à-vis InFormation on the issue of program.

17. Camouflage is often cited as a paradigm of affiliations that smooth. Effective camouflage such as "dazzle painting" is often entirely different from the prevailing influences of the operative context and almost always outside of the dominant modes of the primary discipline (that is, of clothing design or the surface treatment of ships or planes). Yet the effect of camouflage is to smooth the disjoint relationship between site and interloper into another context.

18. For additional discussion of the Jacques-Cartier event structure project, see Bahram Shirdel, Andrew Zago, and Jeffrey Kipnis, "An Urban Place: Place Jacques-Cartier, Montreal," *L'Arca* 55 (December 1991), 32–41.

19. For additional discussion of the Shirdel, Zago, Kipnis project for the Scottish National Museum, see Jeffrey Kipnis, "Four Predicaments," in Davidson, *Anywhere*, 124–131.

20. See Peter Eisenman, "K Nowhere 2 Fold," in Davidson, *Anywhere*, 218–227.

21. To state that the most interesting discussions in architecture revolve around design technique is, to me, virtually a tautology. The most interesting aspect of any and every study of architecture—historical, theoretical, or otherwise—is its consequence for current design technique.

22. For more on the Rebstock project, see Robert Somol, "Accidents Will Happen," *A+U* 252 (September 1991), 4–7, and John Rajchman, "Perplications: On the Space and Time of Rebstock Park," in *Unfolding Frankfurt* (Berlin: Ernst & Sohn, 1991). For Eisenman on folding, see "Visions' Unfolding: Architecture in the Age of Electronic Media," *Domus* 734 (January 1992), 17–24, reprinted in Crary and Kwinter, *Incorporations*.

23. In his studio at The Ohio State University, Eisenman and his students began to develop the implications of the initial Rebstock folding for the building sections and to study its capacity to interlace disjoint organizations.

INDEX